Mort Rosenblum is chief foreign correspondent for the Associated Press and has written widely on the Third World. He is the author of *Mission to Civilize: The French Way*. Doug Williamson worked as a lawyer in South Africa, then trained as a scientist, specialising in conservation. He is currently a visiting scholar at Cambridge University.

By Mort Rosenblum

Mission to Civilize: The French Way

MORT ROSENBLUM and
DOUG WILLIAMSON

Squandering Eden

Africa at the Edge

PALADIN
GRAFTON BOOKS
A Division of the Collins Publishing Group

LONDON GLASGOW
TORONTO SYDNEY AUCKLAND

Paladin
Grafton Books
A Division of the Collins Publishing Group
8 Grafton Street, London W1X 3LA

Published in Paladin Books 1990

First published in Great Britain by
The Bodley Head Ltd 1988

Copyright © 1987 by Mort Rosenblum
and Doug Williamson

A CIP catalogue record for this book
is available from the British Library

ISBN 0-586-08880-6

Printed and bound in Great Britain by
Collins, Glasgow

Set in Times

For Jane and Emily; for Elise and Jane;
and Abdul Rahman Diku wherever he is today.

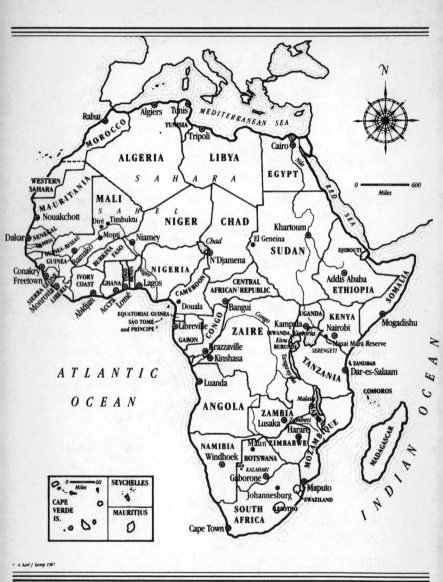

CONTENTS

AUTHORS' NOTE   *ix*

1 AT THE EDGE   *1*

2 THE KALAHARI   *32*
   Obsolete Animals, Obsolete People

3 THE SAHEL   *49*
   Twilight of Timbuktu

4 SUDAN, ETHIOPIA, SOMALIA   *74*
   Horn of Penury

5 CENTRAL AFRICA   *99*
   Crowded Out of Eden

6 EAST AFRICA   *117*
   Good Ideas Gone Bad

7 BRITISH WEST AFRICA   *142*
   Westminster South

8 FRENCH AFRICA   *163*
   Balkans on the Slave Coast

9   PORTUGUESE AFRICA   *183*
     First In, Last Out

10   SOUTHERN AFRICA   *195*
     On the Front Line

11   SOUTH AFRICA   *210*
     Beyond the Politics

12   THE LAND   *232*
     Finding a Balance

13   PEOPLE   *250*
     Women and Children First

14   A WORKING MISUNDERSTANDING   *262*

15   WHAT TO DO   *284*

     BIBLIOGRAPHY   *309*
     INDEX   *315*

AUTHORS' NOTE

We met at work in Africa. Doug Williamson, a scientist, was settled in the Kalahari watching things up close. Mort Rosenblum, a journalist, was covering the continent at large. Over two decades, we discovered, each of us had seen similar things and drawn the same conclusions.

For clarity, we chose a single voice: the "I" in this book is Rosenblum, who wrote the text. But we collaborated on every word. We pooled our notes; between us, we have visited all but a few of Africa's fifty-two countries.

Jane Williamson, a wildlife ecologist, was vital to the project. So was Gretchen Hoff. Our editor was Marie Arana-Ward, whose blue pencil should be bronzed.

We thank especially those Africans who helped us see Africa from their perspective. They are too numerous to name; some will appreciate the anonymity. Other sources are cited in the text, or left unidentified at their own request. We are grateful to them all.

Where frankness nudges aside euphemism, we ask understanding. Our intent is not to plead a case but rather to present the facts as we see them. We realize the subjectivity that can entail.

D.W. owes thanks to the Frankfurt Zoological Society. M.R. is grateful for the support of his employer, The Associated Press, which none of this book engages.

M.R.
D.W.

Photo Credits

Nax the Bushman (Mort Rosenblum)
Abdul Rahman Diku's son (Alexis Duclos)
Kalahari cattle post (Doug Williamson)
Abandoned wildebeest calf (Doug Williamson)
Stranded canoe (Mort Rosenblum)
Tuareg children (Mort Rosenblum)
Tuareg woman (Mort Rosenblum)
Tuareg nomads-turned-farmers (Mort Rosenblum)
Donkey caravan carrying firewood (Mort Rosenblum)
Sudanese women (Wide World)
Terraced well (Wide World)
Pumps in Mali (Wide World)
Refugees in western Somalia (Wide World)
Sahelian farmers' vegetable plots (Wide World)
Mother and child (Mort Rosenblum)
West African children (Mort Rosenblum)
Women in Mali (Mort Rosenblum)
Guinean woman (Mort Rosenblum)
Djibril Diallo (Mort Rosenblum)
Sudanese harvesting rice (Wide World)
Kenyan bus (Mort Rosenblum)

1 AT THE EDGE

Wherever man started, it might just as well have been in the Drakensberg range that rims western Natal Province in South Africa. No archeological evidence suggests this; it simply fits in with creation. The mountains are a blend of space and splendor, rising over rich soils and the native rangeland of wild herds. For perhaps twenty-five millennia, a civilization of Bushmen lived finely tuned to the Drakensberg's natural cycles. They were there when Portuguese explorers passed by in the 1490s and when Dutch settlers came to stay two centuries later. They saw in the twentieth century. Today, the last five of these Bushmen are grotesque plaster statues in a cave museum high up in the Drakensberg.

The vast herds of game that the Bushmen hunted have dwindled to scattered remnants on threatened reserves. And the land itself is dying, defaced by deepening gashes of erosion and spreading patches where nothing can grow.

Damage spreads through the lowlands beyond. Outside Umtata, capital of the Transkei, on what was a thickly forested plain, African fathers take their children to a small nature reserve to see a tree. Three decades ago, millions of Americans and Europeans imagined their first pictures of Africa from Alan Paton's portrait of the land near Ixopo, "lovely beyond any singing of it." Today, much of Paton's beloved country is moonscape.

Bushmen now cling to desert redoubts in Botswana and Namibia. Only a few still hunt and gather. Others work for pennies, tending the cattle that penetrate into the Kalahari and overgraze the Bushmen's last survival grounds into wasteland. And many cluster around villages like Xade, drinking and bickering over handouts from occasional visitors, awaiting the next turn of fate.

The plight of the Bushmen and their land is moving enough as a tale of human and natural tragedy. But it is more. In every ecological system, scientists watch for indicator species in the same way a miner might watch a canary for signs of poisonous gas. Here, the evidence is plain, and it grows plainer by the season. Huge tracts of Africa are dying in stages, as the Drakensberg Bushmen died.

The victims are not only the individuals who wither away waiting for food, but also entire societies, populations of game, prey and predators, and the land they lived on. Fiercely independent peoples who thrived for thousands of years in the world's harshest conditions now huddle in ragged bands by borehole wells, waiting for food trucks. Blame is laid on nature, which persists, year after year, in following its fixed patterns. But man is responsible. We sought to improve on nature in Africa, and we failed disastrously. Rather than repairing damage already done, we are racing full tilt to commit the same errors on an ever grander scale. We will not escape the price.

"There is a little Bushman in all of us," observed Sir Laurens van der Post, in his eighties, after a lifetime of trying to reverse the processes threatening Bushmen. He is right: A massive calamity is taking shape in Africa before our eyes, and we are doing little more than temporarily masking its more obvious symptoms.

Beyond Africa, the direct danger is uncertain. There will be millions more dead on the world's conscience; there may be altered weather patterns, a disruption of vital raw materials, and global political instability. But a frightening question looms for the rest of the world: If we could not respond to save a dying neighbor, are we equipped to save ourselves?

*T*he African calamity is easy to ignore. It is elusive among numbing statistics of dubious reliability. Fragmented news reports swing from gloom to hope and back again. Promise and prosperity on much of the continent often falsify the readings, for better or worse. Sustained attention is hard and depressing work. Instead, the world acts when an "emergency" is declared; it relaxes when the danger is pronounced past.

In between emergencies, Africa is handed back to specialized people with labels ending in "ist." Agronomists. Environmentalists. Nutritionists. Developmental economists. Technical tourists fit Africa onto spread sheets. The human suffering, like the factors that cause it, is seen from a distance in abstraction.

Up close, the calamity is anything but abstract. But even up close it is not always obvious, as in Timbuktu, for example.

From the fourteenth century, Timbuktu thrived as a seat of Islamic learning, a crossroads for caravans of salt and gold. It was set back from the broad Niger River among trees that shielded it from the Sahara to the north. The city lived on sufferance of the Tuaregs, the fabled Blue Men of the Desert. Periodically, they swept into town on camels and plundered whatever they could carry. Mostly, they were mysterious shapes in the blowing sand.

The Tuaregs lived well as nomadic herders. They regulated the land simply. Anyone endangering fragile pastures was moved along at the edge of a sword. But, a century ago, French colonizers began changing the rules. Nomads carried *cartes d'identité* in the folds of their blue robes. Some of their children went to school; a few left their camels to drive taxis in Paris. Fate was no longer in the hands of Allah alone.

Neither the grand designs of France nor the socialist doctrines of independent Mali saved the proud old city. I went to Timbuktu at the height of the mid-1980s' drought and found a crumbling backwater of 10,000 inhabitants, a tenth of its former population. Wooden doors still bore marks of Tuareg swords. But the swords, and the nomads' silver teapots and heirloom jewelry, were for sale. The Tuaregs were starving, camped in miserable scraps of tents on the sand dunes that advance like ocean waves on Timbuktu.

The trees had long since been cut for firewood. Across all of northern Mali, overgrazing and poor farming had turned fields to sand. Modest irrigation projects were failing. The Niger was at its lowest levels in a century because rain forests in the upriver watersheds were disappearing.

The first Europeans to see Timbuktu were put to death by Moslem zealots. Now you can book a room by computer through the French Sofitel chain. At the hotel, an American approached me. He was about sixty, perhaps a dentist from Des Moines, in plaid polyester slacks and a spotless safari hat. He was thrilled to be at the end of the world, and he had a thick wad of postcards to prove it. But he had a question for me: "Hey, those natives in tents outside of town, are they put there as part of our tour?"

No, I replied, they are Tuaregs, starving to death and they are here to beg for food.

"Oh, good," he said. "Then they won't mind if we take their picture."

Most Africans suffer unnoticed, like Abdul Rahman Diku and his family, camped in the dust of a burned-out rice field, a cigarette's toss from the asphalt airport road at Mopti, upriver from Timbuktu.

Diku's crops failed, and he headed off through the sands with his wife, his mother, eight children, and fourteen other relatives. It took a few weeks to reach Mopti, 500 miles south. The last cows and goats died on the way. Diku built a shelter of sticks, with a few goat skins to break the pounding sun. He owned what the women had carried down balanced on their heads: an enameled food bowl, some gourds and sleeping mats, a few rags of clothing.

Each morning, the family scrabbled in the dirt for grains of rice left from past harvests. The Niger was too low for irrigation; there would not be a fresh crop. The women walked a few miles daily to scoop putrid water from a drying well. His children took on the marks of famine: skin stretched tautly over bones, swollen bellies, reddish brittle hair, and oozing eyes black with flies.

The Mopti market was piled high with food, but Diku had no

money. In a town full of refugees, no one was hiring. All day long, he watched the Land-Rovers and Peugeots hurtling past his little camp: technical tourists from the World Bank, Malian government officials, British aid volunteers, U.N. experts on calamities at large.

Somehow, it all missed Diku. Quite simply, he had come to the end of the line. His children had begun to die, and he would probably lose them all.

"What will you do?" I asked him. He considered the question, studying me to see if I might be able to suggest an answer. He was not surprised that I had none. He gently stroked the hair of his four-year-old son. "What will I do? What can I do?"

I had seen Dikus by the thousands in every part of Africa. But his look managed to shatter the carapace, the professional detachment that usually protected me. It was not pleading, not hostile, not even hopeful. It was simply quizzical. He did not know about journalists and scientists or other distinctions among famine groupies: I was another human from a wealthier world, which should not have let this happen.

And I had no excuses to offer. In almost the same place a decade earlier, I'd seen other fathers suffering the same plight. For all the words and dollars that had since flowed into Africa, this time it was worse.

Under Diku's gaze, the calamity was not so easy to ignore. There was the immediate tragic irony: the silos of Kansas and the Beauce held enough surplus grain to pave Mali, and farmers fought for higher subsidies to compensate them for not growing still more.

What might Diku think if he knew the world ended 1986 with 390 million tons of surplus grain? Or that Western governments spent $70 billion in subsidies, price supports, and storage to deal with food they did not need? But that was not the worst part.

Africa could grow enough food for two or three times its population. It could have more wild protein, fish and livestock than it can eat or sell. And its people could be flourishing. Africa was most likely Eden, where man began. It was never a lush garden of food for the taking. Soils were mostly poor, and life was fraught with disease and danger. But there was great wealth and potential. In less than a century, at a steadily increasing pace, Eden has been squandered recklessly. Today, much of it teeters at the edge.

*E*ach year, depending on the rains, there are 15 million Africans like Diku's family, or 6 million, or 150 million. The U.N. Food and Agriculture Organization issues numbers, but they mean little. If Diku's children did not die, they would not be statistics, for all their suffering. If they did, who would report their deaths? In their weakened state, they might succumb to a bad cold. That would put them in the column of disease, not malnutrition.

Two years after meeting Diku, I went back to his rice field. He was gone. Mali had had its first good rains in nine years, and a crop grew. The world's harvest was so rich that American and European officials argued bitterly over price supports. Food aid had flooded the Mopti region. But where Diku's family had camped alone, there were hundreds of new desperate Tuaregs. The emergency was officially over. But no one told the victims.

With the jargon, one can quibble: What is hunger and what is famine? Is it time for relief, rehabilitation, or development? For Africans without food, those are pointless distinctions. The economies meant to support them are largely in shambles. Their governments owed more than they could repay. War is endemic in five countries, and conflict is common in others. At the rate productive land and forests are disappearing, future prospects range from very bleak to cataclysmic. It is not too late for Africa. But it will be soon.

Weather is partly to blame. But African famine is no accident of the rains; it is mostly man-made, and it is getting worse. The underlying causes are politics, greed, and ignorance—in Africa and elsewhere. Even in the worst affected places, few people go hungry if they are not also poor.

Exporting money is not the answer. From 1960 through 1986, Western donors spent $116 billion on aid to sub-Saharan Africa. Better used, that might have been plenty. A lot went back to donors, paid out to experts for dubious advice. Africans stole some and wasted more. Some of it went to badly conceived projects which ruined good land and dispersed productive societies. And even more went to prop up corrupt, tyrannical, or simply inefficient governments.

Clearly, people want to help. When news film brought home Ethiopian suffering in 1984, musicians put the calamity to music. Bob Geldof organized Band Aid, which grew into Live Aid. USA for Africa produced "We Are the World." People worked themselves to an emotional peak. Then their attention moved on. But the expensive part was just starting. Nowhere near enough was done to save the land that would have to feed the same people, and more, year after year.

In Sudan, Bob Medrala, a young relief worker from Chicago, shrugged when I asked him about the spurt of aid. "It is so aptly named. That is all any of us can do, apply a Band-Aid. We can fatten up a kid, but then what? Where does he go? It will happen again and again."

I was in Sudan when USA for Africa directors first looked at the situation they had vowed to resolve. In the western province of Darfur, the first of 3.5 million threatened people had begun to die. On the coast, 360,000 backed-up tons of sorghum were beginning to rot. Relief workers screamed for grain. The trains, however, carried sugar and bicycle parts instead of sorghum. Over breakfast at the "Famine Hilton"—Khartoum's plush Hilton on the Nile—USA for Africa people listened to veterans reeling off the reasons.

Finally, Executive Director Marty Rogol just shook his head. "I never realized $50 million could mean so little," he said. "It is peanuts." A year later, USA for Africa had added $19 million to the billions of dollars from other sources; hunger persisted. Band Aid collected $130 million. That was, coincidentally, how much official donors wasted on a Tanzanian mill that closed because it produced paper at two and a half times the import price.

The musicians did more than raise money. To the amazement of aid professionals, they pricked consciences en masse; they convinced legislators that African hunger was an issue. Suddenly, there was action: 1985 was the Year of Compassion. But 1986 was the Year of Neglect. For Sport Aid, people jogged in world capitals as Sudanese runner Omar Khalifa carried an African torch to the United Nations.

On that day, however, USA for Africa was marshaling people to link hands across America, for hunger at home. Geldof, describing his action as a brilliant meteor flash, went back to the Boomtown Rats.

"Development is boring," Geldof told the *Earthlife News* in Britain late in 1986. "I find it boring. How do you make a compressor pump interesting? I can't go on television and talk about deficits and surpluses and irrigation. People would turn off."

Determination remained but not the wherewithal. As 1987 began, actress Glenda Jackson said of the Ethiopian famine on British radio, "Surely this must be the last famine the world ever sees. I think it is time to stop appealing and start demanding." But as she spoke, people were hungry over much of Africa. A confidential survey by Western agronomists forecast that by the early 1990s Ethiopia under normal conditions would fall 2 million tons a year short of its food requirement. That is twice the amount of emergency relief sent in during the 1984–85 famine.

For most outsiders, saving Africa means giving food. But food aid—even when not stolen, delayed, or spoiled—is only part of an answer. Relief can be a narcotic. The more that is administered, the greater the dependency. Like a narcotic, it cannot be stopped without grief. Once famine strikes, grain shipments are essential to keep people alive. Yet badly timed relief destroys farming systems and subsidizes the policies that lead to famine.

For every Diku, there is an Alex Njorogeh. Alex owns two acres of the once-rich Kenya land that Karen Blixen rode by on her way out of Africa. For him, the question of food aid does not arise. He is one of those marginal Africans whom visitors pass en route to observe the hard cases. We sat in his mud hovel and went over his finances. He would be deep in the red if he could afford ink. Alex needs no agronomist to explain why his neighbor's corn grows fat while his shrivels and dies. The reason is tied out behind the neighbor's hut, contentedly chewing grass into manure.

"I had a cow, too, but I had to sell it to buy food for my kids," he told me. "Now that is gone, and the cow is gone. I cannot pay for fertilizer, and my land gives less and less." He was growing coffee during a world boom, but his family edged toward starvation. Corrupt middlemen took most of his profits. His best hope, he knew, was to try to be a middleman, too.

Abdul Rahman Diku and Alex Njorogeh would appreciate a "We Are the World" T-shirt. But what they need is sustained help, given modestly but regularly, to grow food the way they always have, using new methods to increase their yields, and to protect the land their children must till.

And here is more of the tragic irony: solutions are within reach. In one African capital, a World Bank representative explained to me for two hours how human folly—among donors and recipients—had wasted billions. Foreign aid amounted to a chaotic tangle, paralyzing development. "Finding an answer to this is impossible," he said. "Unless you use common sense. Then it is quite simple."

A *frica* is a big word. Its six letters speak for a continent nearly the size of North America and Europe combined, inhabited since man's beginning. From Casablanca to Cape Town, it is sand, snow, and jungle set among rich farmland and grassy plains. There are 540 million Africans, and in twenty years there will be a billion. They range in hue from coal to cotton. Zaire alone has 200 ethnic groups. Africans speak at least 2,000 different languages and dialects, including English, French, and Portuguese. In fifty-two countries, Africans revere Jesus Christ, the prophet Mohammed, Hindu deities, and carved masks stuffed with animal matter. On a continent where measles is still a fatal disease, surgeons performed the first heart transplant.

One in five Africans lives on imported food. Some countries survive almost entirely on artificial life support from abroad. Overall, Africa is 10 percent less able to feed itself than it was a decade ago. But Africans park their BMWs outside crowded restaurants to dine off white linen, and they breakfast on pastries flown in fresh from France. The continent's combined gross domestic product is less than Italy's. Still, a Nigerian broker not long ago refused to insure a civil servant's bathtub, solid gold, which he valued at $5 million.

A former African head of state, a poet, is a member of the

Académie Française. Another, at this writing, is on trial for cannibalism.

Diku and Njorogeh are Africans, but so is Philippe whom I
sometimes visit in Zaire. He has too many Mercedes-Benzes for his
two-car garage. But his servants take care of that. His house rambles
among banana trees and bougainvillaea, in California jungle modern.
His whisky was distilled when his country was still a Belgian colony
and he was a clerk on meager wages. At independence, he worked
for a state agency and eventually became a cabinet minister at a small
but reasonable salary. Now "in business," he is part of a surprisingly
large new class in Africa.

The Arabic-speaking Mediterranean states—Morocco, Tunisia,
Algeria, Libya, and Egypt—have characteristics distinct from the rest
of the continent. South Africa is a complex blend of sub-Saharan
Africa and the industrialized West. Ethiopia has a separate history;
Emperor Haile Selassie, overthrown in 1974, traced his bloodlines
back to Solomon and Sheba. Liberia was established by freed American slaves beginning in 1822. The rest of Africa was colonized during
the nineteenth century, by England, France, Belgium, Portugal, Germany, Spain. Ghana won independence in 1957, and others followed
over the next twenty-three years. Only Namibia is left, administered
by South Africa.

Statistics abound, and most are suspect. Ethiopia based its planning for the 1980s on a population of 32 million. Early results of a
census suggested the total was 42 million. But some numbers suggest
an overall picture.

In 1983 and 1984, Asia's combined gross national product rose
by 8.6 percent. Africa's fell by 2.9 percent, and it continues to drop.
Of the fifty-two states in Africa, twenty-nine were poorer in 1986
than they were in 1960. It was costing $12 to $14 billion a year to
import food. Altogether, African governments were spending more
than half their income on imported food and debt interest. Sudan
alone had a debt of $17 billion, greater than its gross national product.
Interest payments, if any were made, would require three times the
country's earnings.

Overall, Africa owed almost $200 billion in 1987, nearly half its gross domestic product and twice its export earnings, according to Adebayo Adedeji, executive secretary of the U.N. Economic Commission for Africa. Because of dropping oil and commodity prices, he said, 1986 was Africa's worst year ever for exports. Earnings fell from $60.6 billion in 1985, already a low level, to $44.3 billion.

The World Bank estimates sub-Saharan Africa needs $2.5 billion a year more aid just to inch forward. But in fiscal 1987, the United States reduced its economic aid to Black Africa by a third, to below $550 million, less than half that given to Israel alone. The 1988 request to Congress was only $600 million. In asking for funds, the U.S. State Department noted that, at present rates, it would take a century for Africans' per capita income to double to $700 a year. But, it added, things were getting worse, not better.

In Rwanda and Mauritania, ten times more trees are cut each year than are replaced. Asia has 300 million acres under irrigation; Black Africa has 15 million. For every acre of irrigation put into service, an acre is lost to silt, salt, or waterlogging. Kenya's and Botswana's populations grow at more than four percent a year.

No one can measure the blood spilled. But *South* magazine, in August 1986, cited nearly four million dead in sub-Saharan Africa since 1960—from wars, massacres and famine resulting from armed conflict.

The figures are less eloquent than the reality they represent. In 1967, I first saw Uganda's crisp white Parliament and joked with a guard in a braided blue uniform. "Where is your gun?" I asked. He was aghast. "But, sir," he said, "that would defeat the purpose of a parliament." Less than a generation later, I watched seven-year-olds carry AK-47s through the streets of Kampala.

But statistics and heart-rending charity appeals also mask the vitality, dignity, and humor that characterize Africa. Fantu Cheru, the son of Ethiopian shepherds, is settled as a professor in Washington. He speaks of himself as an American. But he gets homesick. "In Africa, people will help you find your own humanity, much more than here," he said. "In the final analysis, it is they who survive, not us."

From their first contacts, outsiders have tended to overlook the inherent strengths and humanity of most African peoples. Sir Richard Burton pronounced the continent devoid of cultural interest to civilized scholars. But he walked right past the Olduvai Gorge.

African farmers learned to grow millet and sorghum at least 1,500 years before Europeans decided the world was not flat. Great civilizations rose and fell in Africa. When Charlemagne's armies forged Europe's first modern empire, a rich kingdom in Ghana ruled West Africa. Before Westminster Abbey was built, Zimbabwean priests started a mysterious and intricate rock temple of mammoth proportions. While Henri IV built France in stone, Mansa Musa built Mali in mud; both were sophisticated societies of their time. The elaborate court of the Kongo dispatched ambassadors to Portugal. European nations flourished within fixed borders. African states diffused into the space and climate. European empire builders found a raw continent open to their tender mercies.

Wave after wave of outsiders penetrated Africa, blending a mission to civilize with a lust to plunder. Henry Morton Stanley, hot on a story for the New York *Herald*, mounted an expedition of 150 men. In *How I Found Livingstone*, he reports his arrival at a ravine: "We set to work, there being no help for it, with American axes—the first of their kind the strokes of which ever rang in this part of the world— to build a bridge. Be sure it was made quickly, for where the civilized white is found, a difficulty must vanish." And a few lines later, he adds: "After seeing the work properly commenced, I sat down to amuse myself with the hippopotami by peppering their thick skulls with my No. 12 smooth-bore."

Stanley found David Livingstone in a squalid Central African village, just in time. Not long afterward, the British explorer-missionary joined the growing number of white men to expire under the burden Kipling later set to poetry. He offered these last words: "All I can add in my solitude is may Heaven's rich blessing come down on everyone, American, English or Turk, who will help to heal this open sore of the world."

Or Frenchman. A decade later, in 1847, Victor Hugo laid out in an essay* the philosophy that would motivate those who followed Livingstone to the Dark Continent:

> Two aspects to consider:
>   Civilize the people
>   Colonize the land
>   Civilize the people? I would very much like to. But what an enterprise! To meld France to Africa is not only to bring together and mix two peoples . . . it is to bring together centuries. On one hand, we of the nineteenth century, with a free press and full civilization, and on the other, the pastoral and patriarchal, the century of Homer and the Bible.
>   Can these two peoples resemble one another, except before God? Can they mix in any way but in the tomb, where one soul resembles another, where dust resembles dust?
>   In life they reject and exclude one another, and one hunts the other.
>   Therefore, colonize the land.

Europe was way ahead of Hugo. Each colonizing power went to work early, each with a different strategy. Britain ruled indirectly, relying on traditional chiefs; the British provided a wide base of clerks and native policemen with a simple education. France sought to create an elite of black Frenchmen but governed colonies tightly from Paris. Portugal and Belgium wanted as little trouble as possible from over-educated Africans. And all of them wanted cheap tropical produce, timber, and mineral wealth.

Africans, most Europeans thought and believed, were yet another natural resource—of greater value, if more trouble to manage, than mines and fields—that God had placed at their disposal. In World War I, Africans died for France, England, and Germany. Then African sweat repaired the war's damage. But World War II

* As quoted in *La France Colonisatrice*, Nicole Priollaud (Paris: Liana Lévi, 1983).

had a galvanizing impact on colonized peoples forced to watch, up close, Europeans in their most savage and vulnerable state. In Asia, Europe set its colonies free in a process pushed along by American and Soviet statesmen alike. By the mid-1950s, Harold Macmillan perceived the shift in Africa, and he gave it a name that has embedded itself into history: "a wind of change."

The wind gusted suddenly, and no one was ready for decolonization. The Congo (now Zaire) had seventeen college graduates. Or eleven. Or thirty. Authorities were not well enough organized to know for sure. The Belgians departed from the Congo *en catastrophe*, leaving chaos behind. The British balanced their former colonies' books and went home, leaving behind the Commonwealth Secretariat's telephone number in case of emergency. The French hauled down the tricolor but stayed around in force. And the Portuguese gave up only much later, after bitter wars left Angola, Mozambique, and Guinea-Bissau torn almost beyond recovery.

Independent nations started with the deck stacked against them. Borders depended more on the stamina of explorers and the guile of diplomats than on any sensible plan. Brazzaville is French because Brazza trotted barefoot for months through dense jungle to get there; Stanley arrived too late to claim the north side of the Congo River. Sudan speaks English because, during the 1898 Fashoda incident, French minister Delcassé blinked and Lord Lansdowne did not. Frontiers had been sectioned off with compasses on maps in Europe. Natural and cultural boundaries were ignored. Tribes were divided, creating minorities and majorities that would render democracy farcical. Hinterlands were separated from traditional markets.

Colonizers had pushed aside civilizations that were functioning in Africa when French kings ate with their fingers. They ruled African possessions with an authoritarian hand. On departure, they expected fledgling states to adhere to institutions that Europe had not perfected in a thousand years. The result was hardly a surprise. Small elites seized power and kept it. Tribes squared off, and winners took all. Western and Eastern blocs lined up friends by bankrolling the ruling elites. Periodically, some new group shot itself into State House and turned the counters back to zero.

Africa, once the province of district officers and missionaries, was suddenly a hothouse for every amateur development theorist, social engineer, tank salesman, unemployed mercenary, rogue industrialist, and purveyor of unwanted pesticides. Some misguided projects were designed with the best of intentions; others were outright fraud. Often, African leaders were less interested in a project's effect on their people than in the size of the kickback.

Every government, whatever its ideology, depended on centralized control. Its survival depended on it. The more authorities meddled with market forces, the worse things got. Dissidents were silenced, tactfully or with machine-gun fire. Successful tyrants and thugs hired public-relations counselors. Western governments supported them; after all, it was argued, they provided political stability.

Mostly, African leaders and outside experts overlooked the basic component of Africa: the people. Farmers and herders eluded state control. If official prices were low, they smuggled crops and cattle elsewhere. Or they stopped producing. In Botswana, visiting officials were dismissed as the "big bellies." In Nigeria, a local authority admitted ruefully, "To *them*, we are only a cloud of dust behind a big car." As a result, development was designed without the people who were to be developed.

The resulting calamity did not go unnoticed. French agronomist René Dumont sounded the alarm twenty-five years ago in a book entitled *False Start in Africa*. In 1980, African leaders themselves joined the chorus: the Organization of African Unity's Lagos Plan of Action outlined the problems and the solutions. Edem Kodjo, OAU secretary-general, could not have been clearer: "Africa is dying."

Outsiders strained to convey the threat in a language numbed to world crises. C. Payne Lucas, director of Africare and a twenty-five-year veteran of African development work, put it without exaggeration: "World War III has already started, between Africa and its environment, and it will claim more casualties than the first two wars and the exterminated Jews combined."

But, words aside, governments have focused their action on other priorities. Some have wars to fight and opponents to foil. Others are struggling with the barest essentials of running a state. Even in South

Africa, where science and strict laws provide the best potential for land management, erosion is catastrophic. Ian Colvin, at the Natal Parks Board, studies Landsat photographs of once rich forests and rangelands reduced to bare shale.

"Everyone is too preoccupied with politics to think about the land," he said. "But in ten years they will come up with a political solution, and it will be too late. If the land looks like this, they are goners."

Wildlife is going fast, and efforts to save it are diffuse and disjointed. "This is like religion—everyone approaches conservation with his own interpretation and area of interest," observed David Cumming, chief ecologist of the Zimbabwe Department of Parks and Wildlife Management. It is time, he argued, for an ecumenical movement to combat threats on an overall basis.

Zimbabwe is an example of the conflicts. Black rhinos, nearly extinct in Africa, survive in a large population in Zimbabwe's Zambezi Valley. But poachers threaten them from across the Zambian border. Some money is spent on protecting them. But much more is spent on spraying the tsetse fly, in areas where they are no particular threat to humans, so cattle can destroy the habitat that supports rhino and many other species. Zimbabwe's wildlife department, the most effective in Black Africa, can do nothing about it. In a public planning session, Robinson Gapare, of the Zimbabwe peasant farmers' union, offered a reason why.

"I may be an uneducated peasant," he said, with a slight chuckle at his clearly misplaced modesty, "but why should my cattle die to save some wild animals for Europeans who never come look at them anyway?"

*T*his book samples some of Africa's problems. It offers some suggestions. But it does not assess blame for the past. In the face of calamity, recrimination is exorbitant luxury. Workable systems must be found, and Africans must find them. Outsiders can only help at the edges.

Whether colonization was bad or good is beside the point. Black

Africa has been independent a long generation; half its people were born at least ten years after independence. Colonies are not necessarily impoverished. Hong Kong is a colony. With 5 million people on a scrap of land without resources, it generates as much wealth as Zaire, Zimbabwe, Zambia, Malawi, Tanzania, Angola, Mozambique, and Botswana combined, despite their 90 million people and all of their oil, diamonds, copper, and rich land.

A lack of natural riches can hamper growth, but it is no final condemnation. Burkina Faso, Mali, and Chad are landlocked and have no natural resources. So is Switzerland. But Switzerland is better organized.

Anyone who thinks Africa is beyond organization is advised to drop in on Djibouti when the khat arrives. Khat, a deep-green leaf, is chewed in quantity for a light buzz. People love it in the Horn of Africa. Djibouti imports a fixed daily quota, not a leaf more or less. The moment the plane touches down from Saudi Arabia, that khat is sorted, shifted, and carried to the farthest corner of the country. Within hours, everyone has his allotted wad. If food aid moved that smoothly, death tolls would plummet.

Africa's greatest problem may be the enduring myth that Africans are unable—or somehow unwilling—to improve their lot. The continent teems with economists and agronomists, entrepreneurs and investors, peasant farmers and laborers, all anxious to build prosperous states. Most are blocked from above and below, and their frustration is yet another African tragedy.

From below, there is jealousy and a conservative attitude resistant to change. "I fear my own progress in life," a Tswana villager told anthropologist Hoyt Alverson. "I fear *dikgaba*." That is the malevolent envy of others. Some Africans feel held back by tradition. France, Jean Gimpel noted, grew since the Middle Ages because the society believed in progress. He quotes a medieval thinker: "Never will we find the truth if we allow ourselves to be satisfied with what has been already discovered . . . those who wrote before our time were not lords, but guides."

But the most serious stifling is from above.

"Black Africa is a disgrace, politically and economically," George

Ayittey wrote in *Index on Censorship*. He is a Ghanaian, a professor at Bloomsburg State University in Bloomsburg, Pennsylvania. "It hurts us black Africans even more at this time when the world is applying pressure to South Africa. . . . Of the forty-one black African countries, only two (Botswana and Senegal) allow their people the right to vote."

Free expression is stifled so that bad policies cannot be challenged, he argued. People grow rich doing nothing but selling their signatures on useless papers that paralyze real progress. Economic planning is distorted to allow opportunities for corruption.

Chinua Achebe, a novelist and professor, agonized over the problem in a slim book of truths called *The Trouble with Nigeria*:

> Nigeria is *not* a great country. It is one of the most disorderly nations in the world. It is one of the most corrupt, insensitive, inefficient places under the sun. It is one of the most expensive countries and one of those that give least value for money. It is dirty, noisy, ostentatious, dishonest and vulgar. In short, it is among the most unpleasant places on earth! It is a measure of our self-delusion that we can talk about developing tourism in Nigeria. Only a masochist with an exuberant taste for self-violence will pick Nigeria for a holiday.

Late in 1986, Achebe remarked in a television interview that in fifteen years Nigeria had "frittered away $100 billion of oil earnings with no visible result."

Why does he stay? Achebe asks himself. Because Nigeria is his country. In almost every nation of Africa, people talk about inefficiency, corruption, and disorder. And the same willingness to stay and fight for something better. Nigeria has a measure of greatness and no shortage of men like Achebe who stick with it.

Like Wole Soyinka, for example. He won Africa's first Nobel prize for literature, for plays, poetry, and prose that skewered Africans who oppressed their own people. He sat out the Biafra war in prison after trying to prove he could be both a Nigerian and a member of the Yoruba tribe. Earlier, he had forced a radio announcer, at gunpoint, to substitute for a minister's speech a tape damning leaders who subverted democracy. In accepting his prize, he noted that South Africa could call itself a civilized bastion against barbarity by raising "the spectre of a few renegade barons who we ourselves are victims of—whom we denounce before the world and overthrow when we are able."

Or Fela Anikulapo Kuti, whose exuberant, disturbing music stirs juices on every continent. His lyrics blare from roadside transistors and the collapsing dashboards of taxis all over Africa: "Teacher don't teach me no nonsense . . ." or one song that goes, roughly: Democracy is a farce in Africa; why doesn't the White Man denounce this masquerade?

Africans know what is wrong. A Tanzanian named Agnes, who entered first grade the year the Union Jack was hauled down, just shook her head when I asked how realities matched her expectations. Like most Tanzanians, she found it hard to criticize Mwalimu, the Teacher: Julius K. Nyerere. But her country is so poor it bought no bullets to shoot stray dogs during a rabies epidemic. A laborer's monthly wage is the price of a can of spray deodorant imported from Kenya. Civil servants grow their own food or starve. Grain rots in the fields for lack of gas to take it to market. For all the rhetoric of socialist brotherhood, corruption is rampant. Something, Agnes knows, is clearly wrong.

Every country lacks people trained to make modern societies work. I arrived in Bamako, Mali, in 110-degree heat and found my hotel air conditioner spewing hot air. Eventually, I found a maintenance man. He went out on the balcony and gave the machine a mighty uppercut with the palm of his hand. A gigantic brown cloud plumed from the filter. "It was blocked," he announced, leaving without a second look. I thought of that often in the following days, as aid workers proudly showed me their new motor pumps, designed to make the desert bloom.

Philip Jacobson, of the London *Times*, saw the other side, in an amused dispatch on trying to cover the war in Chad. He described his exasperation at the disorder and heat, at people stopping to pray when serious business needed doing. "Why do you get so worked up about things that you can't change?" he quoted his driver as asking, with genuine concern. "I thought about telling him of one's duty to bring readers of the *Times* all the news that's fit to print," he wrote. "On reflection, I realized this would certainly have brought on another of those rich bellows of Chadian laughter."

For far too many outsiders, this condition is simple proof that Africans are "backward." The judgment is hardly new.

Europeans once dismissed the whole expanse as the Dark Continent, an epithet that said more about Europe than Africa. The connotation of inferiority was a slur. But dark as mysterious was well chosen, and we outsiders forget that at our peril. And Africa's.

For a long time, thinking was shaped by such men as Albert Schweitzer, who told visitors to his hospital in the Gabon bush: "I feel for them like a brother, but like an older brother. The Negro is a child in a primitive culture, and nothing can be done with children without authority."

But another foreigner, the English aviatrix Beryl Markham, who was growing up then in the Kenyan bush, saw it differently in her book, *West with the Night*:

The soul is not dead, but silent, the wisdom not lacking, but of such simplicity as to be counted non-existent in the tinker's mind of modern civilization. What upstart race, sprung from some recent, callow century to arm itself with steel and boastfulness, can match in purity the blood of a single Masai Murani whose heritage may have stemmed not far from Eden? It is not the weed that is corrupt; roots of the weed sucked life from the genesis of earth and hold the essence of it still.

In weighing Schweitzer's Africa against Markham's, I come back to my friend James Wilde, a reporter in Africa since colonial days, and his boat trip on the Congo River. He was just below Kisangani, at the bend in the river, when the steamer suddenly shuddered to a halt. The captain had seen the Spirit of the River rising from the current. Everyone else saw her, too; they rushed to the rail and gasped at the same shimmering figure in the water. "Only I couldn't see her," said James, who is convinced she was there. Or maybe not. But so what?

The depths of Africa, Markham wrote, and Wilde knew, "devolve not from edict, nor from rote, but from the preservation of kinship with elemental forces and purposes of life whose understanding is not farther beyond the mind of a Native shepherd than beyond the cultured fumblings of a mortar-board intelligence."

In short, how can you tinker with what you cannot even see?

"*D*evelopment" is increasingly complex in a computerized, high-tech world. But Africans know there is reason to keep the faith. "Every time I come back, I see a continent bustling with life, searching for itself but turned upside down," my friend Djibril Diallo told me. "People are looking for themselves, knowing they will get somewhere. But first, there is a period of searching."

Diallo is a U.N. press officer, from whom one might expect such talk. But he speaks from the heart. He was born in the Casamance region of southern Senegal in 1953 to seminomadic herders. "A car would pass maybe once in two weeks," he recalls. "We would hear it from a distance and run and run and then wave. Parents would put their babies' feet on the tire marks so they, too, would go fast." His goal was to teach school.

At sixteen, he earned a scholarship to the School for International Training, in Brattleboro, Vermont, but his mother made him turn it down. "I hated her then, but she was right; she knew if I went then, I would never come back. 'Take their knowledge,' she told me, 'but be yourself.' " He worked his way through the University of Senegal and got a job teaching French in Nottingham, England. Then he earned a Ph.D. in linguistics from London University and studied at the Sorbonne. He is elegant in twelve languages, has a brown belt in judo, and plays a mean steel drum.

Once, after a ceremonial dinner, the lord mayor of London offered him the signed menu as a souvenir. He was told: "Give this to your mother for her mantel." He replied: "We don't have a mantel. We live in a mud hut in Senegal." Several guests coughed into their whisky. "Well, then, let her read it; she will be proud." Diallo answered, "But she cannot read."

Djibril Diallo loves the story. He has made the bridge. He earns a fat salary in New York, which he shares with the village that helped educate him. He moves smoothly among heads of state. And then, barefoot, he hobnobs with cows. "This could only happen in Africa," he says. "I am a first-generation literate. And I am a living embodiment of the fact that you don't need generations."

You cannot tell Diallo that the continent's best hope is to go back to the bush. He will tell you about his circumcision at the age of seven, a ceremony that lasted days. He fainted from pain. "I could not cry," he remembers. "If I had, I would have brought shame on my family for generations." He is the last of his brothers whose nobility is marked by facial scars—brutally carved and purposely infected by tribal medicine men—and he is glad the custom is dying.

For Diallo, the drought was an electric jolt that awakened Africa. "Otherwise, we never would have questioned our received ideas. You can't sit in a cabinet meeting and give orders downward. You have to go to the farmers, find out what they want. African leaders are realizing now that nobody can come and give them development. It is not something that comes from the outside. African governments know that they will not stay in power if large numbers of people are starving."

The question is whether that is enough. "When you tie a bird to a palm tree, it will fly only as far as the rope, and then it stops," Diallo says. "Africa is in a situation of eternal beginning. We must cut that rope."

Diallo pokes holes in the basic assumptions. African climates are brutally hot and dry. Like Las Vegas, Nevada? African cities must feed themselves with resources grown within national boundaries. Like Tokyo?

In the end, he is optimistic: "No continent that has gone through what Africa has gone through need prove itself further. It is a question of morale. In Central America, I have seen situations without hope. In Africa, I have never seen hopelessness."

Fantu Cheru grew up with shepherds on the other side of the continent. Like Diallo in Senegal, he worked his way out of the Ethiopian highlands to Addis Ababa and then the United States. Now, with a doctorate and a growing reputation, he teaches developmental economics at American University, in Washington, D.C. His optimism is more tempered.

Too many well-intentioned people, he fears, are meddling in Africa without knowing what they are doing. "Before we think about educating the general public, we have to educate our allies," he said. I asked how many U.S. senators and congressmen knew enough about Africa to legislate effectively. He shrugged. "Maybe three or four."

Mainly, Cheru maintains, outsiders speak to the wrong Africans, or to none at all. "There is a silent revolution in Africa, a mass defection of peasants who are dropping out of the system," he said. "They are holding states as hostages by depriving governments of resources. All the talk of new government attitudes is because of this." The wrong sort of aid simply helps leaders hold out. Western governments, Cheru insists, are "sanctioning some of the worst gangsters of the century, one-man rule, kleptocracy and military dictatorship."

Africans will take care of themselves if they can get their leaders to listen to them, he said. Governments must apply their own resources to agriculture and the forgotten peasantry—or collapse. "I would make a case for no aid at all," he concluded.

The psychology of aid is tricky. Most African societies live by the season. Whether their god is Allah or Jesus Christ or a flat rock, He will provide. If outsiders choose to provide in His stead, their gifts are seen as so much manna. But such giving simply perpetuates a mentality that has kept Africa, like Diallo's bird, tied to a tree.

If aid does not support Africans' own efforts to produce, it can reduce proud people to beggars. A colleague once asked Kenyan academic Ali Mazrui what he thought of Bob Geldof's dramatic Live Aid gesture. In his deep gravelly voice, Mazrui recited Kipling:

> Take up the White Man's burden—
> Send forth the best ye breed—,
> Go bind your sons to exile

> To serve your captives' need;
> To wait in heavy harness
> On fluttered folk and wild—
> Your new-caught, sullen peoples,
> Half devil and half child.

At the same time, such talk discourages the help Africa needs. In 1985, for example, the American Women's Club of Vienna earmarked $500 for African relief. But reports of corruption and inefficiency were unsettling. Debate raged for hours: Would the money get to where it was supposed to go? How would the women know who was helped? In the end, they bought playground equipment for handicapped Austrian children. At the same time, the women of Fodiobougou village in Mali were building a dam to catch runoff water and improve their rice crop. Men hauled rocks by bicycle and cart to mix with hardened mud chipped from termite hills. The only outside help was some rusty bailing wire from French missionaries. Five hundred dollars would buy a lot of wire.

But the real concern is over the big money. Too often, Western donors prepare their gifts with little reference to the recipients. This worries Diallo. Africans, he has noted, take on the image of bystanders in a mess of their own making. Worse, he wrote recently, "This will result in a new round of policies out of harmony with primary African needs, and are likely, once again, to fail."

The Africans in charge, however, are not necessarily the sort of people Diallo is talking about. Heads of state, juntas, and cabinet ministers often know less about starving peasants than do the outside experts. Often interests conflict. When governments must decide between subsidizing food prices for a restive urban population or helping out the farmers, the choice is simple: rural people do not riot.

Alverson's soundings in rural Botswana ring true throughout Africa. Villagers told him they thought people in town were corrupt. "They don't obey traditional law; neither do they accept European law," one old farmer said. "They just become wild animals, people caught between two laws." Besides jealousy and superstition, Alverson found, rural peoples' main worry is finding a reliable water supply.

In Botswana, the watchword is *pula*. The word means rain. It is also the national currency, and a greeting among friends. With *pula*, a Tswana can fend for himself. Without it, his cattle and crops die. He can sell a cow. But that is a sign of failure, of being overwhelmed by circumstance, like cashing in the AT&T stock to pay the mortgage. One man told Alverson about his greatest satisfaction: "It is in having complete control over our lives and possessions. Whatever we have or don't have, we have decided how to live and work. This is our great cultural treasure."

That reflects a dignity and self-possession fundamental to much of Africa. Goran Hyden, now at Dartmouth University, argues that only in Africa have peasants escaped "capture" by other classes. By controlling their means of production, they are independent. When rains fail, or locusts attack, they starve. But in normal times, they are free. For many African peasants, development projects have been an arm of governments to subdue them. "Development" has undermined the diversity they need to survive and has made their skills obsolete.

It matters little to most Africans whether scarce development funds are plundered by their own governments or squandered by donors' poor planning. Now, as Fantu Cheru notes, they are going their own way. Rural peasants join with the urban poor in parallel economies which escape government control. In Nigeria and Zaire, among others, the black market economy rivals the official one. In Zambia, official manipulation, internal and external, brought on what it sought to avert: bloody food riots.

African leaders blame international economics, Cheru says, but poor countries elsewhere do far better. They demand drastic redistribution of global resources but do not share wealth within their own national systems. At the same time, African leaders who struggle hard toward reform, risking their own mandates, find Western donors welshing on the promised economic support they need to succeed.

Wole Soyinka put it all into context years ago, in *The Man Died*: "It is better to believe in people than in nations."

No African leader wants to lose control of aid. Aid is power, and power is survival. That is African tradition. Basil Davidson found an aged scholar in Bobo Dioulasso to explain why this is so: "Everybody who attained to distinction spared no effort at extinguishing the flame of his rival. . . . Everyone was in contradiction with the others . . . [while] many a year would drag on fruitlessly because of the numerous quarrels and wars among them."

Newcomers to Africa altered the balances. Slavers bought prisoners from local chieftains in exchange for the weapons used to capture yet more prisoners. Colonial officials brought different sorts of wherewithal to a new elite. Schweitzer saw this worsening sixty-five years ago. He wrote: "According to an inevitable development, tribal chiefs, thanks to the arms and money provided them by world trade, have completely subjugated their people, who have become slaves working for the enrichment of the small minority that controls exports."

Since the wave of independence, not a single group in power in any country has stepped aside for an elected opponent. Military juntas have restored civilian rule. But in almost every case, officers stepped back in again.

In his Nobel speech, Soyinka denounced the Organization of African Unity as a private club set up by leaders for their mutual protection. A few months later, the newest member made that same point. Yoweri Museveni, leader of a popular uprising that brought at least a pause to the butchery in Uganda, electrified his colleagues. Where were they when 750,000 Ugandans were being massacred by Idi Amin Dada and Milton Obote? he demanded. As a result, Museveni thundered on, what moral ground did they then have for denouncing the crimes of South Africa? He got polite applause and no apologies.

Neither recolonizing Africa, nor turning back clocks, offers any glimmer of a solution. Morality and feasibility aside, Diallo is right:

Africans know Africa better. And they are in charge. Donors at least might insure that their contributions are well spent. But even that is not so simple. However much Western and international officials might wish to save lives, aid is essentially political. Except for the marginal amounts given by individuals, money flows through channels. If its purpose is to help a nation develop, it is also to win influence for the donor, or conversion to the donors' philosophy or votes for the donating agency's director general.

The nuances of "bilateral aid" are so numerous that any Western official can defend himself with a clear conscience. But the pattern is indisputable: Recipients set the conditions; donors can object, or withdraw aid, but only with political consequences. The more clever African governments play one donor against the others. In this way, aid often amounts to indirect budgetary support for bad management. In such circumstances, increasing aid risks perpetuating the catastrophe in greater proportions.

"Multilateral aid" might be an obvious way out. The biggest money comes from the World Bank, the International Monetary Fund, and other development agencies. Since their management is mixed, they can avoid some of the politics of bilateral aid. But they are hamstrung by their own ideologies. From the beginning, development bankers pushed a basic policy of trickle-down economics. Wealth created by entrepreneurs and state enterprises was to filter downward to the poor. By Africa's peculiar gravity, however, wealth trickles up, not down.

That leaves the United Nations. The U.N. was designed to provide a corps of selfless, stateless civil servants, organized into such specialties as food and agriculture, health, education, children's needs, population matters, environmental protection.

But the U.N. has 159 mothers-in-law, member states of every political and economic persuasion. Any government can expel a U.N. agency from its territory and roast the director at the Secretariat. Some U.N. officials work hard and well within the system; more relax in the warm still waters and avoid, at all costs, making waves. The result is a tangle of egos grappling for power under the same blue banner. Duplication and waste are enormous.

After the world took notice of Ethiopia in 1984, U.N. Secretary-General Xavier Perez de Cuellar set up a U.N. Office for Emergency Operations in Africa. To head it, he chose F. Bradford Morse, administrator of the U.N. Development Fund. Morse, a former U.S. senator with the manner of a friendly rhinoceros, trampled the underbrush. He took on as hit man a Canadian named Maurice Strong, who had made himself a fortune by hard work and good sense.

The OEOA broke patterns, raising extra billions from Western governments and collaring recalcitrant international organizations. Field offices in Ethiopia and the Sudan broke logjams and cracked the whip. If the Food and Agriculture Organization did not get seed to Chad fast enough, the OEOA swept in. If World Health Organization specialists allowed local officials to disguise cholera, the OEOA blew the whistle. Djibril Diallo, the spokesman, made sure reporters did not forget Africa.

Despite some drawbacks, the OEOA produced results and cornered other agencies' glory. Consequently, it was disbanded.

Afterward, the FAO released a study on African agriculture. It was an impressive work, two years in the making. But it identified problems agronomists had been worrying over for decades. I asked the FAO director general, Edouard Saouma, why donors had taken so little action in the past. Because they do not work in concert, he replied. He said lack of donor coordination was crippling Africa.

Perhaps, I suggested, there might be a coordinating committee. Something on the order of the OEOA, maybe. His mouth tightened. The OEOA dealt with an emergency, and that was over, he said. The FAO was concerned with development. But what was the difference in Africa? I pressed. Maybe not the OEOA; but couldn't there be one steering committee to provide the coordination he suggested? Saouma's Levantine charm disappeared. He stared at me a moment and said: "You are obviously a friend of Maurice Strong's and there is no point in talking further."

In fact, few U.N., multilateral, bilateral, or aid agencies are prepared to align themselves in concert. Nor are they ready to twist arms in Africa.

In 1986, I questioned a U.S. official about a World Bank cattle project—its third in Botswana—that environmentalists feared would devastate yet more rangeland and kill off wildlife in large numbers. If U.S. legislation forbid American aid to damage anyone's environment, I asked, why was the project approved? He said the facts were not clear. "Look," he finally said, "in the end it is Botswana's decision. If they choose to increase their cattle, it is up to them."

But should it be entirely up to recipient governments? Botswana is a good example. Its leaders are elected freely and, essentially, are honorable men. But most of them are ranchers. As elsewhere in Africa, Botswanans do their banking with cows, not savings accounts. A man's value is determined by counting his herd. Few herders slaughter their cattle; they eat grain and wild game. Wildlife, like land, is regarded as an infinite resource available to all. The government knows its fragile land is overgrazed. Farmland is shrinking, and game is harder to find. But who is prepared to relieve the situation by diminishing his herds? Instead, new wells are dug in marginal land, empty but for the last Bushmen and wild herds of game. Cordon fences, used to control cattle movement, cut across game routes. Tsetse flies are poisoned, and new range is opened.

The economics are suspect. Profits from cattle exports go largely to wealthy ranchers, who, by coincidence, often are also government officials. Foreign exchange is pumped into the economy. But the government spends as much on veterinary services, cordon fences, and marketing as it takes in by taxing the livestock industry.

The World Bank had tried two successive livestock programs in Botswana. An internal assessment, noting that abuses had ruined good land, recommended the bank drop cattle projects. Instead, a third one was approved. And in 1986, as the new project was getting underway, President Quett Masire appealed urgently for international aid: five years of drought had killed off crops and livestock, forcing the country to import 90 percent of its grain.

Botswana is an example of only one facet of the African crisis. But it is a dramatic one. Natural constraints limit the productivity of its vast semiarid rangelands. When man surpasses the limits, nature strikes back. But Africans and outsiders together are hammering loose vital links in the ecological chains.

We are only now realizing the irreversible change already brought about and the prospect of deprivation and suffering we are creating for countless people for generations to come. Indicator species warn that we are now on a calamitous course. For one, the Botswana wildebeest.

The wildebeest is a slightly crazed-looking antelope resembling an American buffalo with skinny withers. It shares the Kalahari with the Bushmen. And it is also sharing the Bushmen's fate.

Wildebeest means "crazy animal" in Afrikaans, and one look explains why. It has a long, mournful face ending in a scraggly goatee and the curved horns of a bison. Its head droops on a thick neck, but its barrel chest narrows to meager hindquarters. When it runs, its feet fly off in bizarre directions, like a sunfishing rodeo bronc. It is, by another name, a gnu. The word is from Bushman; it was once *nqu*, which is the sound it makes.

"Mad Mike" Hoare, the mercenary, brightened in a recent conversation when I confessed a soft spot for the wretched wildebeest. "That's where I started out, guiding people to the Kalahari," Hoare said, "and I would see millions of them, maybe 4 million, migrating north for water. It would take two weeks for them all to pass by."

Hoare's numbers were a wild guess, but there were a lot of wildebeest thirty years ago. In 1979, the Kalahari population was estimated at 260,000. By then, however, the annual trek north for water was a desperate pilgrimage. The Botswana government had built long cattle fences across their migration routes. The antelope that did not die tangled in the wire had to find a way around.

In 1983, driven by a fierce drought, the wildebeest streamed north in huge numbers, running for days on end across the sand. As always, they headed for Lake Xau, a wide depression that held water late into the dry season. They reached the fence and turned east, pulled along by the scent of water on the wind. They reached the lake and found it dry. It had been emptied to wash diamonds.

Engineers from the De Beers mine, owned by South African interests and the Botswana government, had diverted the water to

Mopipi Reservoir, deeper and narrower, farther to the west. Doug was waiting there to count the wildebeest.

The few animals with enough strength pushed onward, grotesquely emaciated and crazed with thirst. But Mopipi was surrounded by cattle. Herders drove back the wildebeest with dogs and sticks. Village children fell on the staggering antelope, laughing, bashing their heads in with rocks. Some wildebeest finally reached seepage pools near the reservoir. But the water, thick with salt, only swelled their tongues and fired their thirst.

Months later, Doug and I saw the remains of at least 52,000 wildebeest. They died scattered over the plain, starved and exhausted. Government officers had burned some of their corpses; the ashes were raked neatly into piles. They might have been wood charcoal but for the fragile skulls that emerged intact from cremation. In 1984, only a thousand wildebeest reached Lake Xau.

It is painful to watch part of Africa die. It is more painful still to consider why it is happening. Were the fences necessary at all? If the ranchers insisted on more cattle, why weren't the fences designed to allow wildlife migration? Was it necessary to empty Lake Xau?

In the end, the water diverted to Mopipi Reservoir was not enough anyway. By 1985, engineers had to pump underground water to wash the diamonds.

From the air, the diminishing herds of wildebeest on the African plain look exactly like one might imagine the last of America's buffalo stampeding off to the edge of extinction. The buffalo, at least, gave way to the world's most productive agricultural system. Behind the disappearing wildebeest, there is desolate, barren sand.

2 THE KALAHARI
Obsolete Animals, Obsolete People

*T*he wildebeest were late. It was well past two hours after sunrise, and they had yet to appear on the Xorodomo Pan. For as long as anyone can remember, the wildebeest had migrated north whenever the moisture content of the southern grasses dropped too low. For weeks on end, their routine up north did not vary. By night, they drank east of the Xorodomo; as the burning southern spring sun rose, they headed for shade in the woodlands to the west.

Doug was in his usual spot on the western edge of the Xorodomo, a vast flat depression—a pan, in Botswana—which they had to cross to get from water to shade. Every other morning for three seasons, they had reached the pan by sunrise. He wondered what the hell was going on.

The open stretch, Doug knew, could be a death trap. Hunters in jeeps sometimes raced across the hard smooth surface pumping rifle fire into the herds. The pan was five miles by three; jeeps could return again and again before the panic-stricken survivors staggered to safety in the trees and sand. The raids left the pan dotted with pathetic animals, wounded and abandoned by heedless hunters.

Once, Doug and his wife, Jane, had driven between their camp at Deception Pan and Orapa on a track that drops down from a high ridge over the Xorodomo. As always when they passed, they stopped to watch the wildebeest. That morning, Jane had her own vehicle, and she had gone on ahead. Doug found her standing on the truck, squinting into binoculars and smiling. They were there in force, she said. It was peaceful and beautiful. Doug went to his truck for glasses and returned to find tears streaming down her cheeks.

"They're killing them again," she said. He jumped up next to her and focused on the pan. Three jeeps crisscrossed through the herd, cutting out groups of wildebeest and circling around them at speed. The animals huddled in helpless confusion. It was happening three or four miles away, too far for Doug and Jane to hear the shots.

Doug raced off in his jeep to try to stop them. It took time to cover the rough terrain, and the hunters were gone by the time he reached the Xorodomo. They must have seen his dust plume and thought he was a ranger. All he could do was end the misery of a wildebeest with a leg half blown off.

It was because of hunters that wildebeest drank at night and hurried for cover by sunrise. And, Doug presumed, it was because of hunters that they were late this time.

The sun inched higher, and Doug stewed over another possibility. That morning he had seen a single wildebeest moving slowly across the pan. Doug had camped among mopane trees to the south. Up early, he packed as the tea boiled; by dawn, he was on the Xorodomo. There was just enough light to make out the lone animal heading west toward shade. After a hundred yards, it tottered and collapsed, a flailing heap in the dust. After a minute of desperate thrashing, it got to its feet. Fifty yards later, it stumbled and fell.

After the wildebeest collapsed a fourth time, Doug could stand it no longer. He got his rifle from the truck and waited a few minutes more. The animal could only sit up and look around in terror. He approached to within fifty yards, sat down, braced the rifle between his knees and fired. Up close, he found the animal was an old female, her incisors worn almost to the gums. Grotesquely emaciated, she was starving to death.

Months earlier, Doug had predicted a massive die-off, but was still hoping he was wrong. It was a bad year for Botswana; drought threatened wildlife, livestock, and humans alike. And it was especially bad for the wildebeest.

The migrating herds always drank from Lake Xau, west of the Xorodomo. This year, however, Debswana, the mining company, had diverted the remaining flow of the Boteti River into Mopipi Reservoir. As a result, Lake Xau was dry. The wildebeest had to cover ten more miles between shade and water.

Doug brooded over this that morning, sitting by his camera. Three hours past sunrise there were still no wildebeest.

For a while, he wondered whether the herds had gone down to drink at all. Maybe he was wrong about their migration. In three years of research for the Frankfurt Zoological Society, he had determined that the wildebeest made the grueling trek to Lake Xau only because they had no other source of water. If that was not their reason, he would have to find out what was.

And then several thousand familiar dark specks moved onto the pan. His relief did not last long. Their shuffling, stumbling pace was a sickening contrast to the exuberant craziness that gave the wildebeest their name. They took more than an hour to cover a distance they normally trot in twenty-five minutes. It was not hunters this time; in their condition, they were not worth hunting.

Doug was saddened but hardly surprised. A few weeks earlier, the wildebeest had passed his camp at Deception Pan on their way north. It was a tranquil Sunday afternoon, but he did not hear them coming. Hundreds of animals drifted up soundlessly, the vanguard of many thousands to follow. Then an orphaned calf let out a loud moaning wail. Its mournful and forlorn bellow was as foreboding a sound as Doug had ever heard. The calf seemed to know that, like him, the Kalahari wildebeest was doomed.

The calf was right. That was 1983, perhaps the last great migration. No rain would fall for at least six more weeks, and each day conditions got worse. Withering heat baked the dry ground. Many thousands of cattle had stripped the range bare, leaving a pathetic patchwork of yellow stubble. Their hooves churned the fine clay into dust, which the wind swirled into suffocating clouds. Wildebeest too weak to move huddled together, cringing from herders who chased them with sticks and rocks. Government veterinarians had said wildebeest would infect domestic herds, and cattle owners were taking no chances.

The reservoir's fringe was a macabre battlefield; vultures, marabou storks, and stray dogs picked among thousands of corpses. People made weird statues by propping up dried carcasses and skulls with branches. In the evenings, when a blood-red sun gave the dust a fiery glow, it was like a circle of Dante's hell.

When humans are dying in Africa, one does not reflect too long on animals' hell. Nature, however, does not fix moral priorities on life forms. Affection for wildebeest is not the issue. What kills one species may kill the rest. The victim is the land itself and, therefore, the entire ecological network.

That year, dust storms from Mopipi carried to the camp, seventy miles away. Visibility was so poor Doug often had to abort aerial surveys. Once, a strange billowing plume rose 1,000 feet and spread for miles. It blocked out the sun for forty-five minutes. Exposing huge areas of land to sun and wind at their most fragile time of the year cannot help but have dramatic long-term consequences. It was likely that the productivity of great sweeps of land had been crippled forever. No one knows for sure.

In Botswana, as in the Sahel, the Horn, and much of the rest of Africa, there is endless talk about "desertification." It is one of those United Nations words with too many syllables for television news. Most people do better with the old favorites like *war, famine, cholera.* Like "development," it is a vague term used by a new industry of scientists, international bureaucrats, and a few journalists who don't like gunfire.

Desertification, or desertization, means the turning to wasteland of ground that could grow food or support animals. It is hard to measure on a grand scale. But up close, there is no missing it.

The Kalahari, seen from the air, is patterned with giant concentric circles of varying shades of brown, like a mysterious target range for some celestial lunatic. Each set of circles spreads out from a borehole where cattle drink and then fan out to graze. Toward the outer reaches, some grasses still grow. The center is powdery dust. Since cattle can walk ten miles between water and food, each borehole can destroy a circle totaling 300 square miles.

Elsewhere in Africa, the picture is similar but the patterns vary. Sometimes, rather than targets, they are great broad avenues, or wavy lines. It depends on how herders move their animals, and where vegetation started.

Statistics mislead when they begin, "The desert advances at 150 miles a year. . . ." The mind's eye pictures a steady roll of dunes moving southward, or northward, shifting inexorably toward the great rivers and the tropical belt beyond. One assumes a vast belt of trees would stop it, if only someone would come up with the cash. Or one accepts the immovable will of nature.

In fact, desert forms in great mottled patches in the midst of good land. When trees are cut, the topsoil is exposed to wind and runoff water. When cattle eat away the last grasses, their hooves chop up the roots. If rains are good, and the land is protected, the desert recedes. If not, dunes settle over land that has sustained life for millennia.

Drought has plagued Botswana for most of a decade, speeding along degradation. But there have always been drought cycles. The problem is that nature can no longer take care of itself, and fragile rangeland has been pushed past its limits.

The natural pattern in Botswana was a masterwork. Wildlife thrived in huge numbers in a self-correcting balance. Elephants crashed open thickly forested areas for others to follow. Zebra and varieties of antelope grazed the same grasses at different levels. Kudu and other species browsed the bushes, and giraffe ate high above the rest. Lions kept herds on the move.

Botswanan herders raised cattle, but numbers were kept in balance by limited water and grazing, disease and predators.

Climate and terrain determined mass movements in ways humans did not understand. Doug's job was to learn more about where and why animals moved. Unlike those on the Serengeti Plain, in Tanzania, the Kalahari wildebeest, he found, do not migrate north each year. They leave only when, after a series of dry years, moisture in their grazing falls below a critical level. In the past, they headed not only for Lake Xau, but also for the Limpopo River, to the southeast, and the Orange River, farther south. He wondered why they kept going back to southern Botswana—until he had a closer look. The harsh dry pans were pocked with thousands of pits dug by scraping hooves; the wildebeest had to return for minerals they found nowhere else.

By the time he collected data on the wildebeest migration, however, it was too late. Their route to the Limpopo and the Orange was sealed off by veterinary cordon fences, railroad lines, ranch fencing, and international boundaries. The old trails to the north were blocked by cattle ranches and the long Kuki veterinary fence.

Politics and economics had overridden nature. For centuries in Botswana, a man's wealth was determined by how many cows he had. He seldom ate them or sold them; they were simply the visible tally of his net worth. After independence, however, the ruling elite realized cattle were the key to prosperity. They negotiated to sell a quota of 19,000 tons of beef a year to the European Economic Community at artificially high prices.

At the end of 1986, the EEC had 750,000 tons of surplus beef rotting in storage. That was a full year's sales, representing subsidies of more than $2 billion. Community members, arguing bitterly among themselves, agreed to cut price supports to their own ranchers. They sold beef to the Soviet Union at a third of what they paid to buy it from Botswana. And they paid hard cash to send beef from Europe to Angola, Botswana's northern neighbor. For Botswana, the quota was foreign aid, and it was gratefully received.

But European markets imposed rigid rules against foot-and-mouth disease. Fences were erected to control the movement of cattle across a country that was mostly one giant range. Money was poured into veterinary services. Government officials, the major cattle owners, drilled new boreholes and put in more roads so they could run their cattle into marginal areas.

One fence in Botswana is as crucial to preserving wildlife as it is to protecting cattle. The "buffalo fence" runs straight as a spear shaft below the Okavango, a mirage-come-true across 10,000 square miles to the north of the Kalahari. It is a luxuriant network of simmering channels, reedbeds, and hippo pools, home to 350 species of birds. Tourists fly into remote camps to watch fish eagles plunge from trees and crocodiles slither off the banks.

The Botswana government, with help from European donors, is eradicating the tsetse fly in the Okavango. One of Africa's last great unspoiled ecosystems would be rendered safe for cattle. Each year, millions of dollars are spent contracting air crews to spray poison over the huge swamp.

The government decided it was cheaper to eradicate tsetse at their source rather than spray each year to stop their spread. On paper, no cattle were to be run into the Okavango delta. But no one was fooled. Pressure was so great for more rangeland that no democratically elected government could keep out ranchers. Especially when ranchers were government officials.

Authorities have operated on the principle that damage was not occurring unless it was proven. A few independent studies revealed a serious hazard for fish. Scientists fear that many other adverse effects could be occurring undetected because there is little surveillance. I put the question to Lukas Brader, a Dutch specialist who is the FAO's pesticides expert. "I don't like eradication," he said. "When you remove one thing, something else takes its place." But the issue was essentially ignored.

No one could quantify potential damage to the delta or, for that matter, overall damage to Botswana's rangeland. Thousands of gallons of insecticide were dumped into the swamp with no comprehensive impact study. Elsewhere, fragile land was given over to cattle with no clear idea of what that meant for the future.

But it does not take a scientist to see the danger in stark clarity. Cattle graze right up to the sturdy buffalo fence along the southern edge of the delta. On the north, where there is only wildlife, the bush is thick and rich, with tall grasses right up to the wire. On the south, starting at the foot of the fence, there is desolate moonscape. If the fence goes, conservationists fear, much of the delta is imperiled.

In Botswana, it is the rich, more than the poor, who threaten the environment. And they receive most of the aid.

Beginning in the 1970s, the World Bank lent more than $10 million for two successive projects to raise yet more cattle in western Botswana. At the Bank's request, the International Livestock Center for Africa surveyed the projects and declared them both failures. However good the planning, experts said, abuses and mismanagement had badly degraded the land. Wildlife suffered badly from the ranches, which showed no economic benefit.

Borrowers were supposed to put their cattle on new ranches, taking pressure off communal lands. Instead, nearly all of them kept their herds on common range. When grazing was depleted, they took their cattle onto their new ranches, leaving communal herds on barren ground. Despite record EEC payments, many borrowers did not pay back their loans. Instead, they put profits into new boreholes, threatening more land while the World Bank offered additional credit.

The ILCA report suggested that the World Bank get out of the cattle business in Botswana. Thus advised, the Bank went right ahead with a $17-million loan for a third livestock project.

In 1986, as the World Bank was moving into this new project, President Quett Masire asked for urgent food-aid relief. After five years of drought, Botswana had to import 90 percent of the grain needed to feed its one million people. Much of the land, depleted and used for ranching, not farming, was losing its productivity. The country had cattle, of course. But beef is not food. It is power, status, and personal wealth.

Botswana had bought most of the extra food it needed in the past, even when strapped for cash. By 1986, the government had enough reserves to cover two years of imports; the country was relatively wealthy. But food aid was free. As elsewhere in Africa, it was accepted gratefully as an indirect budgetary subsidy.

Beef sales abroad bring the economy $100 million a year in foreign-exchange earnings, but the profits go mainly to a few wealthy ranchers. A single South African, with vast holdings in Botswana, has exported up to a third of the quota. Much of the rest of the beef is sold by a small group of Botswanans, mostly senior government officials. Meanwhile, the state pays tens of millions of dollars for subsidies and services to the cattle industry.

The greater cost is the disappearance of wildlife that could generate substantial income in tourism, safari hunting, and game ranching. It is depriving Botswana of resources, forms of life found nowhere else.

There is talk of saving the endangered wildlife, but little is being done. Rangers are few, and often without gas if they have vehicles. Ordinary Tswanas would just as soon have wild herds around, but not if diseased buffalo or lions threaten their cattle. Conservation is a new issue, in any case. Wildlife has always been there. Tourism revenue makes little difference to the Tswanas; they never see it.

Authorities hardly seem concerned enough to measure the rate of loss, or the extent of damage to the land. In their thinking, often encouraged by foreign donors, the wildebeest and zebra are obsolete animals. They are in the way.

The same thinking applies to an obsolete people, among the last few hunter-gatherers left in Africa. Like the wildebeest and the zebra, whose fate they appear to share, the Bushmen are in the way.

Potty Thomson first introduced Doug to N!akadio. Potty is a Northern Transvaal farmer who loves to cruise the bush in his ancient Land-Rover. Nax was his Bushman guide. Doug and Jane had just taken over the camp at Deception Pan vacated by Mark and Delia Owens, Americans who had established it. It was hours away from anywhere in the Central Kalahari. Potty drove up to drop off a fruit cake. And Nax.

Doug needed a hired hand, as Potty had suggested. Nax was an exasperating worker; he tried hard but could never remember to do the few routine jobs around camp. And Doug was never happier with an employee or associate.

With Nax, you never knew what to expect. Almost immediately after he settled into camp, he mentioned that something seemed familiar about it. Several times he disappeared on foot into the dunes, offering no clue about what he was thinking. One day he came back volatile with enthusiasm. Into the jeep, he said. He had a surprise.

Nax directed Doug over the trackless dunes without a moment's pause for reflection. For miles, they jolted over sand and scattered woodlands. His parents brought him to the area to hunt, he remembered, and he was going to show Doug their favorite campsite. Suddenly they rolled into a clearing, and he leaped out of the jeep. He showed Doug fragments of a clay pot for which they had bartered a steenbok skin. Nearby were traces of a collapsed shelter.

Then Nax grabbed Doug's elbow and led him into the woods. The family had raided a bee's nest for honey, and he wanted to find the tree. There, he pointed. Doug studied the tree he indicated. The hole had shrunk with age, but the axe marks were still visible. Neither Nax nor his family had been to the campsite in forty years.

"I was born before Hitler's war," Nax said once, when asked his age. Birth certificates are not a cornerstone of Bushman society. He and Doug spoke in Fanagalo, the much-despised pidgin Bantu he had learned as a miner in Johannesburg. Nax also spoke dialects of San, of course, the complex Bushman language enriched by clicks, pops, and grimaces, in which he delivered hysterical stand-up comedy routines. Doug laughed hard at each monologue, and he does not speak San.

Bushmen are more properly known as San, an ethnic grouping that comprises different groups of Bushmen. In common usage, the terms are interchangeable.

Nax had had no trouble working in the coal mines of Zimbabwe, then Rhodesia, or mining for gold on the Witwatersrand. Not overwhelmed, he delivered hilarious mime impressions of the conditions he had found and the people he met. Each time he decided he had enough money, he made his way back to his village, Giom, and then walked to Ghanzi to buy horses. The distance was 150 miles across the remotest part of the Kalahari, with no surface water en route.

Like most Bushmen, Nax could converse about nature for hours without speaking a word.

Once, a pair of sand grouse flew up from a clump of grass. Nax asked Doug if he knew how they brought water to their young. Doug knew but said he did not. Nax explained that adult sand grouse dip their chests in water and fly to the nest. Chicks drink from the wet feathers. Doug had read about this; Nax knew it because his life depended on what he could observe of nature.

Doug found his zoology doctorate to be an academic trifle compared to what Nax had learned the hard way. To hunt with little poison arrows, San must sneak up to within twenty yards of animals which survive by stealth. One of Doug's projects was to study gemsbok, a large handsome antelope that lived in impossible surroundings. For Nax, tracking gemsbok was no problem at all.

Watch, he said once, when they were hidden 400 yards from a gemsbok cow. He made a weird little sound, mimicking a gemsbok calf's distress call. The animal's ears pricked up. Nax repeated the call until she was thirty yards away. He also showed how the gemsbok survived the long Kalahari dry season, by digging up roots, bulbs, corms, and rhizomes. Eland waited until the gemsbok found the buried caches and did the hard digging. Then they chased off the gemsbok. The San did the same thing, but they also hunted the eland.

Doug had had trouble tranquilizing gemsbok in order to fit them with radio collars. Sometimes he would lose a darted animal before the drug took effect. Nax had no such difficulty. He would simply shoot the dart and wait. He could track the spoor, following individual hoofprints through a jumble of others. He never lost an animal.

He knew the natural order of things. It did not pay to be careless among lions, he knew, but he harbored no king-of-beasts illusions. Lions feared the gemsbok's rapier horns and attacked them only when driven by their stomachs. He doubled over with laughter recounting how lazy lions can be. When they gorge themselves with meat, he howled, they piss all over themselves rather than take the trouble to stand up.

There seemed to be nothing for which Nax had no use. If a plant could not be eaten or squeezed for water, it cured ills, poisoned quarry, or provided needle or thread. One plant produced soap. Once, Doug was sure he had him. The Sesamothamnus lugardii is the Polish joke of the vegetable kingdom. It stands ten feet tall and has a bulbous stem, a repulsive blistered skin, and a sparse array of viciously thorned thin branches. All right, Doug asked him, what about this one? Nax was stumped for a moment, and Doug started to grin. Too early. Nax brightened and said: "Oh, yes. We cut sticks from it to hit our donkeys."

The essence of San life was that they used everything they came across. More, they needed nothing they could not find. Laurens van der Post wrote of the Bushman in 1958 in *Lost World of the Kalahari*: "He appeared to belong to my native land as no other human being has ever belonged. Wherever we went he contained, and was contained, deeply within the symmetry of the land. His spirit was naturally symmetrical because moving in the stream of the instinctive certainty of belonging he remained within his fateful proportions."

More than anything else, Nax showed how much this had changed. Perhaps 60,000 San are left: 30,000 in Botswana, 26,000 in Namibia, and 4,000 in Angola. A few are scattered in Zambia and northern South Africa. Of these, only a few thousand are hunter-gatherers in the old sense. And their use of resource is changing fast. Those who hunt with bows and arrows seldom make their quivers out of split reeds. They prefer polyvinyl chloride plastic.

I met Nax at Deception Pan; he was the first Bushman I got to know. Doug was showing me the Kalahari. As we headed toward his little plane, Nax appeared.

Sometimes Nax preferred to work barefoot in a steenbok loincloth. Not this time. He wore a Cincinnati Reds jersey, a black tuxedo jacket, clapped-out Adidas running shoes, and the sort of sunglasses favored by aging Italian movie queens.

I saw immediately what Doug had meant about Nax's ability to track. In the air, Doug found his gyrocompass of limited use above the featureless expanse of the Kalahari. He did better with Nax, as gyro-Bushie. His vision was microscopic, and his sense of direction was absolutely unerring, even from a position that was totally new to him.

As we flew, Nax pointed to an empty patch of ground and folded his fingers into a sharp-faced head with two curved horn: kudu. I strained my eyes until I spotted them. Moments later, his fist changed shape, and his wrist dipped and swayed like a long neck: ostrich.

Many San, like Nax, have shown they can bridge the gap between their ancient culture and modern life, other factors being equal. An airplane or an elevator is simply another new phenomenon to be absorbed and put to good use. Its inner workings do not matter. It exists and, unless the gods were crazy, it was created for a reason.

But other factors are not equal. For a series of reasons, many beyond their control, the San are withering away in the same harsh terrain where they have thrived for tens of thousands of years.

In Botswana and Namibia, the San are victims of severe ethnic prejudice. They are yellowish and small; often, black tribesmen treat them like dirt.

An anthropologist friend once took Doug to visit a charming Herero woman who lives near the Namibia border. She hires San to tend her cattle and speaks their language. They brought some San friends along, and she greeted them cordially. The moment they left, she warned: "You know, you can never trust a Bushman."

Once, Doug flew to Maun, in northern Botswana, with a friend of Nax's. At the airport, a uniformed Tswana guard grabbed the Bushman by the cheek and dragged him over to a group of men nearby. The guard was furious when Doug intervened. All he wanted to do, he said, was show his pals what a Bushman looked like.

Later, Doug took Nax and his friend to fetch water from the borehole at Xobe. The place, normally flyblown and somnolent, throbbed with activity. A team of government technicians was installing a dip at the cattle post. They were an impressive bunch, working briskly in smart blue coveralls. Doug stopped to watch. A tall, handsome Tswana broke away and walked to his truck. He thrust his head in Nax's window, slowly looked them over, and scowled. "What are these bloody fucking Bushmen doing in your car? They should be sitting on the back like dogs."

The San react with deep mistrust of other Africans. Nax, for example, was convinced that Tswana witch doctors murdered his people to cut them up into biltong, strips of jerked beef. He said San biltong was believed to be a potent charm for assuring the fertility of cattle and land. Once when he approached a cattle stockade, Nax announced in matter-of-fact fashion, "This is where the bad guy lives." Doug asked for an explanation, and Nax sailed off in a passionate tirade. The man in question had killed a woman he knew and made her into biltong. There was no way to check out his assertion. But he believed it.

Once, Doug came back to Deception Pan earlier than expected, after two weeks' absence. It was a wild, stormy evening. He dumped his gear and made a fire. While he pottered about the kitchen, he crumbled some biscuits for the tame Marico flycatchers that hung around for food. After a few minutes, a soft voice from behind startled him. It was Nax. He had been in his tent and did not hear Doug's vehicle. But when the wind dropped, he sneaked over to investigate the activity in the camp.

"I thought it was the bad guys come to make me into biltong, so I came very quietly," he said, with a little chuckle. "I found it was just you talking to the birds."

Contempt for Bushmen is a main reason they are disappearing as a people. Another reason is greed. Officially, San are equal to all other citizens. The Central Kalahari Reserve was marked out to protect hunter-gatherers and wildlife, but the expanse of land is tempting. There is money to be made in the short term, and obsolete life forms are being shoved aside.

The San are put to work tending the cattle that ranchers are pushing farther and farther onto the land set aside to preserve their way of life. They live in squalid little hovels and depend upon supplies that arrive, from time to time, by truck. A pittance of a salary buys beer, tobacco, and the honey they once got only by outsmarting bees. The old stories are told less often, more briefly, and with flagging relish. Each time an old man dies, a vast library of bushcraft and folklore goes with him.

Some Bushmen fall victim to their own skills. They are prized as trackers, and their value increases as hunters find big game growing scarce. "I've seen Bushmen trackers pick up a two-day-old lion spoor and then follow it, jogging all day at twelve miles an hour," a veteran white hunter told me. "They are amazing." But, removed from their own societies and not accepted in any other, some drift away into drink and depression.

A few, like Nax, retain enough of the old ways. Watching him, Doug and I each realized there was something missing in our own lives. He enjoyed what came from outside the Kalahari, but he did not need it. When there was sugar, he wolfed it down and then did not worry about it until more appeared. When he wanted something, he worked. But at any time, at no one's whim or order but his own, he could set out alone and on foot across some of the least hospitable land in the world. He could go for hours, or years. It was up to him.

In prehistoric times, evidence suggests, San lived across all of eastern Africa, possibly as far north as Egypt. By the time the Dutch landed at the Cape, they were confined to southern Africa. Perhaps 100,000 were exterminated or dispossessed in South Africa. By 1927, it was illegal to carry a Bushman bow; vagrancy was a crime. Deprived of the means to live, San could easily be recruited as cheap labor. In 1941, Denys Reitz, then South Africa's minister for native affairs, appealed on behalf of twenty-one Bushmen evicted from a national park for hunting game: "It would be a biological crime if we allowed such a peculiar race to die out, because it is a race which looks more like a baboon than a baboon itself does. . . . We look upon them as part of the fauna of the country."

Attitudes have softened, but not a great deal. In 1978, the Johannesburg *Star* began a review of a book on the Bushmen: "Southern Africa's Superdwarf is on its way out: within two decades the Bushman hunter will join all our other relics of the past."

South African authorities whittled away at the San's remaining lands in Namibia. About 2,000 live in squalor at the settlement of Tshumkwe, dependent on army rations and the salaries of Bushmen trackers in the South African Defense Forces. A liquor store opened at Tshumkwe, adding virulent alcoholism to the Bushmen's problems.

American scientists John Marshall and Olga Levinson fought hard against a South African plan to make a game reserve out of eastern Bushman land, where 2,200 Ju/Wasi San live a life balanced between hunting and farming. They wrote: "The death blow of a nature reserve is not a figure of speech. It is not a metaphor for social disintegration and collapsing values. Dispossession threatens their livelihood and therefore their lives."

Conditions are hardly better in Botswana. In 1961, 3,000 people lived on the Central Kalahari Reserve. By 1984, the number had declined to about a thousand. Some live scattered in tiny settlements, where, according to a district officer who inspected the area, they are harassed and sometimes beaten by wildlife personnel. But 80 percent of the Central Kalahari San are clustered in the ramshackle town of Xade.

At Xade, the San have a school, a clinic, and food aid. Like other civilized peoples, they are learning to consume more and more to meet their needs. Teenagers who could not track an eland through soft sand are comfortably at home with mail-order catalogues from Johannesburg.

When Doug and I visited Xade, the women were doing a fertility dance. There was a bizarre mix of bare breasts and fake Parisian lingerie, bare feet and satin high heels. A young man in a buttonless leisure suit and a dirty orange polo shirt pestered us unmercifully for a handout. Beyond him, men sat in the shade drinking, quarreling, gossiping, and telling each other how they will soon go back and be Bushmen.

With striking parallels, the same processes endanger nomadic peoples all over Africa. The rate and extent of loss vary widely, but the reasons are the same. In almost every case, it is man's tampering with nature that dooms them. The land and animals that supported them are disappearing. Boundaries prevent them from moving on. In the end, their choices are narrowed to one: to squat at the side of a road and wait for food relief trucks.

I expressed this view to a U.S. aid official in Mali, a man who knew and loved Africa, and he shrugged. "That is how life works. What are you going to do, cry for the boys?" He may be right. But the American Indians' self-reliance has long since fallen away. New ways have penetrated every other continent. Those who get a vicarious feeling of freedom from people who can live without can openers had better feel it fast.

In Xade, a young Tswana schoolteacher told me: "They are losing their customs, their pride, and their whole way of life. In another ten years, most of it will be gone." She admired the San, and the prospect saddened her. She knew what a loss their passing would mean for Botswana and the larger world.

It takes little reflection to realize the potential loss to the world. If governments could focus on what the San know, rather than on what they do not, ways could be found to learn from them. San could find a socio-economic balance in the world they understand better than anyone. They could harvest wild herds and valuable skins in a balance with nature. They could teach desert lore and lead outsiders on wilderness trails.

But that seems less likely by the year. In the Botswana capital, Gaborone, Doug heard a decent and well-meaning civil servant express an opinion that is far more widely held: "It is time these people stopped running around after wild animals and started keeping cattle."

3 THE SAHEL
Twilight of Timbuktu

*W*hen the current fails at the Djinguerebe Mosque, Imam Ahmadou crawls up inside the crumbling mud minaret and calls Timbuktu to prayer the old way. For a few years in post-independence Mali, his voice was carried by loudspeaker. Now he does a lot of climbing. Electricity is only one casualty of decay and doom in the mystical city that Mali still calls "the Pearl of the Desert." Pearls were always a dubious reference, but the desert part is more evident by the week.

Up north, the Sahel is different desert. The name means "shore" in Arabic; it is the southern rim of the Sahara, stretching from Mauritania to Chad. Hardly anyone penetrated the Kalahari, but the Sahel is crosshatched by ancient trails. Caravan traffic was heavy in gold and salt, slaves and scholars. Timbuktu was a lush and thriving hub. Back in 1327, when the mosque was first built, hippos sometimes knocked over the faithful who paddled up in pirogues. By the time French explorer René Caillié arrived, five centuries later, the Niger River angled southward, and many of its branches and marshes had dried. Timbuktu's port was Kabara, six miles to the south.

Caillié had expected the luxuriant growth described in old Arabic chronicles. In his book, *Voyage à Tombouctou*, he writes:

I had formed a totally different picture of the grandeur and richness of this city: it offers only, at first sight, a mass of earth houses, badly built; in all directions, one sees only immense plains of moving sands, in white tending to yellow, amid the greatest of aridity. The sky at the horizon is a pale red; all is sad in nature, and great silence reigns. There is not a single bird's song. Still, there is a certain powerful feeling in seeing such a large city rising in the midst of sand, and one must admire the efforts of its founders.

The desert was already lapping the edges of Timbuktu, but it was moving slowly. In the 1950s, when Mayor Abbas Kader was young, a thick stand of trees grew between Timbuktu and Kabara. Scattered acacias and shrubs held back the dunes in the north, and wells watered the gardens and shade trees in the courtyards of the rich.

Today, Timbuktu disappears from view in a stiff breeze. Sand swirls into the most intimate folds and crevices. Outsiders suffer most: sand irritates their infidel eyes and grinds up their camera mechanisms. Townsfolk and Tuaregs alike simply twist their turbans tighter and wait for Allah to call a break. But, as the desert advances, the breaks are fewer and farther between.

Kabara is a port marooned by sand. Hulks of old boats sit stranded, awaiting a river that rarely rises. The Niger is not what it used to be. There is an airport, but it is used mostly by aid workers in small charters. Air Mali—Air Maybe—had its last disaster at Timbuktu. An overloaded Soviet-built Antonov took off in February 1986 and lost an engine. All but one of the fifty-two people on board died in the crash. Three months later, the airline was dissolved. By then, drifting sand had covered all signs of the wreckage.

Mayor Abbas Kader is resigned and slightly bitter. "Maybe if the winds shift and start blowing the sand north," he told me, "Europeans will do something."

But Abbas Kader is not expecting much, and neither is anyone else who knows the desert. A U.S. Agency for International Development official put it simply: "Man ain't going to do shit if nature decides to do something else. He has nothing to do with it."

But if man cannot reverse the damage, he can make it worse. The same processes that damage the southern deserts are pushing nature to vast devastation in the north. The effect, bad enough on the land, is changing forever the lives of the people.

As societies go, it is hard to find two more different than the San and the Tuareg. When outsiders probed their desert redoubts, the Bushmen slipped farther inside, like the antelope they hunted. They took to cattle as a last resort, staying put and tending someone else's herds. The Tuaregs swept down on intruders, flailing swords astride galloping camels. They respected their harsh surroundings but did not worship them; Allah and His Prophet had commanded otherwise. Tall and fiercely proud, the Tuaregs built an elaborate culture around sparse possessions: swords and teapots, leather tack, robes and headgear, silver and stone jewelry, and, above all, cattle.

Early travelers called them the Blue Men of the Desert. Their light-brown, sharp Semitic features were tinged with indigo, from their elaborate turbans and billowing robes.

"The men are born to walk as kings," British anthropologist F. R. Rodd wrote early this century. "They stride along swiftly and easily, like princes of the earth, fearing no man, cringing before none and consciously superior to our people."

The Tuaregs left food production to lower forms; Bushmen-style gathering was plainly undignified. In basic ways, however, the Tuaregs' way was always like the Bushmen's. Now, their fate is the same.

"Before, we were masters of the wind," one Tuareg told a reporter at the end of 1986. "Now, we are slaves to it."

*L*ike the Bushmen, the northern nomads picked up nature's rhythm and moved with it. When the range was rich, they took their herds north to the solitude and beauty of stark desert. When grasses died, they moved south.

Cultivators moved as far north as they dared. If they put too much strain on fragile land, the nomads ran them off. Everyone watched the skies and prayed. When crops failed, the desert provided a little emergency food. During the worst droughts, people migrated or died.

That changed over the past century. France and Britain subdued holdout chieftains in bloody, grueling campaigns. They took over the nomads' monopoly on violence and set a new balance. But nomads still traded animals for grain and kept their traditional serfs, blacker tribes from the south. Colonial governments assured them a basic standard of living. Herders moved freely from Mauritania to the Sudan border, all French territory. They had only to stay clear of army recruiters, forced-labor contractors, and taxmen.

Drought and plagues were part of the deal. Locusts caused a vicious famine in 1931, but the French governor in Niger refused to suffer the embarrassment of declaring an emergency. The nomads took it as yet another test by Allah, and they faced it as usual. They dug up mounds and wrestled termites for bits of grain. Women scoured the desert for "drought food," bitter pods and tough grasses they normally shunned. And the weak died in tragic numbers.

In each cycle, new rains brought back food crops. The range grew rich again. When cattle and goats died, or moved south, land restored itself.

At independence, the cycles faltered. Borders were etched sharply across the desert. New armies needed volunteers, and governments needed money. While nomads were shunning the colonizers, southern tribes were learning their ways. Now, equipped with power, former slaves were out to settle scores. In Mali, the Tuaregs fought a brief war of secession, fueling the fears and hatreds. Each nation's development plan contained a generous portion devoted to "civilizing" the nomads. It was unnatural not to depend on the ruling party.

Today, the old rhythm is broken. Timbuktu is only one of a string of cities across the Sahel that draw desperate nomads out of the desert. At the west, a few miles from the Atlantic coast, Nouakchott, Mauritania, has grown in a decade from a settlement of 25,000 to a giant rag-tent slum of 600,000 once nomadic Maures.

At Timbuktu, Tuaregs camp on the surrounding dunes and squat in the courtyards of crumbling mud buildings. Agadez, an ancient crossroads in Niger, and El Geneina, in Sudan, just past the Chad border, each burst with retired nomads. Omdurman, on the Nile opposite Khartoum, is a vast sprawl of refugees from the desert.

Niamey, the capital of Niger, was, for the Tuaregs, a Sodom or a Gomorrah where river people and, worse, farmers mingled with the pillaging French. Now, Tuaregs squat in desolate clusters by Niamey's concrete shopfronts, making tea on the dusty sidewalks and waiting for manna.

At 11:00 A.M. one morning, I stuck my head into a Tuareg tent, invited, and woke up a sixteen-year-old named Mohammed. He had nothing better to do than talk to me. He looked smart in his only shirt, a gift from an American he once knew. His French was good after a primary education, but he had given up hope of finding work. So had his father. The family had left the desert in 1974 and camped in someone's courtyard in Niamey. They are still there. Eleven children and Mohammed's parents live in a tiny rag tent. They have had no income for two years and cannot pay the children's school fees. A Tuareg neighbor, who makes a few bucks a week as a night watchman, helps out with food. The family eats once every other day.

When I left, Mohammed looked sad. "You do not need a watchman?" he asked. "A driver? A gardener?"

Like the Bushmen, many Tuaregs in wretched little bands cling to the edge of the desert that sustained them for thousands of years. In 1986, when I went back to Mopti to look for Abdel Rahman Diku I found Mohammed ag Hamed. He had lost three daughters and all of his animals. At thirty-seven, all he had left was a little girl named Fatima and an air of stubborn dignity. He lived with his wife, an older sister and her daughter. He had no more answers than Diku had had. "Of course, we miss the desert," he said. "And so?" There was no work, and no food. He earned a few pennies selling key rings his sister made from colored plastic strips. I bought one and motioned to his sister to keep the change. She held out her hand for more. Her daughter, about eighteen and beautiful, gently took her mother's hand and folded it back into her lap. With a slight smile of embarrassment, she apologized silently for the begging.

Elsewhere in the camp, desperation had overcome dignity. Swarms of youths found an answer to the question of what to do. "Money, money," demanded a boy of about eleven, locating my hidden wallet with astonishing accuracy. He jabbed at the billfold through my vest: "Give me money. Give me money."

A little girl followed me, pointing to a festering sore on her lip. I paused to look, but a tide of others raced up with their own urgent needs. I was causing a stir, and the cops would show up soon. I strode toward the jeep, and the girl started to cry. She followed, pushing herself in front of me. My frantic U.N. friend motioned me to hustle; the girl wailed in pain. I did what most outsiders have done about African suffering for as long as there have been Africans and outsiders. Nothing. It made me sick to my stomach, and it did her no good at all.

*F*rom the beginning, outsiders have tried to help and, as often as not, ended up making things worse. Mali is a dramatic example. French engineers fantasized about the broad river coursing through the desert. Emile Gautier, a geography professor, wrote of the Niger bend in 1928: "It is truly a second Nile, lacking only management to cause it to fertilize a second Egypt. There is not another spot in the whole Sahara where such financial possibilities are indicated."

Such optimism produced the Office du Niger, a gigantic scheme to irrigate cotton and food plantations. Few people lived near the river, but that did not stop the French. Forced labor built dams and canals. Crops fell far below expectations, and costs were exorbitant. Farmers and laborers were recruited from productive regions farther south. Families, whole societies, were disrupted. By 1961, the project was producing only 1,000 tons of the originally projected target of 300,000 tons. The main result was vast expanses of damaged land.

At independence, President Modibo Keita had no means to develop the Office du Niger. Nor could he abandon it, one of his few potential resources. His socialist order decreed that farmers should try to make it work, and he had hopes for settling nomads among them.

Afloat on their camels, the Tuaregs tried to ignore the modern state. They preferred old Maria Theresa coins and silver bracelets to wads of devaluing francs. When farmers pushed at their fringes, they moved north. But the drought of 1973 and 1974 was too severe. Without water, the nomads' animals died. Then they began to die as well. An international relief effort saved lives, but it was late and chaotic.

Some spirits were broken. One herder told Patrick Marnham in 1973: "If the president orders us home, we will go; if he orders us to stay, we still stay. It is his right. Since we gave up our forefathers' traditions and came here, we now depend on him and will obey him."

Others refused to cede. Ten years of intermittent drought later, a clan chieftain swept his arm north and told me: "Our land is our mother. Would you give up your mother?"

The Great Drought pricked consciences. At its peak, the American ambassador to Upper Volta was filmed pitching grain sacks out of the back of a C-130 transport aircraft. A hue arose, repeated almost every year since, in every part of Africa: We must switch from relief to development. And the outside world set out to save the Sahel.

Sunburned white men crisscrossed the desert in Cessnas and Land-Rovers, each clutching a water bottle and a clipboard. Everyone had an idea and money to spend.

Where engineers found grass but no water, they sunk a borehole. Soon the Sahel was scarred by devastated circles around abandoned boreholes, just like the Kalahari. Tractors were flown in to open new land; instead, they tore up the fragile surface that farmers had protected with their short-bladed hoes. Winds carried off topsoil, leaving behind more desert. Irrigation schemes brought motor pumps to remote villages. But no one thought of spare parts, maintenance, fuel, or marketing. Farmers, encouraged to stay on land that could not feed them, cut down too many trees to cook what food they had.

Experts decided the Sahel needed more trees. The World Bank and other organizations spent up to $6,000 an acre to grow village wood lots of exotic species that sucked down water levels, if they grew at all. Mostly, goats ate the seedlings. The idea caused much mirth at night when the outsiders' jeeps were gone. White men and sleek government officials were telling villagers to pour good water into the ground, on scarce land, for some vague benefit ten years in the future. Foreigners who stayed to listen learned the equivalent in Bambara, Tamachek, Fulani, and Hausa of: "Gimme a break."

Foreign experts told Africans not to cut trees. Hearing that, I could imagine a Fulani in flowing robes at the pumps along the Santa Monica Freeway haranguing motorists: "Don't pour that liquid into your metal box on wheels. Its supply is limited." I have yet to meet an African peasant who does not know dwindling wood is a problem. But what can he do—besides eat raw grain?

And rural families, in need of some cash for cooking oil, sugar, and taxes, have few sources of income beyond selling firewood and charcoal.

For a while the answer was "appropriate technology." Peace Corps compounds were littered with cut-up oil drums, mud hives, and Rube Goldberg solar panels to ease the Africans' lot. Most worked. But a young Tuareg spends months learning to tie his turban according to his clan's tradition. It takes more than a flying demonstration visit to convince him to make gas out of fermented cow dung. A smoky cook fire, where stories are told and bad spirits are banished, is a rural African's family room, kitchen, backyard and, often, bedroom. Few prefer kerosene even when they can find it or afford it.

The big money went to elaborate projects. From the start, foreign aid had its specific purposes. The Soviet Union, looking for allies, gave Mali what it wanted most: military hardware, a football stadium, and a monument. The French, seeking to retain influence, gave money. But the Americans, looking for friends, tried to develop the economy. A decade after independence, the Russians were on the wane, and Mali was fertile ground for Western aid.

Development strategists decided Malians needed more buying power to improve their lives and to give them some alternatives to plundering their environment. Big farms were the answer: irrigation, roads, fertilizer, salaries. If anyone remembered the Office du Niger, he neglected to mention it.

The pattern was repeated across the Sahel. For every yard of new irrigation canal opened, an old one fell into disuse through neglect. Falling water levels left shining new pumps marooned in the mud. Grasslands were plowed once and then assaulted by erosion. By the time the next Great Drought struck, in the mid-1980s, more land than ever was lost to good intentions.

Three problems arose repeatedly. First, donors assumed—or pretended—that African leaders knew their priorities and were concerned with the most needy peasants. Western auditors were satisfied when convinced that aid money was not stolen. That it was thrown away on useless fantasies was someone else's concern.

Another problem was that aid did not cross borders. It was obvious enough that no Sahel economy could develop alone. Each market was too small for local industry. Roads to the coast were largely deep troughs of sand. Beef producers could not export without help; coastal states preferred to buy meat from Europe. But little was spent to develop regional structures. Aid did not work that way.

Third, governments tried to control everything: prices, land distribution, people's movements. The lower economies sunk, the greater the controls. Farmers worked out their own balance. When official prices were low, they sold to black marketeers or smugglers. If it cost too much to plant, they fed only their families. And when their land died for lack of fertilizer, they moved on. Some went to the cities, where they needed grain and firewood, like everyone else. And so on, in a downward spiral.

The nomads eluded government controls but not the damage created. As per-capita food production dropped, donors pressed Sahel countries to grow more food. But there was no money for fertilizer or pesticides. Instead of improving yields, farmers opened more land. They pressed north into marginal rangeland, destroying it. Police discouraged nomads from stealing crops, let alone killing the encroachers.

Increasingly desperate, nomads topped off young trees to feed their animals. As the range dwindled, more livestock concentrated in thinner pastures. Nomads might have survived in the old way, but the rains did not come back. There were sporadic respites until 1983, and then almost no rain fell at all.

As nomads clung to the land, businessmen and wealthy officials came from the city to buy their herds. Men whose families had owned cattle for centuries worked for others at a serf's wage. When no rain fell in 1984, most nomads were beaten.

In the Aïr Mountains of northwestern Niger, in an area twice the size of Switzerland, the World Wildlife Fund is helping the government run what amounts to a game reserve for Tuaregs. "Our first idea was to save the animals, but then we realized we could not do that without saving the people," said John Newby, the Englishman who runs it. A few hundred Tuaregs run their cattle on the protected land, but scouts make sure no one cuts trees or tills fragile land. Several species of antelopes and small predators thrive along with the nomads, Newby says.

He sees the desert people changing. "The Tuareg prime minister of Niger will tell you that their old ways of life are finished," he said. "Look around."

Neither Newby nor anyone else who knows the nomads expects their culture to die out entirely. When new grass grows, herders put together a few animals and go out again. But every African nomadic society has been altered drastically. As with the Bushmen, life will no longer be the same.

At the western edge of the African bulge, Mauritania is disappearing in the sands. Serge Robert, a French anthropologist who spent a quarter-century there, said in 1984: "I used to make it to Tichit from the highway in three hours on a good hard track. Now it can take a day and a half of slogging through sand. In a decade, I have seen a 120-mile band of rich pastureland disappear forever."

And, he said, the Maure nomads are going, too. "The whole system has collapsed and has been replaced with nothing except flocking to cities and looking for help from families or food aid. They won't go back, even if the rains return. Many say they will, but once they move in from the desert, they stay. The old way of life is over. *C'est fini.*"

Abdullah Ould El Bah, a son of the desert turned history professor, nodded assent as Robert spoke. "The old way, the noble self-sufficient nomad with his animals and his freedom . . . that is a memory," he told me. "It is gone."

An American diplomat added later, "The nomads' virtues are turning against them, and those who can save themselves are doing it. Inhibitions which kept people from gross corruption and selfishness are falling away."

That was true enough, starting with the president. A Mauritanian source told me that President Mohamed Khouna Haidalla, since overthrown, was feeding U.S. aid flour to his camels. I asked the man how I could confirm it. Simple, he said, go kick open a camel turd. Before I got around to it, I met one of the truckers who was hired to hijack food aid for officials.

In the mid-1980s, U.S. auditors found evidence that some authorities had used aid funds to build their own houses. The cabinet, outraged, condemned such outside interference in Mauritanian affairs. The Americans were quietly shifted out of the country.

For other nomadic peoples, the problems are similar and sometimes worse. The Toubous of Chad, caught up in a lingering war as well as persistent drought, are changing as fast as the Tuaregs and the Maures. The Fulanis, who stretch from Senegal to Nigeria, are also roaming less, filtering into the cities as their herds dwindle.

Djibril Diallo, whose father was a nomadic herder, sees the small signs. "Once I found a whole cluster of women running toward my jeep tapping their heads; the heat was so intense it made their heads ache. One told me, 'Out here, we have only the trees to talk to, and they are dead.' The whole nomadic way of life is under threat. A lot of governments are putting nomads together, trying to make them sedentary. I see it when I go home; it is really sad. There is a great movement to get the nomads to settle down."

For many Africans, this is not such bad news. Nomadic tribes have often been difficult neighbors. Descendents of people whom they enslaved and terrorized scarcely mask their pleasure at exacting revenge. "We say the only time a Tamachek (Tuareg) bends down is to pick up his shoes," observed a young Bambara in Mali, who works for the state radio advising peasants on how to better their lives. "Now," he added, with a mild smirk of satisfaction, "they are bending over to cultivate."

Besides, uncontrolled bands of independent-minded people are little comfort to insecure states. In Mopti, Ibrahim Sylla, chief aide to the regional governor, told me he was happy that many Tuaregs were settling down. "We tend toward sedentarization," he said. "It has a lot of advantages. You know where people are and what they are doing."

Nomads will not disappear, he said. "Not all of them come to town, you know. A lot of them stay out with their herds, totally untamed." I pressed him on the subject, and he flared up.

"World opinion is more concerned with nomads than anyone else. That is very serious discrimination. We have a dozen different types of societies in Mali. Each time a foreign mission comes, each time journalists come, it is always the nomads. Like we are practicing some form of genocide. There are also the small farmers in the same ecologies. We have a plague of grasshoppers that are eating crops, not livestock. The farmers suffer, not the nomads."

Then I found Noumou Diakite, head of the Mopti Region's Livestock Development Office and a French-trained doctor of veterinary science. He made sense when I saw him in 1984, and I went back to see him.

Nomadic herders were one of Mali's few resources, he explained. Rather than try to make them farmers, he said, they should be helped to raise cattle. Left alone, they took care of rangeland. It was the farmers who put too much pressure on the land.

Diakite's approach is simple and sensible. Farmers should be concentrated along the Niger and Bani rivers, where irrigation multiplies yields. Nomads can be steered by regulating water points. When grass is too dry and fragile, nearby boreholes are turned off. The herds have to move. Markets must be set up so herders can sell cattle quickly when drought threatens. With the cash, they can feed their families and buy new animals later.

With fewer farmers, and with nomads moving with natural cycles, Diakite is convinced the desert will take care of itself. Donors can use the money they waste on exotic trees to help Mali protect the regeneration of acacias and other native species.

Authorities in Mali must work with counterparts in Mauritania,

Niger, and Burkina Faso, he said, since cattle move freely across borders.

"It is simply a question of organization, of political economics," Diakite said. "Look around the world. The people who have made it are those who are organized. Those who are not organized do not survive."

He snorted at the idea of making farmers out of nomads. "We have a saying: 'If you throw a tree trunk into the water, it will not become a crocodile. But it can scare the hell out of fearful animals on the bank.' "

*D*rought is cyclical in Africa; it is never "over." In the two years since I found Abdul Rahman Diku in Mopti, the rains came back and the river rose. Mopti, like the rest of Mali, grew more food in 1985 than it does in normal years. But the dry season again brought its usual crop of refugees. And the river dropped again.

Africa works that way. There are short rains and long rains. Farmers plant if they have seed and harvest what they can. Those not desperate for cash put something aside in straw-roofed mud granaries. A normal Sahel crop produces food until spring, the end of the dry season. Then there is the *soudure*, French for solder, the lean period until harvest in the fall. That is when they ration out what the insects and rats have left in the granaries.

When people run short of food, they buy it. If they can't afford it, they pray for help from CARE or Save the Children Fund or any of scores of agencies who dispense American and European food aid. If that fails, they starve. And then, if nature remains on track, there is a new harvest and grain to sell. The trick is all in the timing.

What happened in Mali was typical. Donors and Malian planners determined the 1985–86 grain deficit would be 104,000 tons. It was pledged and ordered. But food aid moves in mysterious ways. Authorizations go from office to office. Ships must be found. African ports clog. Trucks break down or inexplicably lose their way. Once in the country, it must be shielded from theft and spoilage.

"Frankly, I am completely unable to tell you whether there is enough food or not," the U.N. World Food Program director told me in April 1986, heading into the *soudure*. "Officially, there is a deficit. There is a lot of food in the market, but that may be because people don't have the money to buy it. What is clear is that there are hungry people." A week later, he was throwing up his hands. Another 68,000 tons of food was headed toward Mali, where officials were already having trouble finding money to pay farmers for their projected crop.

The U.N. Children's Fund director was nervous. "With food aid, you have to know your requirements a year in advance to get it on time," he said. "And you can't know a year in advance." UNICEF workers, among others, were still furious over the issue. They had worked hard to convince farmers to plant with the 1985 rains. And then, just at harvest time, American and Saudi volunteer agencies flooded villages with free food, shattering the farmers' market price.

Ibrahim Sylla, the Mopti governor's aide, was also worried. "If food comes in too late, it will depress the market. But if the donors see us stocking food instead of distributing it, they will say it was not emergency relief, and we won't get any the next season."

In such circumstances, it is hard to fix blame. Food aid saves lives. No one can accurately assess needs in countries without roads, let alone telecommunications. The only answer is to grow food where possible and keep emergency stocks on hand to head off serious deficits.

But that leaves poverty. Statisticians add up the tonnage available and divide that by the number of mouths in the country. If it all comes out even, the battle is won. That is like saying there is no hunger in the South Bronx if the neighborhood supermarket shelves are well stocked.

And Africa is notorious for its erratic rainfall. Almost anywhere on the continent, a farmer can stand in his parched fields and watch rain pour down on his neighbor.

Nomads, like farmers, protect themselves by finding a way to put aside some cash. Some families split up; most members settle on a patch of farmland, and a few go north with the animals. Sometimes clans pool their resources to send a son to study in Europe or America. If he lands a decent job, he is a steady source of support.

In Timbuktu, a Tuareg youngster named Alisse hangs out at the Sofitel Hotel hustling the few tourists and aid workers who pass through. At thirteen, he is an institution. I asked him what he wanted to grow up to be. "The minister of finance," he replied. Did he want to go back to the desert on a camel? "Sure," he said. "On vacation."

When I met Alisse, his heyday had passed. In the mid-1980s, he scored big with the tourists who came to Timbuktu, oblivious to the suffering around them. He dressed up in Tuareg finery and served strong, sugared mint tea, three cups at a time, as custom required. Now the Sofitel is empty; its generator coughs to life only when a UNICEF mission or a passing rock star comes to town.

Alisse still had his relief-worker friends, a dozen or so who passed by occasionally for beer when there was any. Sidi, the guide, was out of business. He saw me in the market and immediately sized me up as a lousy customer. He was eleven and in a Michael Jackson T-shirt.

"You want to see the famous house?" he said.

"Whose?"

"If you're French, René Caillié. If you're English, Alexander Gordoon Laing. German? Heinrich Barth. For the Austrians . . ."

He then launched into a blitz history, which I could not stop before the sixteenth century.

On my first trip, a craggy old Tuareg offered to take me by camel across the dunes to visit his camp. I was out at dawn, ready for an exhilarating trot over sands redolent of the old caravans that traded salt for gold when Timbuktu was a thriving hub. He came late and not alone. There was a camel, but also a child to walk ahead and lead it by a rope. Another climbed up behind on my saddle and pestered me without letup to buy his souvenirs.

The camp was authentic, but I should have noticed the carefully arranged artifacts on display. We sat over a small smoking fire in front of an open goat-hide tent. I talked of the desert. My host talked of swords for sale. I spoke of Islamic hospitality. He told me I owed him four dollars for the tea. On the way back, my youthful escort-salesman switched tactics; he shifted to pleading. At the hotel, exasperated, I asked the old Tuareg what had become of the legendary dignity of the Blue Men of the Desert. I regretted the question the moment I asked it. We both knew the answer.

About ninety minutes' jeep ride from Timbuktu is the settlement of Tin Telloutt. In a way, it is hopeful. When I visited in 1984, Tuareg mothers sat starving, surrounded by the inert little shapes of their children. The only well was so low that every few hours a youngster had to be lowered out of sight by rope to haul out mud. The few nearby trees were fast disappearing.

Two years later, the settlement had a gushing borehole, drilled by UNICEF. Families grew vegetables and, in exchange for U.N. food, they carefully tended 1,000 young trees. Mohammed ag Adby, twenty-four, with the angular face that typified the Tuareg warrior, boasted to me about his cauliflower. He was a schoolteacher.

"We did not roam for the sheer pleasure of roaming," he explained. "We had to find pasture for our animals. Now that is impossible, and our animals are dead. We are planting." I looked dubious. He smiled and added: "Cultivation is very decorative. In it, you can find your own survival."

Even if Tin Telloutt bought more cattle and goats, he said, only a few herders would take them. The village would stay and plant.

Two years before, the village chief, Abby ag Hamani, told me he feared the settlement would have to move. Now, he said, it might stay there forever. "The old life is a memory," the chief said. "I would like to live it still: the peace, the solitude. But that is gone."

Villagers were digging a vast hole. It was to be a conical well, like one they saw in Timbuktu, and it would allow them to grow more vegetables. But it was an improbable project. It looked suspiciously like something devised to justify "food for work" rations from UNICEF. By the rules, such aid goes only to malnourished children or adults who need strength to make essential improvements. But Tin Telloutt had figured out the system.

"Look! The same storeroom," said Mohammed Cheikh ag Mohammed, the school principal, unlocking the little green padlock I had seen on my last trip. But instead of a few sacks of World Food

Program grain, there were stacks of cereals, oils, and supplies from a handful of donors. Rain is too scarce and the land is too poor. Except in the best of years, Tin Telloutt and its sedentary Tuaregs live only on artificial life support.

But the government likes places that suggest that nomads can be farmers. To lure nomads toward stability, authorities lend them land farther south. I stopped at a pilot project near San, on the Bani River, a few hours up a paved road from Bamako. Seventeen Tuareg families were camped in half-finished adobe huts. They cleared land for rain-fed farming. A teacher named Inoren ag Mohammed, a Tuareg from a nearby village, spoke for them.

"They are being helped to settle here permanently, to adapt to a level of production that was foreign to them. All of these people were herders, pasturalists. They lived in tents, and now they have constructions in *banco*, a West African adobe. They ate milk and yoghurt. Now they are adopting the diet of regular citizens. The local population came to show them how to do it. It is hard, but they know they must do it."

Has their culture changed? "It is the same, the same songs, the same motifs of art." He admitted some remained attached to the past but added, "People are always nostalgic for the past."

Under a straw tent, women sprawled on mats around a battered brass tea tray. Some wove plastic strips into souvenirs. Others watched a chicken stroll by. I talked to a woman I guessed was sixty-five; she was forty. "In the old days, we lived by a lake and we moved freely. We were much happier, but . . ."

By the river, a young man in filthy gray pants and an old green shirt trudged back and forth with a watering can, hauling up water to spill on his tomatoes. At the well, another former herder put a good face on things. Yes, he said, this was a good life. More stable. Before, his family moved constantly, maybe staying only a night in one spot. He had had a lot of animals, sometimes more, sometimes less. Now things were different. People would develop a new attitude.

But people around him looked dubious. They were in desert turbans and sandals, still clutching their old herding sticks. One was Mohammed ag Jabed, fifteen. I asked what he thought. His lip curled.

Would he go back to the desert if he had a chance? He looked closely to see what fool was posing such a pointless question.

A United Nations expert, an old hand among nomads, pulled me aside and said, "You know what will happen. As soon as they get a little money, they'll buy a few goats, and then cattle. But they won't be able to take them very far. The animals will graze out the land around here, ruining it. Then eventually they will go north."

For me, the question was answered as I walked back to the jeep. I walked through a part of the camp not expecting visitors. An aged couple sat by a straw tent that was not about to be replaced by adobe. The man, on a stool, ignored me and my cameras. He gazed steadily at nothing, slowly working prayer beads through his weathered fingers. The woman squatted in the dirt, hunched forward and watching the ground. She rocked back and forth, as if in mourning.

A USAID friend had warned me not to mix values with facts. But if the values were open to interpretation, the facts were plain. Those old people may never again be herders. But they are not farmers.

The governor's aide in Mopti was right, of course: It is not only the nomads who suffer. In Mali, the Tuaregs and other pure nomads make up 10 percent of the population. They are a like minority in neighboring Niger. But they are linked to the same lifeline as the cultivators and townsfolk: the Niger River.

The natural system is intricate. Rains fall heavily over Guinea's tropical highlands in the spring. Fresh flooding swells the Niger. By fall, as the rains move north, the river broadens in places to a twenty-mile-wide moving lake. It can, at times, carry riverboats from the Malian capital of Bamako, past Djénné, Mopti, and Timbuktu up to Gao. More, it waters a vast inland area, leaving behind naturally irrigated paddies, millet fields, and fish-breeding pools.

From Gao, the Niger snakes south toward Niamey, capital of Niger, and waters the desert down through northern Nigeria. Below Onitsha, it disperses into a wide delta or runs out into the Gulf of Guinea. The Niger's source, at Kissidougou in Guinea, is 200 miles from the coast. Most of its 2,600-mile course meanders through the Sahel. It drains off a basin of 430,000 square miles, nearly twice the size of Texas.

Nature, however, did not count on the chainsaw and bulldozer. Logging and forest-clearing in Guinea have damaged watersheds badly. Water runs off too fast or too slow, carrying with it rich topsoil, which silts up narrow channels. Water finds new courses. With fewer trees, there is less transpiration and, therefore, less rainfall.

Man's efforts to irrigate on a grand scale brought little more food production. Instead, the canals and reservoirs confused the river and threw into havoc traditional water rights and farming systems. They spread waterborne disease. And governments—first colonial, then African—pushed for cotton and other cash crops rather than grain.

The Niger failed to flow in 1973, drying up fields and cutting fishing by half. Tens of thousands of people died of hunger along its banks. It was erratic for a decade. In 1984, the old-timers insisted, the Niger was at its lowest levels in a century. It rose again in 1985, but that brought new problems of flooding. And now, each spring, farmers and nomads alike watch the dusty skies and wait.

After the 1973–74 drought, the *National Geographic* quoted the chief of Sendegue, a river village in Mali: "I pity today's young men to whom a family is one wife and two children." He expected to acquire the four wives allowed by the Koran, and thirty or more children. How do you dare amid such hard times? asked Georg Gerster, the author. "The lean years will soon pass." Gerster found people along the length of the Niger exhibiting the same fatalism toward the river's whims.

After a decade more of lean years, I found the same fatalism. A young father in Mali shrugged and smiled. "There is always famine. But sometimes we have something to eat."

The chief had told Gerster: "Never forget, today we may suffer from the river god's wrath, but tomorrow his mercy will shine again." The fourteenth-century Kingdom of Mali depicted the Niger god as a turbaned figure in a colorful robe, entwined by a serpent representing gold. Placer gold made old Mali fabulously wealthy; salt, brought by caravan to Timbuktu, was worth its exact weight in gold.

Today, Mali's impoverished people are realizing that the river god is no longer a free agent. Nature, Allah, and the gods all must deal with government meddling, individuals' greed, and foreign aid.

Upriver from Timbuktu, the town of Diré is a breeding ground for white elephants. There is, for example, Operation Blé (Wheat). In the first flush of development, USAID airlifted 500 small motor pumps from India. Farmers were loaned money to buy them. Immediately, half the pumps disappeared into private hands. No spares came with the pumps, and the Indian factory went out of the business. Broken pumps were cannibalized. Farmers could not get fuel to run them; when they could, they could not afford it. Often, the river spur was too low, and the pumps sucked only mud. After two years, USAID evaluators declared the project a disaster. They terminated it, leaving the farmers in debt, with useless pumps.

Then USAID contracted a specialist named Linda Smith to dismantle the project equitably. Instead, she found a way to bring it back to life. She organized mechanics to rebuild pumps. She helped farmers set up credit and marketing. Soon, a rice crop flourished along with wheat. Spices, herbs and vegetables brought extra income. When I first visited the project, farmers were hard at work digging a canal in the mud so the falling river could reach their pumps. "She has brought us much," one pump owner told me, when I asked what farmers thought of the only outsider in the project. He did not mean wherewithal.

Farmers prospered under the worst conditions. With his own capital at risk, each man pulled his weight. The self-powered little cooperative promised to flower beyond expectations. That was its downfall.

Since farmers made their own decisions, they cut short the middlemen who once controlled them. Profiteers lost leverage. Authorities sensed a slippage of power. For the first time, farmers complained when outsiders stole their fuel money and credit payments. One traditional chief, with the most to lose, lined up support against the cooperative. Smith, seeking help from sympathetic military commanders and USAID, was caught in the middle. The battle was colorful and swift, an intrigue-laced struggle with *feticheurs* practicing witchcraft and *marabouts* calling on Allah. In the end, Smith was quietly removed from Mali.

USAID called in Africare to close down the project gracefully, once and for all. But Africare, an energetic, often effective Washington-based volunteer agency, was out to help. A fat project report announced Africare would show that the Diré farmers, with access to technical assistance and inputs, "are prepared to produce and consume the food they grow." It would only take seven expatriates and $2.3 million over three years to prove it.

The coordinator's salary was budgeted at $40,070 in the third year, twenty-three times higher than the best-paid Malians in the project. Of the total budgeted, $1.8 million was for salaries, travel, allowances and dependents' education. The $22,700 allotted for computers and electric typewriters was equal to the annual per capita earnings of one hundred Malians. At its most optimistic, the project would involve 840 farmers, at a cost per farmer of nearly $1,000 a year.

Africare's report traced the project's history. "It was discovered," it said, "that farmers had made better use of their pumps than USAID had expected; and they grew rice." Smith was not mentioned. When I went back to Diré, five Africare people had been there six months. Half as many pumps were working as when Smith had left.

The young American manager was not anxious to explain the broader complications, which he seemed to feel, were beyond my ability to understand. It was too early to judge. I asked about Smith. Yes, he had heard of her. But she had not understood Mali. Africare would create the overall conditions for success.

I chatted with the triumphant local chief who seemed to appreciate the spectacle of yet a larger band of perspiring outsiders carting in more wherewithal. The farmers, like me, were waiting to see what would happen next.

Not far from the Diré project, a giant pump sat idle next to 700 dry acres. French government aid brought the pump during the mid-1970s. It was to run on sun. No one had tested it, however, and only when it was installed did experts discover it would not work. Instead, it was converted to diesel. Fuel is trucked up over the desert at outrageous expense. Delivering food would be cheaper, but that is not development.

A third water project might do better. The U.N. Children's Fund brought in a single large motor pump and trained some Malians to run it. UNICEF is neither tinkering with local social structures nor dribbling in resources to be squabbled over. What the farmers need most is water; the pump is supplying it. The rest is up to the farmers—and the profiteers whom they must battle.

Calamity has not spared the Dogon, who are farmers of such skill that they steal topsoil back from the rivers to grow vegetables atop barren rock. Centuries ago, the Dogon moved south across the Niger to flee the nomads. They dug into the jagged sandstone outcroppings of a dramatic cliff face, fifty miles long, and they flourished.

The Dogons' elaborate customs mix daily chores with the worship of water, rock and spirits at large. They pad along their remote paths in richly colored robes and hats like woolen crash helmets. Their roads are often vertical trails no wider than a goat, commanding spectacular views of the plain far below. Women carry fat tomatoes and onions to market in huge yellow gourds balanced on their heads.

Dogons are famed across Africa for their masks and dances, their tightly knit family structures, and, mostly, their wizardry at farming. Granaries like little mud houses keep crops safe for years, cool and free from insects. "They farm dirt," Pierre-Olivier Henri, a Swiss geologist explained to me near Bandiagara. "They collect a two-foot layer, mix it with humus, and close it in with stones. It's extremely productive."

Now the Dogon are leaving their cherished redoubt. First, development brought a road and government agents into their midst. USAID helped on the theory that if Dogons were so good on their own, they would be that much better with the world to help them. But new government regulations complicated their lives. American and European gawpers followed, ferried in by the Malian state tourism agency, known by the ominous initials, SMERT. Heirlooms went up for sale, and young Dogons scrambled for dollars and French francs.

Inevitably, the nomads caught up with the Dogon. Pushed south, Fulani herders are crowding the tightly-knit villagers, camping in their fields and feeding their animals on the dwindling vegetation. Even without intruders, life grew hard: water levels dropped with successive droughts.

It is all too much for the Dogons' social structure. During the 1985 drought, American researcher Sarah Brett-Smith found six to seven fathers a week were committing suicide to escape the shame of letting their families starve. One mother watched her five young sons weaken from hunger and die one by one of measles. Then she killed herself.

Mitch Michaud is worried. He is a Peace Corps volunteer and an authority on the Dogon. "I know families where nine out of ten sons have gone off to the cities to look for work," he said. "They say once a Dogon goes, he does not come back." Michaud is a forester at work on a USAID project. He was not enthusiastic about official efforts to plant trees. Another volunteer put it clearly: "Aid here has been a complete and utter failure. You see the same problems all over the Sahel. For all the money they spent, they could have built a water pipeline from the Amazon."

*F*arther down the river, in Niger, there are other problems. The 1973–74 drought was the final blow to President Hamani Diori, a jovial, polished-ebony father figure who swore no oath of poverty. He took Niger to independence in 1960 and remained close to the French. But army officials charged that his corruption and inefficiency had brought needless suffering during the drought. General Seyni Kountche took over.

Over the next lean decade, Kountche worked hard on agriculture. Niger fed itself in good years. When other states were hungry in early 1984, Niger had an emergency reserve. But, obsessed with security, the government hindered the international agencies that might have helped. Even with surplus grain in some regions, people starved in others. In 1985, Niger was back on the emergency list.

Gerster, arriving not long after the coup d'état, was refused permission to go outside the capital. "The drought is over, so let's not talk about it anymore," an official told him. I went to Niamey a decade later to cover a meeting of eight Sahel presidents, who vowed to fight drought in common. Kountche was eloquent: The dying Sahel faced permanent drought. Only the international community could save it. The world must see firsthand what is happening.

When he sat down, I approached the man who granted travel permits. I said I was there to do just what the president asked. My dispatches would go all around the world. "Call me tomorrow," he said. His tone suggested he did not plan to answer the phone. I hesitated, and he added: "It takes two weeks to get permission." The pass was never granted.

I slipped through the roadblocks, and I learned what I expected. The apparatus is in place to assure that people get enough to eat. But it is so fraught with obstacles and inefficiency that people starve, nonetheless.

*L*andlocked and poor, Niger cannot work out lasting food security on its own. Nor can it solve its other problems. In 1986, I sat next to a senior minister on a long night flight. Guarded at first, he relaxed and let loose.

"Our only hope is to integrate in the region, to work out markets, and more open borders and common industries. But what happens? Niger belongs to twenty-two different regional groups in West Africa alone. Each one has its secretariat and Mercedes-Benz and its political interests. We meet and, after all the blah-blah-blah, nothing happens. It is a waste and a tragedy."

Each government has its narrow interests and fears its neighbors, he said. Few care enough about the future to put these aside. Without regional cooperation, he saw little future for Niger or any Sahel state. And he was not hopeful.

I had just seen why. A U.S.-funded study found that Niger could double grain yields by adding phosphates extracted from its own deposits. That would increase production without moving farther into marginal lands. But the market was too small to justify a phosphate treatment plant. Nigeria had an unlimited market, and a jointly run plant could revolutionize farming on both sides of the border. But Nigeria was not interested.

If the minister was ready for sacrifices, not everyone shared his enthusiasm. At a meeting of Sahel agriculture officials in Niamey, a trip was planned to visit a model project. An argument broke out over who got to ride in the one jeep that was air-conditioned. No one went.

4 SUDAN, ETHIOPIA, SOMALIA
Horn of Penury

*I*f you take enough gas and water, you can drive east from Timbuktu and not run out of catastrophe until you reach the Red Sea. It is not a pleasant trip. In Chad, you must swing south to avoid one of the lingering African wars that is killing as many people as nature is. At the Ethiopian border, Marxist officials will most likely not let you in. And on the way, you will pass through an oasis at dead center of the calamity: El Geneina, Sudan.

In Arabic, *El Geneina* means garden; the name is now a bitter joke. Dry, hot air sucks the life out of almost anything that grows in a garden. Pelting sand grates at the stalks and leaves of plants that sink roots deeply enough to survive. At the height of the 1985 drought, the flyblown little town suffered badly from the cruelties and insanities of well-intentioned food aid.

The details of famine relief in Sudan offer little comfort to optimists in Africa. But they are lessons to be learned well, and remembered.

An alert U.S. official read the signs early in Sudan. Eric Witt, of USAID, saw that the 1984 crop would fail, and he persuaded the mission to demand food from Washington. Other experts disagreed, but Witt's advice prevailed. By the time the need for food was clear, American sorghum was piling up at Port Sudan. Months later, as children died for lack of a mouthful of food, grain was still piled up in Port Sudan.

When I flew to El Geneina, United Nations officials feared that 3 million might starve to death in the Darfur region. Ekber Menemencioglu, a youthful Turk who represented the U.N. high commissioner for refugees, met me at the plane. "How can this happen?" he asked, again and again. "My people are dying, more every day. The crazy thing is that the food we need is here in the country."

We raced across the dunes toward a refugee camp. He feared stalling, because the clutch was slipping, and it was his only jeep. It was one of two that had arrived a few weeks earlier, but someone had rolled the other in the sand. Both were equipped with snow tires, and powerful heaters, for the high Alps.

Ekber was loading refugees into open trucks for a two-day trek over the desert. Some would die of exposure, he knew, but he had no choice. The rains were starting. Riverbeds would run, cutting off El Geneina from the food trucks that should have arrived weeks and months earlier. When that happened, many more would die of starvation. Everyone else wanted rain, to end the drought, but he was praying for enough dry weather to get his refugees to safety.

Ekber's Somali colleague, Mohammed, made up loading lists in a lean-to teeming with desperate people. He was trying to reason with a twenty-five-year-old mother who had gone insane. She insisted on going alone, leaving her young daughter in the camp. No, Mohammed told her, the girl would die if left behind. The woman would not relent. She wailed and ranted, her cries rising above a general din of whimpers and moans. I could not stay to learn the outcome.

The camp sheltered 15,000 Chadians, victims of drought and war across the nearby border. They were a fraction of endangered desert people and among the lucky ones. They had food and medical care. But they didn't look so lucky. The meager food ration was dwindling fast. The two German medical workers were so exhausted and dehydrated themselves that one had to tape a saline drip to her own arm to keep going.

To save the dying, relief workers had to peer inside tents. Nomads often hid their malnourished children, regarding their condition as a mark of shame. Many children would suffer lifelong damage to their brains, bodies, and psyches. Medical teams constantly faced the choice: Who must be abandoned as hopeless so attention can be shifted to those likely to make it?

Ekber struggled to keep up, interrupted regularly by famine tourists such as myself. He had been there from the beginning, and he had no plans to go. "I don't sleep," he said, not boasting. "I think about what is going to happen, and I can't live with it. I'm going to kill people by moving them. And I have no choice if I am going to save the others."

Darfur was the region worst off, but there was famine in Kordofan, and in the northeast and in the south. U.N. organizations and volunteer agencies worked hard to distribute American and European food aid. The spectrum of relief workers was wide. East of El Geneina, we touched down to deliver mail and a woman's swimming suit to a camp watched over by Christian volunteers. "We hope your stay is enjoyable and as brief as possible," said a young woman, glaring at me, obviously an intruder in her private island of suffering. I asked her about conditions in the camp. She grimaced to another volunteer, recipient of the swimming suit we had brought. She said nothing to me. Her look said, "You wouldn't understand."

Good or bad, official or voluntary, relief workers depended on USAID for supplies. The same USAID mission that had the foresight to order the food had taken on the job of moving it. U.S. officials counted on Sudan Railways to carry grain from the White Nile port of Kosti west over the desert to Nyala, from where it was dispersed in trucks. But the railroad worked at a fraction of capacity. Independent local officials stole grain along the way. Mostly, the trains carried sugar. With Ramadan approaching, wealthier Darfur people needed to sweeten the tea that ended their daily fast. Merchants bribed railway officials to carry sugar along with canned goods, bales of cloth, and bicycle parts.

In April, Jonathan Randal reported in the Washington *Post*: "Rail and trucking delays in shipping of American-donated grain are threatening millions of people in western Sudan with famine, relief workers and U.S. officials said today." Randal noted that U.S. officials had complained to the transitional military council that had overthrown President Jaafar Nimeri three weeks earlier. Railway officials said they lacked parts, he reported, but they did not take up a U.S. offer to fly in $3 million worth.

The story ran on page A21 and caused little stir. When I got there six weeks later, sugar was rolling along steadily. American grain moved west at a trickle, and relief workers in Darfur were approaching hysteria.

Save the Children Fund of Britain decided to by-pass the U.S. network and marshal a truck convoy. It was a token gesture. Only weeks were left before rains would flood roadbeds and sweep away frail bridges. "It's too late. We're like Alice in Wonderland, running to stay in one place," grumbled Elbert Gregory, a British road engineer brought in by Save the Children. "I'm starting what I should be finishing."

Richard Copeland, disaster coordinator for Oxfam, echoed a common view: "The Americans should have assumed the railways would not work and used trucks as a backup."

USAID had contracted distribution to Arkel Talab, an American-Sudanese company based in Baton Rouge, Louisiana. It seemed like a good choice. Its mixture of good ol' boys from the bayous and Africa-hardened Englishmen hustled grain from point to point. But it could not break through the bottlenecks.

Independent truckers, angry that the job went to a single contractor, bid up rates to levels that Arkel Talab did not want to pay. U.S. officials neither controlled gasoline supplies nor brought in any of the trucks that sat idle in nearby Saudi Arabia. Nor could they get the new military government to demand action from the state-owned railways.

I went to USAID for some hard questioning. Why, I wanted to know, did they not backstop the railroad with trucks? In fact, they did. They operated a northern truck route. But for the main route between Kosti and Nyala, U.S. officials argued, it was absolute folly to use trucks, rather than trains. A road convoy took ten days to make the round trip over sandy tracks. Sudan's market trucks could carry three or four tons at the most, and each had to carry heavy fuel supplies.

But people were still starving, whatever the logic, I insisted to one senior American. Finally, the official just shook his head, close to tears. "You work so hard to get the food . . . and it just sits. You don't know where to turn. It just kills you. We have passed the point now, and there is no way kids won't die." I pressed him further, and he exploded. Yelling now, he pounded the table in frustration. "How far can an outsider go? Can we come in and run the country for them? They promised the railroad would work. It didn't."

He had a point. USAID had tried to fly in spares and mechanics to get the railroad in shape. But the World Bank had already put $180 million into the railway, and the European Community had tried to help. The railway was short of working locomotives and rolling stock—and of people to run them. Tracks were in bad shape, and bridges washed out with every heavy rain. Food moved along the line, nonetheless, but it seemed to disappear mysteriously before its destination.

At one town along the rail line, an English aid monitor saw ten thousand bags of sorghum stacked in the private warehouse of a sleek local official. Asked what it was, the man replied: "That's our strategic emergency reserve." But, the monitor pointed out, people were starving not fifty feet away. "No, no," the official insisted, "it is *our* reserve." He meant government people, the party hierarchy and their friends.

Earlier, the new military leader, Lt. Gen. Abdel-Rahman Swar al-Dahab, had flown south to sort out the railroads. He strode up to an open-bed freight car and ripped off the tarpaulin. The load was sugar. He upbraided authorities within earshot and demanded new priority for food. Nothing changed.

Ken Willis, the Louisiana loadmaster at Kosti, added a perspective often forgotten: "It's a railroad. You move things on it. How can you stop every other damned thing besides food? You don't shut a whole country down just to feed people." True. But what do you do when half the country is starving to death?

Americans monitored each ton of grain, from Port Sudan to Kosti to Nyala. They knew the problems were political.

Khartoum authorities spent heavily to shelter nearly a million Ethiopian refugees, and they sacrificed to confront their own emergency. But they felt no deep attachment to the nomads and scattered villagers of Darfur, tacked onto the country artifically at the end of the last century. They cared even less about the south; animist tribesmen had battled northern Moslems for thirty years.

Unlike the Ethiopians, the Sudanese provided no trucks to carry food to their own people. Instead, profiteers jacked up freight rates. Private entrepreneurs worked the mounting starvation to their own advantage. Local commanders stole grain to keep their own followers loyal.

While Ekber was struggling for food in El Geneina, 360,000 tons sat rotting in Port Sudan at the end of a functioning road and rail line. At that point, one bitter American diplomat grumbled to a colleague, "There are more people in Peoria concerned about starving Sudanese then there are in Khartoum."

Distribution was no small challenge. Sudan is three and a half times the size of Texas, all desert and swamp, with hardly any roads. "I'm sure the AID director thought Arkel Talab could eat the problem alive," a senior U.N. official remarked later. "But, like a lot of generals in Africa, he found out some hard truths about logistics."

In the chaos of mid-1985, no one had clear answers. The European Economic Community was hard on the Americans for not using trucks. Its answer was an airlift. West German former Luftwaffe crews strutted around the Khartoum Hilton—the Famine Hilton—in brilliant orange flight suits. British and Belgian planes ferried food west. For all the publicity, they could carry only a tiny fraction of the grain and supplies needed. Each landing weakened the fragile tarmac at El Geneina, already battered by Saudi relief teams, who flew in their own bottled water and generator-powered video recorders. Relief professionals dismissed the airlift as a conscience-salving gesture, too little and too late. "That," remarked Willis, "is throwing money down the goddamned commode."

Four donated Libyan transport aircraft sat idle for weeks at

Khartoum's airport. They had not brought their own fuel, and no Western officials wanted to glorify Muammar Qaddafi by lending any of theirs.

Each agency had its strategy. There were the regulars: Save the Children, British and American; CARE, Oxfam, World Vision, Catholic Relief Services, and a handful of others. And every week, a new sticker appeared on the door of yet another Toyota Land Cruiser. I spent most of a day looking for one of them that people swore they had seen: Vegetable Outreach. Its symbol was a huge cabbage with hands extending from it. The agency, according to unconfirmed rumor, had protested Ethiopian bombing of vegetable patches.

An alphabet soup of U.N. organizations and Western government agencies competed for Sudanese staff and the official ear.

Nonstop side shows filled the Hilton, a posh structure between the White and Blue Niles, and the Acropole, a rough but friendly inn run by two Greek brothers. Relief people gathered to plan, plot, and socialize. One star was Fred Cuny, a Dallas-based consultant known as the Red Adair of disasters. The government had hired him to advise on refugee camps. He was not impressed with relief operations. Volunteers were mostly well-meaning amateurs. No one was running things, and U.N. agencies were getting in each other's way. "I have rarely seen a good U.N. project," he told me. "They just are not efficient."

Cuny had seen it all before. "We should have paid attention to famine warning systems and learned how to stockpile or move buffer stocks," he said. He was being modest in saying "we." He was not among those who ignored the signals. "The basic logistics were not in place. We haven't learned anything about the economics of disaster relief or crisis in an economically bankrupt country."

By then, lumbering C-130 aircraft were carrying small loads to the worst-hit remote areas. But Cuny, like most other logistics experts, dismissed the airlift as mainly a conscience-soothing gesture. He concluded, "Whenever you see C-130s headed someplace, you know somebody fucked up."

Another disaster regular was Nils Enquist, a weather-lined Swede working for the World Food Program. His staccato speech was punctuated by a cough brought on by breathing dust everywhere from Biafra to Uganda's Karamoja. "One bloody word ruins everything," he said. "Prestige. Everyone wants to show his success and take credit. It goes on and on. You know, you can spend fifteen years in Africa and not learn a damned thing."

Enquist agreed with Cuny. Why wasn't there a team of professionals who could handle the logistics and unspring the political booby traps? Why did every agency have to have its own radio, motor pool, charter flights, and supply chain? But, after nearly two decades of banging his head against the same walls, he knew the answers.

Another old hand, who asked not to be named, was despondent. The Sudanese, he said, were victims of more than the weather. "They're getting ripped off by an elite, and that is at the expense of posterity." With a sad shake of his head, he added: "The whole bloody country may die, with that great bloody river coursing through it. What we've got here is a gentle atomic bomb."

*E*very plane brought more short-term famine groupies. Late into the night, earnest people scrambled to work deals. Band Aid and USA for Africa were in town the same day but did not meet. A truck salesman cruised for business. I met an American charter agent from Frankfurt who was frantic. World Vision wanted to rent five C-130s, but the agent had not been able to get Los Angeles—or anyplace else—on the phone for two days.

At the Acropole, a young Englishman struggled to organize the Save the Children convoy from Kosti. "But it's too bloody late," he fumed, smacking a table for emphasis. "We've been telling USAID for three bloody months this would happen." Then he turned on me. "Why didn't you write about this before?" It was no comfort to answer, "I did."

In fact, I had met his father sixteen years earlier, during yet another African calamity. He was a volunteer transport officer, trying frantically to get food to starving children in Biafra. Not much had changed.

I sat up late with Kevin Jenden of Band Aid, soon to be Live

Aid. He was on a roll; he had found a million dollars' worth of Sudanese trucks to buy, in Sudan, to feed the Sudanese. And I had breakfast with Ken Kragen and Marty Rogol of USA for Africa, just finishing their first two-week look at the African catastrophe they had promised to alleviate. They were casting about for ways to spend money in areas where others had wasted billions.

Side effects of famine were obvious in Khartoum. Able-bodied victims came to the capital, a chaotic city held in place by Islamic values and family discipline. For many, survival meant violent crime.

In government offices, meanwhile, machinery ground on at its snail's pace. In mid-catastrophe, officials worked normal hours, allowing urgent matters to sit for days and weeks. The government finally commandeered trucks, but it did little with them. By then, the rains had started. There was nothing left to do but call in the aircraft. An air bridge took the grain from Khartoum to Nyala, El Geneina, and El Fasher. U.S. military helicopters dropped it in bundles to clusters of starving people across Darfur. A lot of people were missed; others died waiting.

In hindsight, Winston Prattley, the U.N. coordinator, summed it up: "It was a marvelous feat of logistics, but no one should ever want to know what it cost."

Neither Prattley nor anyone else knows how many Sudanese died in the famine. "It would be irresponsible to even make a guess," he said. "I saw a lot of people who, I know, died later, and they were spread over a wide area." More than 100,000? "Certainly that. Whether it was over a million, that's something else. We just don't know."

Another U.N. official, who asked not to be named, called Sudan typical of relief operations in Africa. He put it like this:

You start with interagency rivalry, not only within the United Nations but also USAID, the EEC, and the voluntary agencies, who don't like each other that much and head each other off. You have the fresh new cowboys, who are used to walking around in purple smoke, and the rock stars, people with no experience. It is great fun for them, rushing around with walkie-talkies, but the job is vast. Then governments are in shambles, if indeed they exist, and there is usually a civil war going on. The basic infrastructures break down, if they ever worked at all. You can't get a two-engine Cessna to work, let alone transport aircraft.

If you think about moving 400,000 to 500,000 tons of grain over a million square miles of desert, without roads or communication, it is a miracle, in a way, that anything at all was done.

The U.N. official noted an ironic sidelight. For all the criticism, it was American help that broke the back of the Sudan famine. And in early 1986, after President Reagan bombed Libya in reprisal for terrorist acts, a U.S. diplomat was shot. Others were beaten up by Sudanese, who went unpunished. The same Americans who helped save millions of Sudanese lives fled Khartoum to save their own.

But the main irony came later. In the eastern Sudan, rains fell steadily, at well-spaced intervals. Golden grain waved over the horizons, and Sudan grew nearly 2 million tons more than it needed. The surplus was nearly as much as all the grain needed the year before in Sudan and Ethiopia together. Farmers, short of silos, buried grain to try to save it. Tons rotted in the fields. And in Darfur, people were starving.

The Sudanese had yet no way to distribute food within their own country. They asked for foreign grants to pay local truckers, who continued to bid up their rates. And Sudan could not export its surplus: How would it look for a food aid recipient to be selling grain?

And then in August, war flared to new intensity in the south. The Sudan People's Liberation Army accused the government of sneaking down arms on relief flights. To make their point, they aimed a Soviet-made SAM-7 missile at a Sudan Airways Fokker Friendship. Sixty people were killed. All flights stopped. Truck convoys halted as well. Each side blocked food aid for fear the enemy would seize it. With a bumper crop, and donor agencies pleading to deliver it, yet another 2 million Sudanese faced death by starvation.

A ranking official of the U.N. World Food Council had a simple word for it, on both sides: *genocide*.

As in most of Africa, the roots of Sudan's crisis reach back at least a century. When Africa was colonized, Sudanese desert warriors fought off all comers. Charles "Chinese" Gordon defended Khartoum in 1885 until followers of the Mahdi stormed his palace and hacked him to pieces. Eventually, Sudan's borders encompassed the biggest single chunk of Africa.

In 1986, the nation elected as prime minister Sadiq el Mahdi, great-grandson of Gordon's nemesis. He was Oxford-educated and less fanatic, but a devout Islamic leader. The south was still dominated by the tall, ebony Dinka, animists whose culture was a planet away from the northern Moslems'. An array of ethnic groups in between saw life in different ways.

War in the south has taken at least 1.5 million lives, draining resources from a country with none to spare. Sudan could feed most of the Middle East, and Arab governments joined the World Bank in pouring billions into its agriculture. Instead of a bread basket, they got a basket case.

Skilled Sudanese were lured to jobs in the Persian Gulf and in Europe. Local authorities plundered the economy. Distances, inexperience, and torpor stalled plans. Foreign advice was faulty—sometimes purposely so, with fast profits in mind. Farmers had no markets, fertilizer, or pesticides. Many ended up in the cities.

Middle-level officials saw the squandering but could not stop it. Saaed Abu Kimbal, the planning officer for Kordofan Province, knew exactly what went wrong.

"The British introduced shelter belts in 1938," he said. "They were quite aware of the dangers of the desert. We wanted to carry on their work, but since 1980, the government did not raise a finger. Rural people did not pose any threat to the protected palace in Khartoum, so the government didn't give a damn about them. They had no voting power. If they died, so what?"

Meanwhile, he said, the World Bank and others pushed mechanized farming over vast areas. Tractors chopped up fragile rangeland. Topsoil was blown away or carried off with the rains. Machinery broke down, and fertilizer did not arrive. Small farmers abandoned their own productive fields to work for wages. Artificial settlements brought new social problems. A few entrepreneurs made money at the expense of the peasants and the land itself, Abu Kimbal said.

"That was the World Bank's philosophy," he said. "If you concentrate wealth in the hands of a few, they will reinvest. Unfortunately, instead of reinvesting, they built big houses in Khartoum and enjoyed themselves in Cairo and London. Farmers gave up and moved to the city. They ate bread baked in ovens that needed more and more wood as fuel."

Abu Kimbal stopped for a moment and concluded: "That is what is wrong here. We ate our forests and built houses. We wanted to match the white people, and we created all sorts of white elephants, most of which have died. Now what do we do?"

He shrugged, helpless. It was not enough to be a planner. His capital, El Obeid, was one of Sudan's major cities, a desert crossroads of several hundred thousand inhabitants. Engineers had figured out a water supply, but no one maintained it or removed the silt. As we spoke, El Obeid had been bone dry for months. The only water was brought in oily tankers from a hundred miles away.

Failed development created a downward spiral that assured more failure. Sudanese hopes are pinned regularly on the Gezira cotton project, the world's largest farm lying between the Blue and White Niles. It usually lets them down. Even when the crop is good, it is marketed poorly. In 1985, hopes rose again. But the food crisis was on. Transportation was too bogged down moving sorghum to deliver fertilizer to Gezira.

When Gezira was conceived, its soil was so rich it needed no phosphates. Years after the minerals have been depleted, farm managers still brag that they don't have to add phosphorus. Centralized management means the entire project suffers from a single wrong move. When I visited Gezira, an official complained of a vehicle shortage. That day, I saw a fleet of Mercedes-Benz jeeps mysteriously parked unused behind a barn, all thick with dust.

The billions of dollars spent on Gezira and the dubious Kenana sugar project left little for developing food production. In the early 1980s, food deficits began to slide toward famine. "I pleaded with Khartoum to declare a famine emergency in Kordofan," Kimbal told me. "But Nimeri answered, 'We are the bread basket of the Middle East. We cannot have famine.'"

By 1984, famine had declared itself. But it was a little early for the outside world. People were caught up in Ethiopia; public opinion has trouble handling more than one catastrophe at a time. The World Food Program in Rome pushed hard on alarm buttons, but Sudan would have to wait its turn. In November, a month after news film finally alerted the world to Ethiopia's lingering famine, a WFP coordinator remarked to me: "It is easy to track public interest. For example, we already know the next crisis will be Sudan. Senator Kennedy is taking television crews there over Christmas."

He was wrong. Sudan was seen mainly as a place where Ethiopian refugees suffered in border camps. By the time world pressure geared itself up, the rains had come. Reporters wrote of little green sprouts covering the desert. Those who cared heaved a collective sigh and went on to the next crisis. In fact, the rains came too hard in Darfur and washed away the seed. Rainfall was badly spaced.

But those are the breaks.

Late in 1986, I asked people I trusted to look back. An American diplomat who lived through the catastrophe answered without a pause. "The truth is that [the authorities] don't care. They care about Kassala [in the east]; they care about Khartoum and some areas along the river and maybe a few other parts. But they don't care about the west. Or the south. They just don't care."

But some cared, I argued. He agreed. "And what can they do? There is so much corruption in the railways, in other sectors, the government could not fix it even if anyone wanted to."

I pressed him. But how do you help people in those circumstances? He shrugged helplessly. He was an economist, not God.

It is hard to assess blame without defining values. As the Koran prescribed, Sudanese authorities offered hospitality to desperate brethren on their doorstep. They did their best. But starving masses in some remote place were the will of God, beyond their concern. The map says it is all Sudan. But the government in Khartoum did not draw the map.

In Rome, I talked to Tarekegne Taka, an Ethiopian economist who directed African development for the U.N. Food and Agriculture Organization. I raised USAID's dilemma: How far can outsiders go to help? He had the best answer I had heard on the subject. Political and logistical chaos were simply part of the problem. Some governments condoned theft and incompetence, neglected agriculture, kept food from foes, and hid famine to save embarrassment; those were obstacles to be overcome. "If donors are not equipped to handle the crisis, the recipients are even less so," he concluded. "Either you want to save lives or you don't."

*D*uring 1984 and 1985, Ethiopia overshadowed Sudan, but the Ethiopian situation needed all the attention it could get. It was about time the world noticed.

Anybody who cared to watch had had decades of warning that the Ethiopian highlands would continue to produce steadily worsening famines. For years, Ethiopia's major export has been topsoil, swept along in chocolate-brown torrents after each rain. In the Ethiopian Highlands, soil loss each year runs to twenty-five tons an acre. And it is getting worse. Tall trees covered half of the Highlands at the turn of the century. Today, 3 percent is forest. Raw hillsides and valleys are plowed over and over by farmers who cannot afford to replace nutrients. When it rains, they lose land. When it does not, they starve.

The rains failed in 1973, and people died in hamlets miles from the nearest road. Starvation spread, but news of the catastrophe did not. Emperor Haile Selassie, King of Kings, Conquering Lion of the Tribe of Judah, outlawed famine in his realm. American diplomats joined their European colleagues, U.N. representatives, and other foreigners in sparing the emperor embarrassment. It was only when refugees reached Addis Ababa, hollow-cheeked and stumbling with weakness, that an emergency was declared.

By the time food shipments were mobilized, tens of thousands had died. Whole villages expired while the emperor's table groaned under delicacies flown from Rome. Largely because of the famine, Haile Selassie, the seventy-fourth descendant of the Queen of Sheba, was bundled into the back of a Volkswagen Beetle and later humiliated until he gave up and died. A Marxist military junta dismantled Ethiopia's feudal system. Henceforth, the plan went, socialist Ethiopia would feed itself with cooperatives, state farms, and shared labor. And the country would unite in peace.

First, the new leaders had to get organized. Thousands were murdered in the Red Terror. Colonel Mengistu Haile Mariam, in a new twist to board-room politics, strode into a meeting and shot dead his nearest rivals. What followed was the pattern known so well in Africa: the ritual changing of totems. In the place of the emperor's lion, there was a giant bronze statue of Lenin striding off in some unannounced direction. A small group of opportunists and pragmatists put on the revolution's uniform—a blue V-necked suit, such as what might be worn by a hospital orderly—and learned a new litany. And the overwhelming majority of peasants did what they have done for a thousand years in Ethiopia, and elsewhere in Africa, at each such change in course. They went about their business of trying to stay alive, keeping as much distance as possible between themselves and government.

Ethiopia's problems went unsolved. Land taken from the old nobility produced little for the new collectives. Peasants took badly to the African version of Soviet Utopia. Tools, fertilizer, and pesticides did not appear as promised. As before, farmers burned off trees to clear land and chopped firewood at alarming rates. A U.S. Embassy report estimated the Highlands were losing a billion tons of topsoil a year.

The bitter and unending war to retain Eritrea worsened, and it was joined by another struggle for autonomy, this one in the northern province of Tigray. In his first decade in power, Mengistu imported $3 billion worth of aircraft, artillery, and ammunition from the Soviet

Union. Much of it went to create hungry refugees in Somalia and Sudan. Crops were destroyed as a weapon of war. Little was spent on Ethiopia's own ravaged land.

The Save the Children Fund of Britain first noticed trouble ahead for the Highlands in 1982, and relief workers started a small feeding program. The next year, Catholic Relief Services, based in New York, appealed to the U.S. government for emergency grain. Other volunteer agencies, and then United Nations organizations, banged the alarm bells.

It took Washington six months to dispatch grain for CRS. A General Accounting Office report later blamed this on American reluctance to help a Communist government. Other grain trickled in. But, in village after village, desperate families left their homes to wander in search of food. In March 1984, Ethiopia's Relief and Rehabilitation Commission made an urgent plea for help, warning in elaborate detail of the impending suffering.

But 1984 was the tenth year of the revolution, and leaders were torn. They had peasants starving in the hinterlands, but they had a success to proclaim to the world. It was an embarrassing contradiction.

In June that year, the U.N. World Food Council met in Addis Ababa. Ministers from around the world gathered for their annual session to discuss ways of combatting hunger. Mengistu, welcoming them, did not dwell on the millions of Ethiopians whose lives were in danger.

In the following months, perhaps as much as $250 million was spent on festivities to celebrate the anniversary of the revolution.

Discreetly, but clearly, the Ethiopian commission kept up its appeal. Foreign relief workers in Ethiopia hammered at their governments. And then on October 1, an umbrella group of relief agencies met to assess the calamity. It was the Christian Relief and Development Agency, run by Augustine O'Keeffe, Brother Gus.

He is one of those Irish Catholic priests found invariably at the heart of African calamities. He was in Biafra in the late 1960s, and he was in Ethiopia all through the famine of the mid-1970s. His gentle, jovial manner is counterbalanced by haunted eyes. He works smoothly, is not given to drama and overstatement—and he smokes like a fiend.

His agency's cry of alarm could not have been plainer:

> Ethiopia has not experienced a food shortage of this magnitude within living memory. In terms of geographical extent and population affected, it vastly exceeds in severity the drought and famine of 1973, when three regions were affected. Today 12 of 14 regions are affected by drought, and death by starvation is occurring in six of those. More than six million people are estimated to be affected by food shortage. . . . We are taking the unusual step of contacting governments, the U.N. and donor agencies directly out of the conviction that only immediate and massive action can arrest this famine.

And the response, Gus said later, was minimal. What saved millions of Ethiopians was a simple fluke.

A Nairobi-based cameraman named Mohammed Amin did work for Ethiopian Air Lines' in-flight magazine, and he knew the information officials. He had arranged for a rare visa—most reporters were refused entry—and he included a British Broadcasting Corporation radio reporter on his trip. Then he negotiated for permission, rarer still, to visit the town of Korem, in the stricken Highlands. At the last minute, a BBC television reporter named Michael Buerk insisted on coming along. Amin fixed it. On October 24, British television viewers heard Buerk say: "Dawn, and as the sun breaks through the piercing chill of the night on the plain outside Korem, it lights up a biblical famine—now, in the twentieth century. This place, say workers here, is the closest thing to hell on earth."

The news film was yet more electrifying. Wherever Amin aimed his camera, the lens filled with stunned mothers clutching children with limbs no thicker than an adult's finger. Huge round eyes fringed with flies stared blankly. Babies sat lifeless in small pools of greenish fluid. The quiet dignity of victims contrasted with the frantic activity of the small group of people who sought to help them.

Network editors in New York turned down the film, arguing that Americans were fed up with pictures of starving Africans. After they saw the reaction in Britain, and still with reluctance, they changed their minds. Suddenly, when it was too late to save the million who eventually died, Ethiopia had a famine.

Any relief specialist could have predicted the immediate result. Food aid poured into the little port of Assab and paralyzed it. Ethiopia, at war in the north, was desperately short of trucks. Many roads are little more than lines on a map, rock-strewn tracks gouged deeply by ruts.

Bitter conflict arose as relief officials bargained for more trucks. Arguments arose over who would receive food. Humanitarians said everyone should eat. Military strategists pointed out that Eritreans and Tigrayans, if potential famine victims, were also rebels who were shooting at the Ethiopian Army.

By the end of 1985, one billion dollars' worth of relief supplies had gone into Ethiopia—a million tons of food—and the United States had paid for a third of it. No one knows how many Ethiopians died. Uncounted thousands never made it to relief camps. The figure of a million is a handy round number, and it might be the right one. But, without question, millions were saved.

Aid veterans in Ethiopia are bitter because ideology makes their job so much harder. Western nations responded massively when attention was focused on starvation victims. But aid began to dry up as soon as camera lenses turned elsewhere.

For all the verbal assaults on Ethiopian authorities, even conservative Americans admit that they ran the cleanest relief operation in Africa. Most foreigners agree that less than 5 percent of relief supplies there were stolen or commandeered. In Sudan, up to half disappeared in some areas. Sudanese officials supplied no trucks, even when millions were dying and food was backed up in warehouses. The Ethiopian RRC marshaled convoys day and night.

And in Somalia, Ethiopia's eastern neighbor and a U.S. ally, corruption and inefficiency were worse than in Sudan. U.N. officials estimated privately that in the early 1980s, at times 70 percent of food destined for refugees was taken by the army. "Officers would come up and put a gun to my head and simply hijack convoys," remarked a friend of mine who worked for the U.N. World Food Program in Somalia. When he complained to authorities, they expelled him. To obtain more aid, the Somali government reported double the number of refugees actually in the country.

Somalia, forming the tip of Africa's strategic horn, is a reliable East-West barometer. The Soviet Union signed a treaty of eternal friendship in 1975 and then dumped Somalia for Ethiopia two years later. The two neighbors were fighting bitterly over the Ogaden region, and Moscow could not keep both as allies. After the Russians began putting 18,000 Cubans and $2 billion of weaponry into Ethiopia, Somali President Siad Barre decided he was a friend of the United States.

Somalia is a handy staging base for the U.S. Rapid Deployment Force. But, despite Barre's urging, neither the Carter nor Reagan administrations showed much interest in using the huge naval base at Berbera. Budget cuts reduced aid to Somalia. Late in 1986, however, the Soviet embassy in Mogadishu suddenly sprang to life again. And so did U.S. interest. The State Department requested $52 million in aid to Somalia.

In Ethiopia, a controversial sidelight was the government's decision to resettle nearly 2 million people from the Highlands to more productive land farther to the south. The move was widely attacked as political, a crude maneuver to reduce the population of a rebellious region with the desirable side effect of killing enemies in the process. The French voluntary agency Médecins Sans Frontières (Doctors Without Borders), declared itself spokesman for the detractors.

Without discussing its methodology, Médecins Sans Frontières declared that 100,000 people died in the process of resettlement. People were herded into trucks, with families separated in the process, and carried for days to be dumped in malodorous swamps. Soldiers moved stragglers along with clubs and whips. It was a needless political move, the report said.

In hindsight, nearly every veteran relief worker I spoke to in

Ethiopia dismissed Médecins Sans Frontières' numbers as French hysteria. There were cruel abuses, and the Ethiopian government apologized for them. Perhaps thousands of people died, according to sources whose judgment I trust. But, said one, "you've got to ask yourself whether it was more humane to move them to better ground or let them stay where they would have died anyway."

Even the Americans admit officially that there were strong ecological reasons for reducing the Highlands' population. "Hell, we drew up our own plan for resettlement under the emperor," acknowledged one senior U.S. diplomat. Their objection was the timing and the toughness with which it was carried out. "When you're up to your ass in alligators," the diplomat put it, "it is no time to drain the swamp."

One Amharic-speaking American, who had had a close look at the results of resettlement, pronounced it "brutal paternalism."

Under so much pressure, Ethiopian authorities suspended resettlement after moving slightly fewer than 600,000 people. They poured resources into some resettlement sites to prove to visitors that they had achieved their goal. I was to have a look for myself. Top officials of the RRC and the Ministry of Information and National Guidance encouraged me to go, and they issued me a permit in record time. But a low-level RRC official, apparently offended that someone had bypassed him while he was out of his office, canceled my permission at the last minute. I learned nothing about resettlement, but a great deal about the functioning of Ethiopian bureaucracy.

Instead, I drove out of Addis Ababa to investigate yet another controversial program: villagization. In order to provide better services, the government declared, three-quarters of Ethiopia's 42 million people are to be regrouped in neatly plotted new villages near access roads. It is not a bad idea on paper. But Tanzania has collapsed in ruin largely because it attempted exactly the same sort of thing. For centuries, Ethiopians have clung tightly to their isolated patches of land, living in their great-grandfathers' houses.

An Ethiopian who advised the government told me, in a conversation he was assured would not be attributed to him by name, "This is a very unwise move, I am afraid. It cannot work here any better than it worked in Tanzania. The real reason is political, to educate the people in socialist ways and to control them better with cadres."

And a Chinese diplomat put it differently at a cocktail party: "The Ethiopians are determined to make every mistake every socialist state has ever made."

At the edge of Addis Ababa, it seemed obvious at a glance that Ethiopia had hardly changed, for all the Stalinist breast-beating. In the early morning, women out of the Book of Solomon trotted along rutted donkey tracks under gigantic loads of twigs. Bakers, barbers and butchers were hard at work in falling-down shacks. The air was spiced by eucalyptus that Emperor Menelik planted a century ago when he realized the forests were shrinking. But there was a more powerful scent: woodsmoke.

I stopped to look up a friend of a friend, a highly educated man who was lying low under the new Stalinist order. He decided to trust me. "You know," he said, "we don't like the Russians. We love Americans." I expected him to tell me it was because we were such nice guys. In fact, Ethiopians had a much more practical reason to like the West.

"Russian families don't hire anyone," he explained. "Americans have a cook, a maid, a nanny, a driver, night watchmen. Each family has ten servants, maybe. And each one has ten people dependent on him. So every American feeds 100 Ethiopians. We love you."

Prevented from visiting a resettlement site, I checked around for the best sources I could find. One was an Ethiopian driver who knew the north well. "Up to half the people have already sneaked away to go back to their homes," he told me. "Truck drivers help them out by hiding them in their loads. Sometimes soldiers at road-blocks close their eyes. Ethiopians are very attached to their own homes and their own way of life."

*E*thiopian authorities might succeed in relieving pressure on the land, and increasing food production in the process. But their heavy-handed social engineering and hard rhetoric are unlikely to win them much help from the outside. Western distaste, particularly in Washington, for hostile ideology augurs badly for the future of people caught reluctantly in the middle.

I saw this in Sekota, in 1986, where I went to talk to survivors of Buerk's biblical scene. The dusty brown hillsides were thick with new green growth. Men emerged from a World Vision warehouse staggering under heavy sacks of seeds. Most had already planted sorghum, their first crop in five years, and they were about to grow teff, the grasslike grain that Ethiopians love. Others waited patiently to be given oxen, brought in on old-fashioned cattle drives. Women drew water from village wells, full again, to cook for their recovering families.

Kassaway Aweta, fourteen, might have starred in Amin's film from Korem. He was back home again, and healthy, playing with an elaborate toy car he had made by bending wire over scraps of wood.

"Sure they look well and healthy," remarked Pat Banks, of World Vision, "but if the food stops for two weeks they will be skeletons again." She was right, of course. Food was still dropping onto the muddy runway nearby, pushed out of the back of C-130 cargo planes chartered for the International Committee of the Red Cross and for World Vision. After a while, the region would grow enough food for itself, perhaps with a surplus.

But every year, as always, everything would depend on the rain. At the slightest drought, people would suffer. With another major one, the whole horror would begin again.

Western donors planned to do little about the land. The United States, for one, was banned by law from putting development funds into Ethiopia. Americans had saved lives during a passing emergency. The rest was up to the Ethiopians and their Communist friends.

At the office in Addis Ababa of the U.N. Office for Emergency Operations in Africa, a remarkably successful little team that was to be disbanded at the year's end, coordinator Michael Priestley told me: "The generous response to the famine and the compassion it represented will be brought to naught, indeed made mockery, if there is no follow-up to bring Ethiopia back from the brink of famine."

Down the road, I spoke to Brother Gus, who by then had seen

it all twice before. He praised the RRC, and the donors who eventually responded, but he noted that interest was already flagging fast. In his gentle lilt, he observed, "If we are to avoid a situation like what we have witnessed last year, there has to be long-term development and food-security stocks. But the donations are very small indeed."

He was troubled that he could not say how many people had died. "A million? No one will ever know. However many it was, it should not have happened."

I asked him if the lesson was learned. "It will happen again. If things turn around badly, in two years' time we would probably face the same problems in getting response and organization." He lit yet another cigarette, and his eyes grew more haunted.

"You know, unless you attack the root causes, it is really rather sad."

Sure enough, in 1987 the ominous signs returned to Ethiopia. Relief officials asked for 409,000 tons of aid for 2.5 million threatened people. Outside experts warned as many as five million would be in danger. Once again, the specialists said, Ethiopians were minimizing the danger to avoid criticism of their agricultural failures.

Rains had come back—but too hard. Fields were washed out. Locusts and other pests damaged the crop. "If development aid is not forthcoming, then all they have done over the last two years is postpone the deaths of every child, woman and man they helped save," said Yemane Berhan Debre-Michael, an Ethiopian executive of World Vision. As Priestley told donors: "The emergency is emphatically not over. Another serious famine can be expected within the next few years."

A survey by Western agronomists concluded that by the early 1990s, Ethiopia would face a "structural food deficit" of two million tons. In a normal year, the experts agreed, the country will have a grain shortfall twice that of the 1984 famine. The land is washing away, at an annual rate of a billion tons. It is as though a yard of topsoil is stripped from 200,000 acres, every year. Emperor, Communist junta, the result is the same: peasants suffer.

Some Western diplomats argue that the people and the land should be protected despite the government, for humanitarian purposes. They reason that those who suffer most are least able to protect themselves. Such thinking goes nowhere in Washington. Early in 1987, I went to a press conference by Toby Roth, a Republican congressman whose personal issue was Ethiopia. He had introduced a bill making it a crime to trade with Ethiopia or offer its government any aid or comfort.

Roth insisted the Ethiopians had put to death at least 100,000 people during the resettlement program. His source was the discredited Médecins Sans Frontières report. Pressed, he admitted the figure might be much lower. Moments later, he was citing 100,000 deaths as gospel. If he was protecting human rights, I asked, had he considered including Zaire or Liberia or other offending countries where ideology was closer to Washington's? "I suppose others might be included," he said, "but to be frank I only know about Ethiopia."

When I asked Roth who supported him, he waved a sheaf of letters. It was a tempting comparison. Here was an anti-Communist legislator from Wisconsin, no less, brandishing documents while he played fast and loose with the facts. But this was no McCarthy. Roth seemed to be a sincere and good-hearted American doing his best for a cause he believed in. Hard luck for starving Ethiopians.

Afterward, I spoke to Roth's staff person. I wanted to know why the congressman was so confident; had I missed something? "We have our sources," she replied, with ice. "Go back and check *your* sources." It was like some silly Washington media game; one person is right and another is wrong. I tried to suggest we might pool information; I had been places Roth spoke about secondhand. After all, millions of lives were involved. By then, however, she was gone. I was not a possible source for the lawmaker; I was a threat to the candidate.

*I*n Ethiopia and Sudan, professional hindsight was remarkably close to what experts had said in advance. A few well-timed stocks of grain could have headed off hunger before it bloomed to famine. Instead, people panicked and took to the road. They ate their seed and abandoned their land, assuring a second year of failure. On the move, their access to food diminished. Children and old people died first. Then men left their women in search of a miracle.

The early-warning systems did not work because they were based on expected harvest levels. They did not take into account how people would respond to bad harvests. Satellite photos gauged the fields but not the local markets and families' granaries.

Now the experts are growing increasingly alarmed. When a five-year-old child who survived the famine reaches the age of forty-five, Ethiopia will have three times its present population. Or it may not. Nature may have had enough by then.

No small number of people in the wealthier world argue that nature will take care of itself. There may have to be what scientists call "a massive mammal die-off." It is nature's way. Why bring health and hope to people who face such a bleak future anyway? There is, of course, no moral answer to someone who can look at his own kids and make this argument. But there is a more pragmatic one: Desperate wildebeest will not be at their doorstep, demanding redress or at least revenge. Humans might.

*T*arekegne Taka, the FAO official in Rome, is convinced that Ethiopia will drop from the world's agenda. "The West thinks once the rains come, it is over," he said. "That's not true. Africa is like a man dying. When vital organs go, the rest follows. Drought hit hard because the body was so weak. But even an end to drought is no end to the crisis."

He insisted on his main point. Corrupt or incompetent or ideologically awkward governments might make development harder. But they must be regarded as an obstacle, like the lack of rain. People with the means to help must find a way to do it.

"You have to do it," he said. "If you don't, our children will never forgive you. They will never forget."

5 CENTRAL AFRICA
Crowded Out of Eden

*I*n the mountains of Rwanda, forests rise sharply from the valleys and disappear into mist. Compared to the arid lowlands and much of the Horn, the heart of Central Africa is Shangri-la. But the continent is most crowded here; Rwanda has 450 inhabitants to every square mile, swamps and jungles included. Villages cling to every slope. Corn is planted at angles so steep that farmers stand up straight in one row to weed the next.

If there is little room for man, there is less for the mountain gorilla, the hulking ape whose last home is a few peaks of Rwanda and neighboring Zaire. In its battle against extinction, the mountain gorilla attracted two devoted allies with starkly opposing philosophies. The first was Dian Fossey.

I first heard of Fossey in 1967. I had gone to find a band of white mercenaries holed up in the eastern Congo (now Zaire). Someone told me about an American woman who had gone up into the mountains alone to study gorillas. Wherever she was, I was warned, she wanted no visitors. The story at hand was more pressing; there would be time later. When I went back eighteen years afterward, I was a little too late.

Fossey started her research in Zaire (then the Congo). She had persuaded anthropologist Louis Leakey to support her. She was no scientist, but Leakey thought that might make her more patient and less biased.

Only the dedicated or the reckless lived then in the Congo bush. From the moment a young Congolese snatched Baudouin's sword at the independence ceremonies in 1960, the former Belgian colony was in turmoil. Katanga seceded in a bloody war that United Nations forces had to quell. Prime Minister Patrice Lumumba was murdered by opponents after the CIA botched an attempt to poison him. Rebels massacred civilians, black and white. American diplomats were seized at Stanleyville, and Belgian nuns were raped and tortured. Joseph-Desiré Mobutu seized power in 1964 and quelled uprisings with white mercenaries. In 1967, the mercenaries turned on him.

Fossey set up camp in the midst of this. She had hardly found the gorillas when Mobutu's soldiers grabbed her as a mercenary. After two weeks, she escaped, only to be captured by rebels. With all her equipment lost, she started again in Rwanda.

Her camp was 10,000 feet up, on a saddle between Mont Karisimbi and Mont Visoke, on a misty meadow where it rained or hailed 300 days a year. Her guide left her with rudimentary Swahili and an African woodcutter. When the woodcutter asked, "Do you want water?" she ran into her tent in panic. She had heard: "Do you want me to kill you?"

Fossey approached her work with single-minded zeal, even in later years, when severe emphysema made her pause for oxygen every few minutes. A suitor appeared one day and announced that he was taking her back to America. He went home alone. Later, she was engaged to a French doctor from the hospital down the mountain. He would not live at her Karisoke Research Center, and she chose her gorillas.

She gave each gorilla a name: Uncle Bert, Beethoven, Macho, Icarus. One morning a young male named Peanuts ambled up to her and touched her fingertips. "I've finally been accepted by a gorilla," she exalted that night, tapping away at her portable typewriter.

Fossey demolished the King Kong myth, revealing gorillas to be gentle vegetarians—intelligent and shy—that prefer to walk away from a fight if they can manage to. She habituated some to humans, allowing researchers to watch them up close. She stood nose to nose with 400-pound males, trading bellow for bellow. "One feels a fool thumping one's chest rhythmically, or sitting about pretending to munch on a stalk of wild celery as though it were the most delectable morsel in the world," she noted in one of her many reports back home. But there was seldom anyone around to notice. Over the years, she earned a doctorate from Cambridge University.

Fossey's eccentric behavior became legend. The Rwandans called her Nyramacibili; it means "small woman" but was meant ironically to describe her determination. Some translated it as "woman who lives alone in the forest without a man." It did not bother her. In 1985, she told a visitor: "The more that you learn about the dignity of the gorillas, the more you want to avoid people."

Trouble started when she decided that protecting gorillas was more urgent than studying them. Little red-painted wooden markers were beginning to grow numerous in the graveyard not far from her hut. For decades, poachers had supplied baby gorillas to zoos. They killed whole families to get them. And Europeans and Americans paid heavily for skulls, to use as gigantic ashtrays. The hands and feet sold well as curiosities. Also, small-time poachers set snares for small quarry; gorillas stumbled into them and died of wounds, often from legs severed by the wire.

By 1980, perhaps 250 were left on the volcanic peaks of Rwanda and eastern Zaire. At the rate they were disappearing, they faced extinction by the twenty-first century. Fossey organized an anti-poaching squad with the Mountain Gorilla Project, a group of private donors. She did not like their meddling. And some contributors worried about her methods.

From the start, Fossey had taught the habituated animals to run from Africans. She created racist gorillas on a black continent. She explained it simply: There were no white poachers. And she was rough on poachers.

Once, her trackers showed up with three wanted men, tightly bound and snarling. She paid a handsome reward and sent them down the mountain to the police. But an African helper told her she had been conned. He led her to the poachers' shack, where the trackers and their captives were drinking up the reward in a raucous party. Furious, she seized a flaming log from the cook fire and flung it at the house, which burned to the ground. In the turmoil, a poacher's four-year-old daughter ran to her for protection. Fossey took the girl home, and then insisted that the child did not want to leave her. The poachers had her arrested briefly for kidnapping.

After poachers killed her gorilla friend Digit, Fossey threw herself further into the battle. Almost an invalid from emphysema, she stayed in the dank forest, chain-smoking local Impala cigarettes and rasping to catch her breath, to marshal her guards. She cultivated her reputation as a white witch, twisting bits of grass and making fetishes to strike fear among poachers.

The Digit Fund, an international group of sympathetic donors, sent money. In 1984, her teams cut down 2,264 traps in 347 days of patrols; seven poachers were arrested, and none of the seventy-six gorillas under watch were captured.

It was an uphill struggle. Rwanda had 6 million inhabitants. By 2000, there would be 10 million, in an area the size of Massachusetts. The volcanic soil yields three crops a year, and the Agriculture Ministry took 20,000 acres of it from the Parc des Volcans just before Fossey arrived. Herders, farmers, and woodcutters nibbled at the remaining 30,000. Fossey had little faith in local authorities. She had her own army.

Late in 1985, the guards brought in a Zairean gold smuggler and poacher. She wrote to a friend, "I gently examined his clothing to find . . . three packets of *sumu*, bits of skin and vegetation looking like vacuum cleaner debris (nasty lady). . . ." *Sumu* means poison, or fetish, in Swahili. She took the packets away, and the poacher lunged for them. He was hysterical, scratching and flailing, until three guards subdued him. Then he went limp. "It was like taking a nipple from a baby," she wrote.

The poacher was taken to jail, but he kept in touch with his men. The night after Christmas, Fossey went to bed after a number of nightcaps. In the morning, her cook arrived at 6:30 with her warm milk. He found her body, slashed six times by a panga, a heavy machete. The hut was ransacked, but $1,300 in cash and $1,000 in traveler's checks were not touched. Nor were her passport, her cameras, or any other valuables. Her friend and colleague Ian Redmond came from England to pack her personal effects. He found the *sumu* hidden where no one in a hurry would have seen it.

Rwandan authorities later convicted *in absentia* Wayne McGuire, a young American researcher who was living in the camp. He wanted to steal her research, they said. U.S. officials were unconvinced. Investigations were so sloppy, one noted, that a dozen people handled the murder weapon before anyone thought of lifting fingerprints.

Fossey's last thoughts were mailed to Redmond a few days before her death. What she wanted most in the world, she said, was the knowledge that the fourteen gorillas buried nearby—where she now lies—"were still on this earth propagating their kind, stripping thistles, pulling galium vines off hagenias, sunning and purring on the rare sunny days and even shivering and steaming on the long rainy days."

Fossey's philosophy was that gorillas had to be protected from humans at all costs. She died trying to protect them.

The gorillas' other ally was William Weber. He and his wife, Amy Vedder, are scientists from the University of Wisconsin. Both worked at Karisoke until the thin air grew too tense. Fossey, they said, was much like her gorillas. She blustered and bellowed; if one was patient, there were rewards. But she was a loner, and it was her camp. After eighteen months, Weber and Vedder moved down to Ruhengheri to work on their own.

"Dian had discovered a desert island, and she felt it belonged to her," Vedder said later. Vedder and Weber each paid tribute to Fossey's work, acknowledging that she made it possible for others to study the gorillas. But they believe the gorillas can only be saved if humans around them decide to let them live.

The gorillas' frightening mien was protection enough before firearms and radios tipped nature's balance. They had room to run before woodcutters marooned them on a few mountain peaks. Now, Weber feels, humans will spare them only if they pay their own way. That means tourism. He is not happy about it, but he is a realist.

"Tourism for us is a sort of compromise with the devil, but it is better than having 5,000 head of cattle move into the gorillas' habitat," he said, pointing out on a detailed map where humans had penetrated gorilla country.

He worked out a careful plan. Three groups a day are allowed to look for the few gorillas habituated to humans. None can spend more than an hour watching the animals; tourists put in a very hard morning in mud and thistles—and pay heavily—for the privilege. At first, the government insisted on larger groups. But a huge male gorilla, upset by too many people, bit Weber in the shoulder, wrestled him to the ground, and rolled him down a hill. "That is the best thing that could have happened, for the gorillas," Vedder said, with a sympathetic chuckle for her husband's broken shoulder. "Now the government understands what has to be done."

Weber's sociological research suggests that African societies can learn quickly to protect endangered wildlife communities they once cared little about. When he first sampled people in the area, few had thought about the gorillas. Most said they would not miss them.

Then he mounted a massive campaign. He brought film shows to every village in the region, reaching 100,000 people. He spoke in schools and sat with elders. Rwandans saw tourists come and go, leaving money behind them. A second sampling five years later showed a complete turnaround. The gorillas were a resource, even a point of pride, which made Rwanda unique, and people wanted them protected.

Encouraged by this, Rwandan authorities renewed their efforts to build up national parks and attract tourists. In Kigali, I went to see the director of wildlife and tourism, but he was at the airport. Authorities had decided Rwanda once again needed a giraffe. One was being flown in from Tanzania by Air France.

Weber's lesson is not restricted to Rwanda. Animals are not treated well anywhere humans are treated badly. Little room is left in Africa for large private zoos. Africans know that a dollar spent on animals is one not spent on people. If wildlife and tourism are supposed to earn money, people at the edges want to see some of it.

Emotional and esthetic arguments appeal to outsiders, and they raise money for the World Wildlife Fund. But they do not motivate Africans who suffer from reserves. Masai tribesmen delivered the message with chilling clarity when the borders of Ambroseli National Park were defined in Kenya. The Masai were ejected from lands their ancestors' herds had grazed. They were forbidden to hunt animals they had lived among for centuries. From the late 1950s to 1977, the rhino population dropped from 150 to 15. Many were found dead from Masai spear wounds, with their horns still in place. The Masai were making a point.

Africans tend not to murder animals for the pleasure of it. Unless they kill for the pot, their hunting is business. That is why the African black rhino is nearly extinct in the wild. Asian pharmacists believe powdered rhino horn lowers a fever; some Indians think it raises a penis. As Asian rhinos disappear, pressure mounts on those in Africa. But the real threat came, in a twist of world economic interdependency, during the Saudi oil boom.

Yemeni youths, home from oil-field jobs, could suddenly afford the traditional symbol that proved their manhood: a dagger with a handle carved from polished rhino horn. From 1970 to 1979, North Yemen imported the horn of 8,000 rhinos. The wholesale price of horn rose from $15 a pound in 1970 to $300 in 1986. A single rhino carried on his nose the equivalent of three years' earnings for a typical African peasant. In Singapore, a pound was worth $7,000.

David Western and Esmond Bradley Martin for years have kept careful track of African rhinos. Western is a Kenyan ecologist working for the New York Zoological Society. Martin, a Kenya-based American geographer, is a sworn foe of the wildlife trade. At tea in Western's backyard, a scone's throw from a rhino path in Nairobi National Park, they laid out horrifying numbers.

Kenya's black rhinos dropped from 20,000 in 1970 to fewer than 500 within fifteen years. Nearly all of Africa's surviving few thousand black rhinos are scattered in groups of fewer than fifty, too small for reproduction. The last sizable herd is in northern Zimbabwe, but poachers sneak across from Zambia. Guards shot dead thirty-one poachers in two years. But rangers found nearly 200 carcasses in the same period. Fewer than 400 black rhinos are left there.

Martin has waged an intense campaign to dry up the world rhino-horn market, with some spectacular success. But, he allows, he is mostly just winning time. "The African black rhino is finished in the wild," he told me late in 1986.

Elephants are another problem. Their numbers are disputed. Western and Martin agree they are between 750,000 and 1.2 million. Iain Douglas-Hamilton, a renowned elephant man, agrees with that range. But Ian Parker, a maverick among wildlife authorities, refuses to guess at numbers as a point of principle. For all we know, he argues, there may be 5 million. But legal and clandestine ivory exports are easier to estimate. Africa is losing up to 70,000 elephants a year, a pace that cannot go on for long.

Pressure on consumers can reduce the demand. Spotted cats were once in serious danger, until women's coats began attracting more scowls than admiring glances. Now leopards and cheetahs thrive again. But ivory is used for more than piano keys. In Japan, status is enhanced by a personal seal carved from ivory. Demand is steady for ivory jewelry and artifacts.

The ivory trade is hard to control because much of it is legal. African governments earn foreign exchange by selling tusks of elephants dead of old age. But who decides what ivory is legal? For years, the little state of Burundi, south of Rwanda, has been down to a single elephant. He is an old bull living on an island. And each year, Burundi has exported the ivory of 18,000 elephants. Tusks from Zaire, the Central African Republic, and Sudan are smuggled into Burundi, where it is certified. European airlines then fly it to Asia and the Middle East.

Burundi finally agreed to curb the trade in 1986, under pressure from outside conservationists. An international quota system, organized in 1986, seeks to control exports. But African ivory always seems to find its way to market.

From tusk weights, it is clear that young males and females are being slaughtered indiscriminately. Ivory grows more quickly in old elephants, and income is greater when the animals die of natural causes. But poachers do not wait. They sneak in with automatic weapons and take what they can.

The easy, hidden profits have been too much for some African officials to pass up, even at presidential levels. In Zaire, a director of national parks was jailed for trafficking in ivory. Top generals in the Central African Republic aided poachers. Rangers and wardens can find it profitable to look elsewhere at the right time. But even when efforts are made to catch poachers, rangers are seldom a match. In Tanzania's Selous National Park, gas is so scarce that some rangers walk three days to reach their posts. They are not about to chase heavily armed poachers in jeeps.

Poaching is serious enough, but a worse problem is habitat encroachment. If the vast Kalahari is not big enough for wildlife and livestock, the forests of Central Africa are even less able to sustain a balance.

Officials work out what is reserve and what is rangeland. But herders are loath to let good grass go uneaten. To farmers needing land, the parks are land. They push hard at the edges. Reserves are mostly unfenced patrolled areas, and the animals carry no maps. As seasons change, some animals migrate. Others filter into humans' settlements looking for food and leave unnoticed. But elephants, for one, are not known for their stealth.

Clashes are inevitable, since a herd of hungry elephants can ruin a planter overnight. A British farmer in Kenya put it to me simply: "I like elephants as much as the next man, and I do what I can to protect them. But not when the bastards turn my fencing to spaghetti and eat up my entire corn crop."

Lazier leopards and lions have discovered that cows run slower than your average gazelle. This also tends to annoy ranchers.

As Weber showed in Rwanda, the only real answer is an intelligent compromise between man and nature. But indifference, ignorance, and greed too often get in the way.

George Schaller, research director for the New York Zoological Society, has given as much thought to these problems as anyone. He was among the first to look closely at mountain gorillas, and he studied the Serengeti Plain in Tanzania. He tracked the snow leopard in the shrinking wilds of Tibet. He has seen vast tracts of natural habitat razed in Brazil and Pakistan. I met Schaller in China, looking for pandas. He explained how much pandas and mountain gorillas had in common. Small populations of each are isolated on mountain peaks, stranded by human settlers moving up the slopes. Natural corridors linking the groups are razed for farmland and pasture. Food supplies are threatened. Worse, when separated groups can no longer meet to mate, they will disappear forever.

The big lovable mammals are only individual species in a network, vulnerable and essential to others. They seldom go alone. Schaller made the point he repeats again and again:

"Pandas and gorillas are useful symbols because no one will give money to save the leech. But we have to protect entire environments, not single species within them."

*R*wanda is proving Schaller right. Herdsmen and woodcutters have degraded part of the Parc National des Volcans, the gorillas' habitat, and someone has seized an opportunity. Instead of letting the forest regenerate, local entrepreneurs—not far from power—had a plan. The World Bank put $21 million behind it.

The damaged forest would be cleared entirely and replanted in pines and cypress, to be harvested as timber. Fat milk cows would graze in the empty spaces. The project fit well into the latest development rage: agroforestry. It seemed natural for Swiss money to be involved: the idea was to create a little piece of Switzerland. The gorillas, not native to the Alps, were out of luck.

The World Bank hired Amy Vedder as environmental consultant but did not listen when she showed why it was a bad idea. The U.N. representative in Rwanda hit the roof. He wrote a blistering letter to the Bank, warning of severe ecological damage.

The obvious occurred immediately. As soon as crews cut down the remaining trees, rainwater ripped away topsoil, which clogged the watershed. There was the inevitable surprise: Rats loved the phosphorus in cypress bark, and they killed young trees getting to it.

The hubbub of razing a forest and handing out new land threw traditional societies into uproar. There would be winners, but no one was clear about who they would be. The losers were more numerous.

As ecologists warned, the environment shifted to a different mix, and the natural forest was finished. As sociologists warned, once cattle were run into the forest, they could not be kept within the defined limit.

In Kigali, a World Bank official defended the project with charm and logic. Yes, he allowed, choices had to be made. But repairing the degraded forest would be expensive. Rwanda needed money now, and the project could generate income. Individuals would profit and reinvest in the country. Rwanda, and then Africa, would flourish.

I asked if timber and dairy products were not available elsewhere at prices low enough to avoid selling off the nation's future. What had convinced the Bank that profits gained from the project would be spread around? Experience suggested the contrary. If the park was invaded, Rwanda would lose a much greater resource, one that benefited more people.

But Rwanda has its own separate economy and debts to repay, he said. It had to make money and save foreign exchange now; the future was later. He challenged my ecological projections. Was I aware that sixty years ago people had calculated that at the rate horses were increasing in New York City, the streets would be waist deep in horseshit by 1980? Good point, except that Rwanda was already up to its knees.

An American official joined the discussion. He, too, believed in little countries earning their keep with whatever they had to sell. With some condescension, he asked me: "Do you know what agro-forestry is?" It is, we agreed, when someone makes money harvesting trees and products grown among them. Who, I went on, might that be? And at the expense of whom?

Others will doubtless agree with the banker and the American aid official. And that is what worries most scientists who look hard at Africa's future. Major donors and lenders are helping African governments tear up their environments without any real understanding of the price to be paid. And often it is for dubious gains, which, even in the short term, might be losses. It is partly a holdover from the days when Africa's land was thought to be infinite. It is partly the greed of people who know they must make their money fast. And it is partly a blind attachment to a new Western financial religion.

One thing was clear: If the World Bank man was right, twenty years hence a few more Rwandans will have made a few more bucks. But if not, some of Central Africa's richest forest will be wasteland, unable to feed burgeoning populations; waterways will be severely damaged. And the world's last mountain gorillas will be hanging on for dear life in American and European zoos. The stakes are not comforting.

On the drive into Rwanda, the predominant scenery is people. They stream along the roads that wind through green and jagged mountains. On a back road near Ruhengeri, I stopped to pick up a nattily dressed young man heading toward the highway. His name was Apollinaire Ndagisimana, and he worked in a bank in Kigali.

"My father has fourteen children and three acres he inherited from his father," he explained. But the family's plot is a fraction of what his grandfather had owned. It was split up among the sons in the same way that he would share the remaining land with his brothers. Up to now, the system had worked well enough. But this is the last generation: Ndagisimana can expect less than an acre.

And what about your sons? I asked. He reflected a moment, as if he thought it was a good question. It had not occurred to him to worry about the future. For the moment, the present was enough. "I was lucky and found a job in the city," he said. "I come back on weekends, and my salary helps my family get by. My brothers and sisters stay here." What about his neighbors who are running out of land? "Most young men find no jobs," he said. "Some offer to be your houseboy and then steal everything when you are gone. They have no choice. The city is getting to be like that." But what will happen when Rwanda runs out of land? He shrugged. That was the future.

Ndagisimana was a Hutu, like most people in Rwanda and in Burundi to the south. Some are pygmies, the Batwa. The rest are Tutsi, the tall, lanky people known to Americans as the Watusi. For 400 years, Tutsi herders held the Hutus in feudal semislavery. Germany and Belgium kept the peace in twin postage-stamp colonies. But independence brought a bloody reordering of societies. In Rwanda, the 90 percent Hutu majority rose against the Tutsis, who tried to re-establish their former power. Many thousands were massacred. Hutus swung pangas at the ankles of towering Tutsis, quite literally cutting them down to size.

Nearly 100,000 refugees fled to Burundi, which the minority Tutsi still ruled. In 1972, an army of Hutus and Zairean rebels attempted a coup d'état. In the bloody vengeance that followed, at least 80,000 Hutus were shot or hacked to death. Since then, the two neighbors have kept a guarded peace, each more concerned with making a living while fitting ever greater numbers onto shrinking land.

There is plenty of land in neighboring Zaire, along with copper, diamonds, cobalt, uranium, and a river capable of lighting up half the continent. And Zaire's people are among the most miserable in Africa.

A visit to Zaire is recommended for anyone who takes seriously references to morality in U.S. foreign-policy rhetoric. Mobutu Sese Seko, *le Guide*, took absolute power in 1964 with no small help from the Central Intelligence Agency. Nearly a quarter-century later, after having pocketed perhaps $4 billion and murdered opponents under the benevolent gaze of Washington, he is still there. During two rebellions, the Americans took an active part in keeping him there.

I lived in Zaire (then the Congo) in 1967 and 1968. Mobutu, one must admit, had a flair. A former rebel named Pierre Mulele had sought refuge in Brazzaville, across the river. Mobutu invited him back in the name of national unity. He gave solemn assurances to the president of Congo-Brazzaville: Mulele would be welcomed as a brother. He sent his foreign minister over to escort the prodigal son home. Mulele stepped from the ferry, smiling and waving, into the arms of Mobutu's thugs.

The traitor would go before a military tribunal at midnight, Mobutu announced. Radio Kinshasa would give regular reports. I stayed up all night, monitoring the bulletins. At dawn, the verdict was announced: Mulele would be executed later in the morning. In fact, I learned later, soldiers had cut him into small pieces, slowly, and dumped him into the river several hours before the trial began.

In truth, I would not miss Mulele. But the incident taught me about Mobutu's tactics, which I saw later applied to people whom I would miss very much. There have been more bloodthirsty leaders in Africa, and perhaps more corrupt, but seldom do they evoke warm praise from Western politicians who regard themselves as honorable men.

It is not only Americans. Jacques Chirac, just before he became prime minister of France, called Mobutu "a respectable and profoundly Francophile man who is ulcerated by the attacks of certain media." He took over during a time of anarchy, Chirac said, which required "a particular charisma."

But Mobutu is known widely as a close friend of Washington— by 1986, U.S. aid was running at $70 million a year—and no one takes pains to deny it.

The American government had its reasons for supporting Mobutu. Among other things, the Zairean president helped U.S. agents support Jonas Savimbi's Unita guerrillas in Angola. A first chunk of $15 million in aid was channeled largely through Zaire. And in early 1987, James Brooke of the New York *Times* reported Americans used the old Belgian air base at Kamina to fly down arms in C-130 transport and Boeing 707 cargo jets painted, "Santa Lucia Airways." Mobutu, who signed a non-aggression pact with Angola, denied it. U.S. officials declined to discuss it on the record. Eyewitnesses, however, leave little doubt.

Zairean authorities detained Brooke briefly after his Kamina visit. Two days later, U.S. ambassador Brandon H. Grove, Jr., advised

Brooke that the Zairean government had said if he wrote about the Zaire-Unita link, he would never get another visa. Grove stressed he was merely conveying the message. Before long, the Pentagon pressed for negotiations to use Kamina as a permanent facility in Central Africa.

Support for Mobutu is nothing new. In 1981, I asked a ranking State Department official how the United States could back Mobutu with such enthusiasm. He shrugged and smiled, a reply that said: How do you want me to answer that one? What he said was: "He maintains stability. What would happen without him?"

In 1986, the question rose again, at a higher level. Whatever Washington thought about hypocrisy, hadn't anyone learned anything from the Shah of Iran or Ferdinand Marcos? This time, no smile. "It is policy" was the answer.

At the end of the year, Mobutu made yet another trip to the White House. President Reagan gave him a broad smile and a warm handclasp. Mobutu, he said, was "a voice of good sense and good will."

The sad implication is that what Western governments crave in Africa is stability. Their concern is not over what a tyrant does within his borders. It is that he will not disguise it well enough, and let his people get out of hand. The French do not even mind Communist rhetoric so long as it doesn't mean anything. The Americans demand at least a pretense of free enterprise.

Unquestionably, Mobutu delivered stability. He took over after four years of chaos during which U.N. forces fought a war against the secessionist province of Katanga. Rebels, with savage methods of warfare, threatened to break the young nation into pieces.

From the beginning, Mobutu did not mask his style. African societies needed strong leadership, he declared. When President Alphonse Massamba-Debat, of Congo-Brazzaville, gave himself the humble title *Frère*—just one of the brothers—Mobutu sneered, and then thundered: "I am not Brother. I am not Comrade. I am Chief."

Mobutu's esteem soared among American bankers in the mid-1980s. Having run a rich country into the ground, and having put aside enough to assure the comfort of the next ten generations of Mobutus, the president swallowed his IMF salts with a smile. The signs of recovery were positive. Shelves filled with imports, and the currency black market withered. Small entrepreneurs were risking profits on new investment. I went back for a fresh look at Zaire.

Sure enough, there was a new spirit among people who had money. The same hands were extended at the airport. The simplest operation, such as getting your bags cleared, had a price. But you did not get the feeling anyone would remove your fingernails if you refused to pay it. Diplomats and businessmen were enthusiastic. The fancy part of Kinshasa, where the Belgians had lived, was in reasonable repair, and someone was regularly filling the potholes. But something felt funny. Then I went to the Cité Africaine, known since independence simply as the Cité.

The outdoor tables of Cité bars measure Zaire's temperature as accurately as mercury shows a fever. Normal is a raucous din of electric chank-a-chank and the clatter of Primus beer bottles. Whatever their problems, Kinshasa people love to dance until dawn and drink until they puke. I had never seen the Cité the way I found it. No one was dancing, laughing, or even staggering around bumping into doorways.

Men sat glumly around the tables, chins hovering just above spilled puddles of beer. There was little conversation. I took an empty chair next to two young men. One drank himself into a blind stupor, not saying a word. The other waited to size me up and then opened the gates.

"This is what we have. What you see. There is no politics, we can't say anything. So we drink. You can't feed your family. . . ." He launched into a list of prices and salaries that suggested more poverty than I had seen in Zaire. I knew enough not to translate them into dollars, or reality. Too many hidden factors go into the Zairean Miracle. Whatever happens, however bad it gets, people squeak by. And some don't.

By late 1986, Mobutu had abandoned the IMF agreement, in any case. He limited debt repayment to ten percent of the country's earnings, setting a precedent for other hard-pressed states to follow.

The distressing part is that it is so unnecessary. At first, few Africans were trained to run the former Belgian colony. Political sensitivities forced the new leaders to run the whites out of town; perhaps that was just as well. But that was more than twenty-five years ago. Now Zaireans capable of exercising almost any skill in virtually every profession live almost everywhere but Zaire.

The country itself could be wealthy from agriculture alone, but its minerals are enough to enrich a nation several times its size. Its wealth and most of its potential have been stolen.

Into 1987, American officials were insisting that at least Mobutu had mellowed on human rights. Amnesty International did not agree. Neither did Buy-Niembes Mbisha. In January, Belgian authorities rejected Mbisha's appeal for asylum. He was pushed onto a plane and handcuffed to his seat. Before the aircraft took off for Zaire, he swallowed poison. Or he was murdered.

For a while, a crusading Zairean promised to deliver the goods on those responsible. He was Nguza Karl I Bond, who resigned as prime minister and fled to Brussels. In a book entitled *Mobutu or the Incarnation of the Zairean Malady*, he described his first cabinet meeting as foreign minister. Mobutu, he said, gave his definition of a statesman: "A statesman knows how to keep a secret. If we decide to kill someone today for reasons of state, it must remain among us."

Nguza told how he was arrested falsely, tortured, made to eat his own feces, and sentenced to death. He was eventually pardoned and, in the style of Mobutu's Zaire, later named prime minister. With detailed figures, he estimated Mobutu's family income at $136 million in 1977 and 1978 alone. He showed that top party officials earn twenty times more than government doctors. His language was cool but damning, and he had testimony and documents to support his case. He warned that Zaireans might revolt violently and turn on the United States for supporting Mobutu.

"If my suffering served to open the eyes of the world to an inhuman absolutism, if it served as a lesson for history and our people, then I will say that I have not suffered for nothing," he concluded in his preface. "This suffering legitimatizes my struggle of today."

The book was published in 1982. Four years later, he had a different forum to tell the world about the Incarnation of the Zairean Malady. He was Mobutu's ambassador to Washington.

*J*ust before my last trip to Zaire, Mobutu had been reelected president. He polled 99.97 percent of the popular vote. I raised this subject with a senior journalist for the state-owned broadcasting service. He seemed straight enough with a sense of humor and a realistic view of the world beyond Zaire. How did one explain the vote count? In most democratic states, I suggested, popular leaders are seldom elected by a vote of more than 70 percent.

He replied without the slightest trace of a smile: "Maybe *le Guide* is more popular than other leaders."

6 EAST AFRICA
Good Ideas Gone Bad

On Tank Hill outside Kampala, I pawed through videotapes in a drawer at the Hotel Diplomate. The one marked *Rise and Fall of Idi Amin* was well thumbed but already forgotten at the bottom of the pile. Another was more popular but had lost its bitter irony: *The Killing Fields*. It was deep into 1986, and Uganda's fragile new peace and economic chaos were better reflected by the title on top: *Staying Alive*.

While based in Zaire, I sneaked off frequently to Uganda, the country Winston Churchill enthusiastically nicknamed "the Pearl of Africa." But it had been eighteen years since my last visit. In that time, three-quarters of a million Ugandans had been spattered with bullets, hacked to death by machetes, or forced to starve by soldiers who burned their crops.

Under Idi Amin Dada, officers and soldiers took what they wanted, including at times their victims' vital organs for ritual cannibalism. Toward the end, in Milton Obote's last years and under Tito Okello, soldiers took to raping girls of ten. No one moved about Kampala, or even less in the lush Ugandan bush, without considering the consequences.

Now it seemed to be over. Maybe. The National Resistance Movement imposed its control during February 1986. Henceforth, decreed President Yoweri Museveni, Ugandans would die only of natural causes. Each soldier had to account for every bullet given him. Sticky fingers at a roadblock, or a misdirected lewd glance, could mean harsh discipline. No one, least of all Museveni, knew whether the shattered nation was capable of cleaning up the mess. At the very least, most Ugandans were trying like hell to do it.

In the 1960s, Uganda was an enlightened country. True, President Obote, a northerner, had quashed the traditional monarchy of the Baganda, the powerful tribe that peopled much of the south. The Kabaka, King Freddie Mutesa, was exiled to London, and his palace was profaned as a repository for prisoners. But Obote kept most of the trappings the British had left in Uganda.

Cabinet ministers wrung their hands before question time in Parliament; politicians feared the power of the press. If a reporter wanted to see Foreign Minister Sam Odaka, he simply went to Sam's nightclub on the Entebbe Road and danced and saw him. Newspapers were active and nearly free, with black and white editors. *Transition*, run by an Indian Ugandan named Rajat Neogy, was perhaps Africa's finest literary review. It was read at Makerere University, in Kampala, in courses taught by V.S. Naipaul and Paul Theroux.

Even trying, it seemed Ugandans could not go hungry. Most of the country was so lush you could stick a broom handle in the ground and find it sprouting papayas in the morning. Coffee grew rich on small farms, bringing cash to families and the national treasury. Well-maintained roads, lined with the gasoline pumps that were so rare elsewhere, led to idyllic parks, teeming with game.

In the 1970s, Uganda was linked to Kenya and Tanzania in the East African Community. The three former British colonies had worked out complex accords to help them prosper together. They used a common currency and protected its international standing. East African Airways, with its familiar zebra-striped luggage labels and barf bags, was dependable, comfortable, and ubiquitous. So were the railways, carrying passengers and freight smoothly across borders.

Shelves were stocked, restaurants were excellent, and night life was raucous.

A traveler could rent a car at Mombasa, on the Kenyan coast, and drive straight through to Uganda's spectacular Murchison Falls without worrying about clean hotels or, least of all, security. East African friends would laugh at me when I came cringing out of the Congo for a break in Uganda. It meant something more to me than a vacation spot.

In Kenya, die-hard whites could argue that only their presence made the place work; if they left, it would collapse. Not so in Uganda. There was proof—if anyone needed it—that Africans could thrive in a modern state on only what they grew and what their industry could produce. That Africans had to wait generations to develop was so much racist claptrap. Look at Uganda!

I reflected on this to Obote in Singapore in 1970, at a reception during the Commonwealth Conference. He smiled. The next morning, he was nowhere to be found. His semiliterate army commander had seized power.

Idi Amin distrusted men who were brighter than he was, no small number. Many were put to death. Still more left the country, applying their skills to developing countries as far away as Papua New Guinea. To the world, Amin appeared half buffoon, half lunatic. He was neither. With brutal cunning, he dismembered the society. He drove out the Asians, who laced together commerce and provided technical skills. He drove away Europeans, and their investment capital. And he massacred Acholi and Langi tribesmen in his own army, heightening ethnic animosity to blood hatred.

Each time Amin needed to divert attention from problems at home, he selected a target from among Uganda's dwindling circle of friends. Israelis had trained him as a paratroop commander and lent aid in other fields. But, seeing more potential with Libya and other Arab states, he converted to Islam. Hitler was right, he declared. He arrested a British teacher who had criticized him and demanded that

Queen Elizabeth II come personally to plead for his release. She did not.

During Amin's time, the East African Community melted away. It broke up mainly over differences between Kenya and Tanzania, but for Uganda it meant the loss of a vital crutch.

A Tanzanian army ran Amin out of Uganda in 1979. With the arrogance of foreign invaders, they looted and raped on their own account. Great chunks of Kampala collapsed to rubble, still not cleared away. After a brief transition, Obote was back. But, spewing revenge and fearful of a second fall, he became a despot. Museveni broke with Obote and built the first elements of his resistance in a wedge of rich land north of Kampala, the Luwero Triangle. His source of strength was the Baganda, still bitter toward Obote for abolishing their monarchy.

Obote's tactic was simple enough. It was genocide. Northern soldiers, mainly Acholi and Langi, murdered villagers who did not flee the Luwero. They killed women and children, arguing that Museveni used women and children to fight them. They burned crops and blocked relief convoys. Systematically, they destroyed towns, villages, and homes. In 1984 and 1985, Obote's Ugandan People's Liberation Army killed an estimated 200,000.

It was afterward that I returned, with great trepidation. The country was still full of desperate men with automatic weapons, but that was not my worry. I was most afraid I would find the people I had liked so much brutalized and bitter.

*U*gandans were stunned, beyond bitterness. The few disconnected remnants of a modern state contrasted starkly with the devastated countryside. Most people lived the way John Hanning Speke found them a century before, on his way to find the source of the Nile.

In better years, villagers had lashed together small roadside tables of sticks, on which they displayed papayas and tomatoes for sale. Throughout the Luwero Triangle now, the tables were stacked neatly with bleached human skulls and severed arm bones. Skulls littered fields. Banana trees were choked with elephant grass and coffee plants gone wild. People who had returned lived in leaf shelters and under loose sheets of tin, staying clear of the roofless hulks that had been their towns. In places, short blackened columns of twisted metal stood near tattered red signs reading CALTEX.

I drove around with Stephen Ofori, a Ghanaian civil engineer who worked on roads and schools for the International Labor Organization. He took me to Kalege, the remains of one of the hundreds of wealthy little coffee villages in the Luwero.

A cobbler was back at home, with tools supplied by the ILO. The blacksmith also got tools, but he was dead. A rabid dog bit him. Ofori showed me a shallow hole in the tangled undergrowth, from which children scooped putrid water. It was the old well, to be replaced by a new borehole and hand pump.

The U.N. Children's Fund was already at work across the Luwero, sinking boreholes and installing Indian-designed hand pumps at blinding speed. Crews worked so fast that the supervisor, a hardworking Australian from Alice Springs named Tony Espie, could not keep track of his rig.

Over and over, I was struck by the conflict between the lingering damage and the energy people devoted to overcoming it. The old Uganda I had known was still there, living among its ruins. But for years it would be far from clear what might eventually emerge.

At the airport, a smartly dressed immigration officer could not have been more polite. He asked if I was a journalist. I replied that I was, wondering if that meant I would be taking the same plane I came on back to Nairobi. "Have a nice stay," he said, stamping my passport. The air was relaxed and friendly. People joked and smiled as they once had. The hotel had a car waiting; no one had lost my reservation. Businessmen and even a few tourists settled down for the Entebbe-Kampala ride, which, not long before, was a constant harrowing brush with death. Good old Uganda, I thought, here is proof of Africa's amazing ability to spring back from anything.

I looked closely at the hotel car. Someone had etched the car's serial number into all of its windows, a slight measure of protection from free-lance expropriation. A single side-band radio maintained contact with the hotel, just in case.

And then we stopped at the first roadblock. A barefoot soldier in a frayed khaki shirt and torn jeans peered into the window. He cradled a Kalashnikov that he clearly knew how to use. Steadily, deliberately, he studied us, as if deciding whether to raise the muzzle and fire. His piercing eyes gave no clue about the direction he was leaning toward. He was, I guessed, nine years old. He waved us on to the next checkpoint down the road.

At the Diplomate, I met a young woman named Veronica who had finished a science degree at Princeton and had come back for a while to help rebuild Uganda. But it was not quite that simple. The cup of tea I ordered was listed on the menu at two dollars. That was the equivalent of 12,000 Ugandan shillings, or one-third of a high-school teacher's monthly salary. If Veronica was lucky, she might earn a cup of Hotel Diplomate tea a week.

The minimum wage in Uganda was 6,000 shillings a month, enough to buy two beers in a bar downtown or a half-cup of tea on Tank Hill. Cabinet ministers earned the highest salaries, the equivalent of fifteen dollars a month. At such wages, people either moonlighted when they were supposed to be at work, or stole, or lived in excruciating poverty. Most ate, since even the flimsiest shacks in Kampala have flourishing little gardens around them. But there are sixteen-year-old Ugandans who have never tasted sugar.

"You know," Veronica said, "there are a lot of Ugandans who say, 'Sure, I love my country, but . . .' When you're making $50,000 a year at Du Pont, coming back is a hard sacrifice to make."

I went to the library at Makerere University. Someone had swept up dust and debris from the stacks. A few green plants had reappeared in pots in the courtyard. The only things missing were books and magazines. By counting racks and rows, I calculated the periodicals section had 2,100 neat little cubbyholes. Many bore labels for internationally known and African magazines; specialized journals for every discipline and from every part of the world; literary reviews. Every box, in each of fifteen rows, was empty.

In the stacks, shelf upon shelf was empty. Upstairs, by what had once been a microfilm collection, some of the remaining books were locked behind a wire cage. I caught the titles of two of the treasures: *Water Resources of the Wheeling, Steubenville Areas, West Virginia and Ohio*; and *U.S. Government Organization Manual, 1954–1955*. A tattered poster warned of a 1983 campaign to prevent vandalism: "Unpleasant steps will be taken against those who do not comply."

I pulled open an index drawer, not noticing which one, and flipped at random to a file card: "Obote, Apolo Milton, Pres. Uganda. Proposals for New Methods of Elections of Representatives of the People to Parliament. Kampala. UPC Hq. 1970."

But in the downstairs reading room, serious-looking students were poring over what was left. Among other volumes, there was *Electronics: Fundamentals and Application* from 1970, a Bryn Mawr catalogue from 1975, and three aged copies of Gustav Kobbé's *Complete Opera Book*, edited and revised by the Earl of Harewood. I found what was likely the latest star of what had been one of the best libraries in Africa: a 1985 *World Almanac*.

The Makerere Medical School, at Mulago Hospital, was far more depressing. I went to the Department of Psychiatry in search of a specialist who had studied the effect of stress on Uganda's children. It was a small red-brick building with no labels on the doors. Someone pointed out the secretary's office. No one was in the smelly little room; in fact, it looked as if no one would ever be back. The scarred table was bare but for an old-fashioned telephone, which was dead. The bookcases and shelves were empty. A battered old filing cabinet was open, with someone's medical records tossed loosely in the bottom.

I knocked on the only other unlocked door and found Dr. Freddie Kigozi. Yes, he said, Uganda had experienced quite an upsurge in psychiatric problems. Older people suffered badly from anxiety and depression. But the problem was the children. Youngsters had seen their parents gunned down. Many had grown up displaced, with no sense of values or belonging. Still, Kigozi saw hope.

"The majority of young people I see here are eager to go back," he said. "They want to go to school, join society, and they can do it with help, rehabilitation."

But that, of course, was the problem. Who would rehabilitate them? The head of psychiatry at the University of Nairobi was a Ugandan. But at home, Uganda had perhaps nine active specialists. "How much do we earn?" Kigozi, young and ambitious-looking, chuckled. "Let's just say, nothing." His monthly salary worked out to about fifteen dollars, hardly enough to cover his cigarettes. Even by taking private patients on the side, he could barely put gas in his car.

His tiny office was remarkably uncluttered. "That's how the cleaning staff get by," he explained. "They take any paper they find and sell it." What is for sale is not the content, but the paper itself. Occasionally visitors find secret government documents rolled into cones to hold a few cents' worth of peanuts.

The hospital had no drugs. If he prescribed an antidepressant, his patient could find it downtown. A week's course would cost only a few dollars. That is, a few months' minimum wage. No one was hopeful that drugs would arrive anytime soon. The hospital had not even had running water for a decade.

I talked about the kids with Cole Dodge, director of the U.N. Children's Fund. We spoke on his veranda by candlelight, because the lamps were packed away. It was his last night in Uganda after five years of internationally recognized work. Dodge did not say it, but friends said UNICEF had nudged him along to a promotion elsewhere. He had made waves about the *kidogo*, the 3,500 to 7,000 child soldiers still in the army.

When Museveni fought in the bush, his officers took in young boys who lost their parents. The youngsters were trained to handle assault rifles and, often enough, they used them. Some were as young as five, Museveni told a BBC camera crew, obviously proud of his prototype for the new Ugandan man. The president made oblique references to putting them in school, but he made no clear promises.

In the same BBC documentary, Dodge argued that the child soldiers were too young to make life-and-death decisions. They were growing up with no love and warmth. And, in any case, the Geneva Convention banned the use of soldiers under sixteen.

That last night at Dodge's, we ate *matoke*—banana paste—with our fingers from a large pot. Talk was optimistic. One guest was

Betty Kinene, thirty-four and crippled from polio since childhood. She had lost her husband in the Luwero Triangle and been left with six children. Cole's wife, Marilyn, had helped her set up a shop in the UNICEF building to sell crafts made by handicapped women. The business thrived, and Betty was a star. She was looking hard for funds to build a training center for handicapped women near Kampala.

Another guest was William Senteze-Kajubi, a Makerere professor who had lectured in the United States. He joked easily, poking affectionate fun at his country's crushing poverty. A few mysterious shots echoed from the distance, and the conversation turned serious again.

Dodge repeated his concern about child soldiers. The word *orphan* did not apply in Africa, he noted. Extended families can always find room for one more. Senteze-Kajubi, who had studied the problem, took an uncharacteristically grave tone.

"These children are growing up without any sense of values," he said. "They know nothing but the gun. We are creating in Uganda another generation of Idi Amins."

*E*arly in 1987, the kids were demobilized and sent to two special military academies for some formal education. But a lot of them, it was clear, were already lifers. The army was their family. And even the ones headed for school and a new life were deeply marked.

While in Kampala, I had tried to interview *kidogo* (the word means "small" in Swahili) with no success. Few spoke English. Those who did glared with cool hostility at my feeble efforts to engage them in conversation. What do you say to a kid with a Kalashnikov? On my way to the airport, going home, I had no choice.

My taxi was stopped by a boy who looked like he had just come from the set of a *Little Rascals* film. A baseball cap sat low over his eyes. His khaki pants were out at the knees, and he wore oversize rubber flip-flops. Instead of the cliché catcher's mitt, however, he had his AK-47. He wanted a ride. My driver spoke Swahili and interpreted.

He was from Masaka, south of Kampala. His parents had fled, he said, not elaborating. He left school in the third grade and had been in the army two years. Had he killed? "Of course." He said he was nineteen; more likely, he was ten. I asked what he wanted to do when he was older. "Get a job like normal people. Not in the army."

We had reached the airport, and he jumped out of the car. He swung the heavy assault rifle behind him with such practiced ease that it was hard to imagine that it would not always be part of his life. And, perhaps, Uganda's life.

In Tanzania, guns are strangely absent. That is partly because of the society shaped by Julius Nyerere. And it is also because the country is too poor to afford them. When a rabies epidemic threatened Dar es Salaam in 1985, the Health Department could not afford bullets to shoot stray dogs.

I visited Tanzania before going to Uganda, and I spoke to an office worker named Martha. "That is a TP," she warned, referring to a mutual friend's vow to organize a meeting with sources for me. "Believe it when you see it." A TP is a Tanzanian Promise. As she suspected, the meeting did not come about. There was no bad will on the friend's part. Things happen that way in Tanzania. Against all logic, everything goes wrong. A country with every reason to have prospered as an African example has crumbled in ruins, a monumental TP.

Tanzania's tragic collapse claimed far fewer lives than Uganda's, but it was just as unnecessary.

Like many outsiders, I had marveled at the good sense and moderation of Nyerere, Tanzania's beloved *Mwalimu*, the Teacher. When other new leaders sketched out their impossible Utopias, he spoke of simple sharing in the African way. His model for Third World socialism was to be open to the West and the East. Everyone would have access to education, health care, and a full plate.

Agronomists raved at the potential of Tanganyika and the island of Zanzibar, which had merged into Tanzania. Soil was deep and rich, with rivers, lakes, and regular rains. Vast plains, forests, and high plateaus were thinly populated. Colonial farmers had proven the land's value but had hardly begun to develop it.

As a member of the East African Community, Tanzania could expand markets for small industry, import agricultural tools and chemicals, and build up a communications network. Tourists reaching Nairobi, in Kenya, could cross the Great Sand River to the fabled plains of Serengeti, Mount Kilimanjaro, and the Ngorongoro Crater.

Tanzania seemed a natural outlet for Zambia, the former Northern Rhodesia, landlocked and dependent on rail links through Portuguese territory or, worse, South Africa. China gave money and men to build the TanZam Railway, a monumental project meant to strengthen Tanzania's links with Central Africa. Zambia could export its copper, and Dar es Salaam's port would prosper.

The socialist governments of Scandinavia were especially enthralled with Nyerere, and they contributed heavily to his plans. Other Europeans pitched in, as did the World Bank. Not to be left behind, the United States committed sizable chunks of their hard-pressed foreign-assistance budget.

Altogether, Western donors gave more aid per capita to Tanzania than to any other country in Black Africa. Commercial lenders poured in new money, ignoring clear evidence of what was happening to it.

Twenty-four years after taking Tanzania to independence, Nyerere chose a successor as president and retired. His reputation as a statesman remained strong. His people loved him. And his bold experiment, long since shown to be a catastrophe, hurtled forward.

*J*oseph the photographer answered with a chuckle when I asked how he survived. Articulate as he was, how could he explain the African Miracle to a *muzunqu*, a white man, who did not live with it? He tried his best.

"I finish work at 2:00 P.M. and catch the bus for my *shamba*." Like most Tanzanians, he had a little patch of land, a *shamba*. By "catch a bus," he meant he waited up to an hour until a bus appeared, squeezed himself aboard and rode for forty minutes. "I walk thirty

minutes to my land and pray to God that I have the strength to work."
His government job is six days a week. "Being a religious man, I do
not work on Sunday. That means I must spend every daylight hour
working my *shamba*."

The figures are dizzying, and they mean little in dollar terms.
Between this writing and the first proofs, they will slide dramatically.
What they mean to Joseph has not changed in a decade and may not
change in his lifetime.

For example, at the time, a U.S. dollar was worth 16.3 Tanzanian shillings officially, but any decent black marketeer would pay
200. A government clerk's monthly wage of 1,000 shillings was the
price of a can of spray deodorant made in neighboring Kenya. But
deodorant was for the middlemen who make fortunes amid such chaos
and sneak them out of the country. People like Joseph worry about
corn, cooking oil, school fees, and, rarely, an item of clothing for
someone in the family.

By rising at dawn and working until late at night, Joseph supported his family. A shortage of food in Tanzania meant that his wife
could earn extra money by selling produce from the little plot. Since
Joseph produced no surplus, selling corn and bananas would mean
cutting the family rations. Luxuries like medicine threw the whole
budget into a spin.

The *shambas* are precarious safety nets, steadily less secure,
along with many others: stalls in the market, banditry and petty theft,
creaming from the boss or the state treasury, bribe-taking. Tanzanians like Joseph have given a whole life to the cliché "eke out a
living."

Joseph, well educated, has a firm grasp of macroeconomics. He
knows the IMF has a point. Tanzania can never survive until it
restores its monetary balance, starting with a ruthless elimination of
unnecessary government jobs. But which jobs? Joseph's?

Nyerere's dream was built on a cornerstone called *ujama'a*, pulling
together. He felt that village life was essentially socialistic; by ex-
panding that idea into a modern state, everyone would approach
moderate wealth. Tanzanians were allowed to choose their own lead-

ers, as long as they were candidates of the single party. All worked together and each was to receive according to his need.

The government could never educate and care for families spread haphazardly in the bush, Nyerere decided, so he grouped Tanzanians into *ujama'a* villages. Each would work on communal farms, sharing tools, fertilizer, and pesticides. In their spare time, farmers could grow a few things in small private plots.

Peasants were reluctant to abandon good, productive land. As elsewhere in Africa, their roots were deep. Land meant tribal identity, respect for ancestors, and a link to the universe. That, argued party officials with giant clipboards, would change with education.

Once relocated, peasants found themselves crowded onto land that soon wore out. Fertilizer did not arrive to restore it. Tied to villages, farmers could plant only as far away as they could walk in a day. Crops did not reach the market, and rewards were small. With no one around to tend the trees back home, the export cashew crop plummeted. Everyone caught on fast to a basic weakness of socialism: Those who worked supported those who did not. Soon enough, no one worked.

The problem was obvious. Traditional African societies may have a communal structure, but they are made up of separate pockets of capitalism. Families amass cattle or crops by their own labor. Common structures work only when they are practical. Leaders, sanctified by custom and religion, have power but also responsibilities to people they must regularly look in the eye.

The new common structures, neither practical nor necessary, did not deliver. Those in power were not traditional rulers but, rather, politicians. They could not create wealth; they could only interfere with its being created. Tanzanians discovered that making a lot of people poor did not make anyone rich.

Tanzania's links with Kenya could not withstand the divergent policies of their leaders. Nyerere fell out bitterly with Jomo Kenyatta. Not only was the East African Community dissolved, but their common border was closed for years, a self-inflicted wound for Tanzania. Tourists stopped at the border of Kenya's Masai Mara reserve and went back to Nairobi without a look at the Serengeti.

The socialized state required a vast apparatus of ministries, planning boards, state enterprises, enforcers, and spies. As production steadily fell, operating costs rose. As foreign currency grew scarce, imports were cut to save money. In the cities, shoppers could look for days for a light bulb. Then Tanzania felt the 1973 oil shock.

While Western motorists grumbled over lines to get gas, Tanzanians scrambled to find enough fuel to run tractors and haul crops to market. Power plants stopped. At the same time, the only products Tanzania could export—coffee, palm kernels, sisal—bought dramatically less of the hardware a modern state needs to survive.

That was the time for reality, a lot of Tanzanians argued, but Nyerere was not giving up his dream.

To survive, every Tanzanian worked the angles. People who needed papers to move through the endless chain of bureaucracy had to make small gifts for nearly every signature. Pilfering was rampant.

The port was all but paralyzed by theft and corruption, which were also jamming the railway from Zambia and drying up a source of foreign exchange. Cash crops evaporated across the borders; farmers preferred immediate hard cash to the hopeless process of contributing to the socialist state.

The last tourists vanished. Often, the national airline was grounded for lack of fuel. Visitors had to bring even their own water. Canada built a modern treatment plant, but Tanzania had no foreign exchange to bring in the chemicals needed to use it.

Drought struck in 1980, bringing the ultimate of indignities. The country with enough rich land to feed much of the continent had to import corn from South Africa. One crisis brought another. To unite the country, Nyerere decided to build a new capital at its center, at Dodoma. Without enough gasoline to collect grain harvests, Tanzania ran air shuttles and truck convoys to an artificial city where only a few government offices were established. The main result was ravaged land as yet more trees were cleared on fragile land.

Nyerere admitted to mistakes, but he made his position clear in a speech to the Institute of Social Studies at the Hague:

> I am tired of being told that Tanzania's present condition
> arises out of our own mistaken policies, our own inefficiency,

and our own overambition. I am tired too of being told that Africa's present condition is the result of African incompetence, venality, or general inferiority in capacity. . . . Our mistakes in Tanzania and Africa's mistakes generally have made an impossible situation worse; they do not account for the situation itself.

Tanzania survived it all because of foreign aid. With consummate skill, officials played one donor against another. Even when aid money was not stolen, it was rerouted into the economy at large to provide the foreign exchange necessary to sustain the bloated bureaucracy.

"This government doesn't really worry," a Tanzanian journalist remarked to me with a snort of laughter. "They figure if they run short or the harvest is bad, they can just shrug and say, 'Ring up Sweden.' "

But the United States had closed its aid mission by then, and even Sweden was losing patience.

*L*ate one night, I lay on a beach house lawn under a Tanzanian moon, getting drunk among the Hash House Harriers. The Harriers are a floating brotherhood of part-time runners and full-time drinkers found throughout the Third World. Though largely British, they include any brand of expatriate willing to put up with their rituals. Their common bond is, in ways more subtle and up-to-date than Kipling had in mind, shouldering the White Man's Burden.

Often Harriers are company representatives bent on making money. In Tanzania, however, most are in the development business.

It had gotten late and raucous singing had given way to the venting of common frustration. The presence of an outsider spurred them on.

"You don't know what to do," said a young Swede whose job was to inspect health clinics his government had built across Tanzania. "I go to these places and see brand-new clinics with no medicines, nothing. Building materials disappear. They are stolen; we know it. But do you stop building clinics? Do you bring in policemen? Yes, it is so frustrating you could scream, but you don't know what to do."

A Canadian transport officer told me, "It's the same thing all over. You can't get any trucks. If you do, there are no batteries, or tires. And if by miracle you can get together working trucks, with reliable drivers, it still doesn't make any difference. You can't get gasoline."

A West German professor talked about training bright young students who starved for lack of work. At the university, incompetent teachers elbowed aside good people because of their political or family connections.

And an aid coordinator told me how the government carefully worked one Western donor against the others to side-step agreed priorities.

"They are masters at the game," he said. "Some aid money is going into private pockets, but that is not the major problem. We are duplicating grants and spending money in ways that simply subsidize their gigantic, inefficient system. Because of us, they can keep an enormous staff of useless civil servants, and nothing changes."

The conversations had a monotonous tone, varying according to the specialty of the speaker. A U.N. agriculture expert told me about potatoes he saw on the high southern plateau. "Any farmer in Idaho would have been proud as hell to grow such potatoes. Fabulous yields, good fat potatoes. And 60 percent of them rotted. The farmers have no way to get them to market. One man offered me a sack free if I would take a second one to the nearest village. This country has no trucks and less fuel."

A few Heinekens later, I sat on a rock over the waves with Abdul, one of the few Tanzanians there who was not hired to barbeque chicken.

"It is rotten, the whole thing," he said. "Anything you need, you go to the black market. If you want cooking oil, it is finished. But if you pay two times, three times the official price, it suddenly appears. Many things you don't find anywhere, at any price. If you need a signature from an official, you can't find him. When you do, you pay. No one works. People take salaries from the government but they only work for themselves, on their *shamba*. Who can blame them?"

*T*here is a brutal side to Tanzania, as occupation troops showed in Uganda. But, in a lot of ways, it is hard not to like the place. The day I arrived, Jimmy Carter flew in on a four-nation swing through Africa. Carter, no longer president, was in his role as statesman-farmer. With money provided by a Japanese ship magnate, he was trying to help Africans grow more food with a project called Global 2000. I went to the airport VIP lounge for his arrival. In Africa, such occasions are high anxiety. I had no local press credentials; there surely would be a half-dozen checkpoints bristling with gun barrels. Security police might carry me off for hours of unpleasant questioning. But this was Tanzania.

A lone policeman waved me through the gate. I introduced myself to local officials, who were happy to see me. Carter came in, chatted, and headed for State House. In a photographer friend's car, I joined the motorcade. Halfway into town, my friend pointed to an eight-year-old Volvo. Its left front fender was mashed and corroded, and one back wheel wobbled dizzily. The whole car slumped sideways on dead shock absorbers. Faded paint was streaked with rust and great billows of dark smoke belched from an exhaust pipe dragging precariously under a twisted bumper. "What about it?" I asked. "That is the chief of traffic police for Tanzania," he said.

We reached State House long after Carter and President Mwinyi, but no one stopped us at the gate. We parked and walked into the vast German colonial mansion, in rich deep woods and white columns, facing a majestic lawn leading to the Indian Ocean. I accepted a drink and relaxed. Suddenly a plain-clothes officer bumped into me, and, experienced in such situations, I braced for the confrontation. "Excuse me, sir," he said, and he moved on.

Carter was there with a simple idea. By showing Tanzanians how to use fertilizer, pesticides, and better strains of crops, yields could improve dramatically. There was no need for tractors and modern technology, he argued, just good farming.

But his chief adviser had an even simpler idea. Carter had come with Norman Borlaug, who won a Nobel prize for his work with the Green Revolution in Asia. He was a distinguished professor of agricultural science at Texas A & M.

No farmer, in Tanzania, Tasmania, or Texas, is going to waste his labor and capital on food he knows will rot in the field, Borlaug told me. The problem was not agricultural; it was political. With the slightest encouragement and support, he said, Tanzanian farmers would do just fine on their own.

Tanzanians who look hard at their problems are gravely worried about the future. Years of cutting corners has scarred the land, deeply lessening its potential. Farmers know they are turning vast, rich forests into desert. Their own topsoil boils away at each heavy rain, and each season takes away more nutrients they cannot afford to replace. But what, as corporate strategists like to say, are their options? Corn must be cooked, and cooking requires fuel. There is only wood to burn. For cooking oil and cloth and school fees, they need a little cash. There is only charcoal to sell.

People know wildlife is threatened in much of the country. But the last few rhinos and the elephants mean immediate income for families who are desperately hungry. Antelopes are meat. Tanzanians, by and large literate and sophisticated thinkers, grasp very well the philosophical argument of game-viewing. Tourists bring foreign exchange and provide jobs. But for whom? And when? A government that cannot move food has little to spare on its wildlife.

Officials admit their problems with disarming honesty. In Paris, I met Gertrude Mongella, minister of natural resources, who was attending a conference on threatened forests.

"We are terribly worried about deforestation and land degradation," she said. "It is a serious problem, and it is getting worse." She ticked off the regions and assessed damage in alarming terms. And then she added: "But what do we do? People need the wood."

Officials have promised to replant trees and enforce better range management. They have also promised to reorganize the economy, redress social imbalances, and make the country finally prosper.

As always, there is hope in the air. The *ujama'a* system is being quietly dismantled, and villagers are receiving title to land. Prices are rising for farmers. Tanzania is finally taking the IMF shock treatment in full force. There is still plenty of land and energy, if only someone could organize the economy. Most Tanzanians, however, are waiting to see. They know about the TP.

Along the shores of Lake Tanganyika, not far from where Stanley found Livingstone, another intrepid woman scientist does lonely battle on behalf of large lumbering primates. Jane Goodall, an Englishwoman only slightly younger than Dian Fossey, has studied chimpanzees at Gombe stream since 1960. She and Fossey were friends, but they disagreed over methods. "Dian was faced with this horrifying situation where her gorillas were being poached," she told an interviewer. "I haven't had to face this situation. I wouldn't be brave enough to carry on a vendetta on a personal level the way she did. I think it was a mistake but I think it was incredibly brave—and I can sympathize with her absolutely."

But Goodall and her chimpanzees face much the same struggle. During 1986, Tanzanian authorities wanted to channel too many tourists into Goodall's research area, endangering her work. That was resolved. But habitat destruction is taking its toll in remote parts of Tanzania as everywhere in Africa. "We're going to end up with practically no chimps at all in the next hundred years," Goodall said.

Kenya, by most measures, is a success, still marked by the grizzled old lion who conceived it. Jomo Kenyatta was known as "Mzee," meaning "the old man" in the best of its senses. He fought the British during the Mau Mau uprising and then worked out reconciliation.

Mzee believed in democracy, African style. There were elections and a parliament, but he was chief. During a banquet for visiting U.S. Vice President Hubert Humphrey, a waiter spilled soup on Kenyatta. The old president, about eighty at the time, rose and knocked the man flat with a right cross. An official floated up to the only foreign correspondent in the room. Print that, he said, and pack your bags.

Independent Kenya was fiercely capitalist in practice, with a substantial ration of white farmers, former British civil servants on contract, and die-hard colonials who never left their heavy wooden chairs at the Muthaiga Club. Departing British officials worked out a careful plan to transfer land to Kenyans, according to a complex tribal balance. The government bought some land from departing Britons and divided it among Kenyan farmers. Mostly, wealthy Kenyans bought the farms and kept them.

A senior Englishman involved in the process told me later: "It wasn't the up-and-coming African farmers who bought us out but, rather, the rich bastards from the city, government officials often, who came out in their Mercedes-Benzes and bought three and four huge properties. If you didn't want to sell, they found ways to persuade you."

But non-Kenyans still own rich estates around Nairobi, up to the Ngong Hills that Karen Blixen made so famous. Whites and Asians, residents and tourists, move comfortably about Kenya with little racial conflict. The *wananchi*—black Kenyans—are more equal than the rest, but other communities learned to live with that.

By the 1980s, the poorest one-third of the population earned 6 percent of the national income. The richest 2 percent earned 33 percent.

Kenyatta died peacefully in his sleep a very wealthy man, and he was succeeded by Vice President Daniel arap Moi. Kenya is not now what one would call a full-fledged democracy. Moi found Mzee's shoes a few sizes too large, and people made some unflattering comparisons as the country edged deeper into economic difficulties. But Moi consolidated his power with a semblance of parliamentary cover.

In 1982, Moi crushed a coup d'état attempt within the Kenyan Air Force and strengthened his hold. In 1986, he cracked down on an underground political organization, known by the Swahili acronym Mwakenya: Union of Nationalists to Liberate Kenya. Its leaflets denounced Moi's "dictatorial rule" and accused him of, among other things, economic mismanagement, corruption, and forced family planning.

Neither politicians nor the press criticized the president in public. Authorities jailed two dozen people, mainly teachers or students who wore the telltale beards of intellectuals. "No ordinary Kenyan is a member of Mwakenya," Moi said, "and you should be careful of these bearded people because they are serving foreign masters. When you see bearded people, you should know they lack something."

And lest anyone assume he was acting arbitrarily, he declared in a speech: "Kenya is a free country and only those who commit evil against the state are jailed."

In pursuing dissidents, Moi cut deeply into Kenya's substantial capital of international good will. After Kenyan writer Ngugi Wa Thiong'o criticized government heavy-handedness from abroad, the Kenyan Embassy in Washington said he and all other self-exiled Kenyans were welcome to come home. Salim Lone, a Kenyan journalist working as a U.N. information officer, tried it; he had official assurances that he would be welcome. He was held incommunicado for two days, expelled and stripped of his citizenship.

U.S. Secretary of State George Shultz visited Kenya in January 1987, and carefully skirted human rights issues. But Congressman Howard Wolpe, who followed shortly after, did not. The Michigan Democrat, chairman of the House subcommittee on African affairs, watched police break up a church leaders' rally. He denounced harsh government methods. Moi responded by forbidding cabinet ministers and members of Parliament—even the foreign minister—from seeing diplomats without his permission. The daily *Standard* berated Wolpe for "a conglomeration of lies and allegations against the country."

Moi went to Washington in March 1987 at a delicate moment. A Nairobi court was investigating what U.S. Embassy officers called "Ruby Ripoff, Part II." Witnesses said Kenyan officials in 1984 stole ruby ore worth up to 1.5 million dollars from a mine belonging to Elliott W. Miller, an American geologist and investor. It was Part II because Miller had been through it before in 1974 under Kenyatta's presidency. In the earlier incident, U.S. officials say, important Kenyans including Kenyatta's wife, Mama Ngina, illegally seized the mines. Miller and an American partner were expelled; Kenyatta called one of them a "hyena." The episode did little for investors' confidence in Kenya.

Moi was welcomed to the White House, but President Reagan raised the question of human rights. The Kenyan president was not happy. The morning's Washington *Post* did not make him any happier. Blaine Harden, citing court documents and Kenyan sources in Nairobi, reported that the police had used torture repeatedly for a year to extract confessions from accused dissidents. Moi canceled a private trip to New York and left Washington early.

Politics grew touchier by the month. To avoid any unpleasantness, the association of *matatu* bus operators in Nairobi decreed that anyone heard talking politics on their public carriers would be handed over to police.

For a brief moment, Rwanda had a taste of Kenyan touchiness. A batch of tourism posters arrived in transit showing a giant gorilla face over the words: "Protect me." But the caption was in French and said: "Protège-moi." Kenyan customs police seized the posters and demanded to know who was calling their president a gorilla.

Moi is regularly accused of amassing a fortune. In 1986, papers reported the Tanzanian Parliament had raised President Hassan Mwinyi's salary by $25 to $150 a month. At the same time, the London-based newsletter *Africa Confidential* estimated Moi's real-estate holdings "conservatively" at $100 million, along with companies in construction, transportation, fuel distribution, banking, wholesale foods, tires, films, and "a myriad of other high-earning businesses."

Human-rights organizations accused Kenyan police of some torture and arbitrary arrests. When Wole Soyinka won the Nobel prize, Ngugi wa Thiong'o toasted him from exile in New York, where he had gone after his release from jail at home. His book *Petals of Blood* depicted how the postcolonial elite exploited common people.

In 1986, a University of Nairobi law student named Tirop arap Kitur was sentenced to sixty-one years for sabotaging the state. He told the court: "A vulture, a bird of prey, is not to blame for landing on a carcass. It is the state of affairs that brings about the presence of the carcass that is to blame."

But foreigners who know Kenya tend to like it. Compared to

most of its neighbors, they say, Kenya is paradise. It is pragmatic, generally efficient, and a pleasant place to visit. I arrived at Jomo Kenyatta Airport in Nairobi after leaving the Organization of African Unity summit in Addis Ababa. A policeman tried to hustle a handout, but he was polite and his uniform was clean. He scurried away when I suggested that importuning the public was bad form.

At the summit, Kenya had joined the chorus in demanding total isolation of South Africa. But I was back to reality. A lilting voice on the public-address system announced, "Olympic Airways for Johannesburg is boarding at gate number four."

In the comfortable hotels, lavish restaurants, and immaculate game parks, life can approach the idyllic. I visited a friend in the Ngong Hills, and hiked around the neighborhood. Gardens were lush and the unmistakable African air was soft and peaceful. Night fell, and I flicked on what I thought was the light. A bloodcurdling howl arose, sending every neighbor within earshot leaping for his elephant gun. I had turned on the burglar–bandit–Mau Mau alarm.

Kenya grapples with its identity with a blend of pain and panache that only Africa can manage. It is a modern state, with the trappings of high technology. But in 1987 the cold chamber at Nairobi's morgue held a man locked in an ancient tribal conflict. Silvano Melea Otieno, a highly respected Kenyan lawyer, died of a heart attack in Nairobi. He was a Luo. His wife is an aristocratic descendant of Kikuyu chiefs. When she ordered the body buried in family ground in the Ngong Hills, Otieno's family objected bitterly. The body had to be buried in Luo territory, where survivors could make sacrifices. Luos did not leave their dead to wander alone in the bush.

The case went to the high court. Each day, Luos in traditional dress sobbed and danced outside the courtroom. Each evening, an anchorman in coat and tie reported the news on national television.

Kenya seldom appears on the emergency list for famine relief. But few tourists stop to visit the impoverished little *shambas* where peasants teeter at the edge of starvation. The problem is that there are 4.2 percent more Kenyans every year—the country has perhaps the world's highest birth rate—and there is steadily more pressure on the land.

Nairobi has grown from a sleepy little railhead with dirt streets to a traffic-choked metropolis that could have 5 million inhabitants within a generation.

Around the country, habitat encroachment threatens the animals that once roamed freely. Overcultivation has depleted soils. Too many trees have been cut in places, and marginal rangeland is under pressure. Life has changed drastically for once fiercely independent peoples like the Masai and the Turkana.

But much of the land is well used, and Kenya lives largely off the land. In 1987, Kenya was deep in debt, but it was making money. Its coffee brought high prices, and its oil bill was down. The maize crop was a record.

As wildebeest disappear in the Kalahari, they approach record numbers on the East African plain. Every July, herds totaling over a million thunder down the hills of the Serengeti, cross the river and stream into Kenya's Masai Mara reserve. They graze for months, snorting and grunting like so many bullfrogs, and then head south again to Tanzania.

Lance Morrow, in 1987, wrote an appreciation of Africa's disappearing fauna in a *Time* magazine essay. He stayed in Masai Mara, where I had been not long before. His Masai friend was Moses; mine was Joshua. I met Joshua late one night when I headed back to my tent alone from the well-lit, cheery lodge. Joshua stopped me. "Very dangerous, many wild animals," he pronounced. "I take you." He was armed with a flashlight. I asked Joshua what he would do if a dangerous animal presented itself. He lifted the khaki blanket he wore as an overcoat, revealing a short knife. With a light chuckle, he suggested that was all he needed.

Hardly anyone misses the wonderment of Morrow's unnamed "American visitor," the overwhelming awe of MMBA: miles and miles of bloody Africa. And few escape the anguish he felt over their future. Morrow recalled John Donne's question: "Was not the first man, by the desire of knowledge, corrupted even in the whitest integrity of nature?" And he concluded: "The animals are a last glimpse of that shadowless life, previous to time and thought. They are a pure connection to the imagination of God."

Michael Norton-Griffiths, an old hand in East African ecology, describes himself as more optimistic than most. Kenyans terrace their fields when they have to, he maintains. If they own their land, as they do in Kenya, they take care of it. The predominant Kikuyu tribe has produced good farmers from its earliest history, he said, and they are adapting with the times.

I asked him about the Masai. "There are no more pastoralists; they are rich farmers," he replied. "Maybe there are a few in those flea-ridden *manyattas* they keep for the tourists. And I think they are as happy about it as the government. The Samburu? They are changing. I love pastoralists, but today they belong in a zoo."

Norton-Griffiths acknowledges that a lot of Kenya has been badly degraded, but he insists there is plenty left. "I don't see a system rushing to disaster which has to be changed," he said. "Millions of small farmers have shown how inventive they are and with a little help they can do even better." Kenya's 20 million inhabitants are no threat, he concluded: "I would feel very happy with 60 to 80 million Kenyans."

At the rate the population is growing, he should be proved right or wrong within a generation or so. And then what?

7 BRITISH WEST AFRICA
Westminster South

The moldering old port of Accra, Ghana, is the flip side of Dar es Salaam. Its signboards are also in English, but they reflect a different style. Like the one that reads: FIASCO GENERAL TRADING COMPANY. West Africa is in a mess, but West Africans who get by each day still manage to laugh about it. The overriding philosophy is emblazoned in Day-Glo letters across the bumper of a ramshackle Nigerian truck I once saw: "Oh, Don't Worry."

With television cameras pointed more often at hungry Ethiopians and rioting South Africans, outsiders tend to forget about the western coast of Africa. But West Africa is where most people live, with much of the continent's possibilities. And it is where the potential for catastrophe is the greatest.

Before Machiavelli thought about politics, West Africans had worked out elaborate systems of state, and they dispatched ambassadors to Europe. Before Michelangelo learned to paint, West Africans mastered sculpture in bronze and hardwood.

Caravans across the Sahara had linked the African west coast to Islamic civilizations. Gold and slaves were traded for rich textiles, salt, and sabers.

A century ago, when white explorers set forth from Zanzibar and Mombasa to settle in East Africa, five generations of gravestones bearing European names were already sinking into the west coast mangrove swamps. Many of the names were British.

East African settlers came to stay, and some still refuse to go. In West Africa, however, Britons put up with the mosquitoes for God, queen, and cash flow. Colonial officers came and went, camping in wooden-slat houses open to sea breezes and termites. Tin roofs kept off rain but not rust. Each big wind meant breaking out a new keg of nails. Serums and bug sprays wore away the coast's fame as the White Man's Grave. But amusements ran to gin and the cockroach races Graham Greene described at the City Hotel in Sierra Leone.

What was meant to last, in British West Africa, was institution. The schools and courthouses, the warehouses and customs sheds, were built of heavy stone. African police were dressed in smart khaki shorts and taught to respect order. In steaming heat, judges wore heavy woolen wigs and black gowns. Barefoot or not, a clerk was a gentleman of power.

By the late 1950s, when independence was inevitable, many Europeans could not get out fast enough. Britain would leave behind four states, with borders drawn arbitrarily across the crazy quilt of traditional tribal lands. The Gambia was a misplaced little enclave surrounded on three sides by French Senegal. Sierra Leone, farther down the coast, was larger and richer. Nigeria was huge, a cornerstone of the continent. But the first was the Gold Coast. In 1957, it led the way for Africa as independent Ghana.

For Britain, Ghana was a towering source of pride. Freedom was granted when Harold Macmillan's wind of change was still a gentle breeze. The colony had flourished. Cocoa farmers organized cooperatives and dominated the world market. A thick belt of coconut palms planted on the coast generated income and protected the interior. Britain left a well-stocked treasury and a smoothly running civil service. Above all, there was a parliament. And the queen.

The prime minister was Kwame Nkrumah, a forty-eight-year-old teacher turned politician, who decided from the start not to be a black Englishman. He knew he was leading a parade, and in a book entitled *Africa Must Unite* he mapped out the route. With all of its disparate pieces rejoined, he wrote, the African continent would be an industrialized modern superstate, a vital participant in any world forum. And Ghana would set the example.

Africa Must Unite, meant as a manifesto for Africa, was a significant book; Nkrumah should have reread it.

"In our struggle for freedom, parliamentary democracy was as vital an aim as independence," he wrote. "The two were inseparable. It was not our purpose to rid the country of the colonial regime in order to substitute an African tyranny."

But in the same book, he argued the contrary: Ghanaians were not capable of democracy. The opposition sought "to vilify and attack us as a means of destroying our young state." There were laws, he noted, but "to have served writs upon them for libel would have kept us busy in courts to the exclusion of our proper duties."

He said unity was essential to a young nation, but he defined unity as following the chief's orders. "How could our people pull their weight with zeal and dedication when it was ceaselessly being drummed into them that their government was unscrupulous, inept and corrupt; that their leaders were venal and power-thirsty, and that the national effort was invoked, not for the greater glory of Ghana but for the personal glory of Kwame Nkrumah?"

He set about proving his critics right. He dismantled the apparatus of Westminster. Why, he asked, did Ghana need a British queen when it had Kwame Nkrumah? And why a confusing multiplicity of parties? Or a free press? Or niggling auditors and judges? Didn't everyone have the same goal?

Ghanaians were caught up in the heady rhetoric. Kenyan academic Ali Mazrui tells of a young accountant at the time who was trained in England and then returned to help his country. Discovering evidence of fraud, he rushed to tell his boss. The man placed a pitying hand on the youth's shoulder and explained: "Kwame Nkrumah has killed a very big elephant, and there is plenty for everybody·to chop."

Nkrumah was not immediately concerned with the size of the elephant. His dictum was, "Seek ye first the political kingdom, and all else shall be added to it." Ghana had begun with towering optimism. "If we get self-government," he had written, "we'll transform the Gold Coast into a paradise within ten years." It did not work out that way. Within three years, when other states were set free to follow Nkrumah's example, Ghana had little to offer. To escape Western trade routes, Nkrumah had bartered away cocoa for Russian fishing boats suited to cold northern waters, heavy machinery, and national monuments of Stalinist grace. Scant revenues went into flying a luxurious road show around Africa and Asia, where Nkrumah boasted of accomplishments that rang empty at home. Far too many state employees did nothing at heavy expense.

Economics were based on politics. Factories operated behind high protective tariffs, replacing imports with shoddy substitutes. Cocoa farmers' profits, instead of improving agriculture and related industries, were burned up in useless investments.

In 1966, Ghana provided Africa with an example of a phenomenon already catching hold with wildfire popularity: the coup d'état. Ghanaians perfected the art of the African overthrow. Generals told Nkrumah not to come home from a trip to China, and he was kept out while others took over. And then others. And more after that.

I went to Accra in 1969 for what was to be a return to democracy. Kofi A. Busia, kindly and gentle, was campaigning against a jolly and articulate former Nkrumah sidekick named Komla Gbedemah. It was good old-style stumping. Tribes lined up for one or the other just as Irish-Catholics and Jews do in New England.

The candidates pounded hard on the issues and made sensible promises. Laughter and beer-drinking lent charm to the proceedings. Busia won a relatively fair election, and I left feeling good about Ghana. Soon afterward, yet another general was in power.

Ghana slid from poverty to misery to desperation. Its cocoa wealth was squandered. The fishing fleet had sunk long since in the harbor. Factories shut and rusted away. On its fine old road network, cars all but disappeared from sight into the potholes. It took five hours to cover the thirty-three-mile stretch from Asankrangwa to Bawdie. Even if farmers grew food, it stayed where it was. The gentle grew pushy, and the weak starved.

Forests were cut away for wood, and they were not replaced.

Without fertilizer, farmers abandoned depleted soils and burned off bush to clear new land. Waterways silted up and clogged the dams. Hungry people thinned out the wildlife nearly to extinction.

An Englishwoman I know left Accra in 1981, bitter and sad. "It was such a fun-loving, easygoing society, and people were so polite," she told me. "Now it is a vicious fight to survive." People scrambled to get out. When her plane was announced at the airport, she was engulfed in a screaming, frantic tide. "A woman tripped and I stopped to help her," my friend said. "A huge Ashanti man behind me shoved me aside and scowled, 'Move, bitch.' "

Each new government had a different idea. In 1979, Ghana fell to a thirty-two-year-old air force flight lieutenant named Jerry Rawlings, known best as J. J. He was a dancer and a lover, a man of the people who favored peoples' solutions. For example, J. J. decided that the economy was choked off by the market mammies, the women who sold food and essentials in the Accra Market. On New Year's Eve, he sent in sappers with dynamite and blew up the market. The mammies were back the next day, trading among the rubble. Not long afterward, J. J. turned over power to an elected civilian.

At the end of 1981, Rawlings came back to stay. He abolished political parties and all the other nonsense of a struggling young democracy. Ghana was mortally ill, he said; it was time for the cure.

The witch doctors of Western finance now point to Ghana as evidence of their skill. Rawlings and Ghana took the International Monetary Fund dose without a wince, they say, and it is working. The Ghanaian cedi stopped its vertiginous skid against sensible currencies. Goods have returned to the shelves, at relatively stable prices. Cocoa is earning money, and farmers grow enough food to feed the country.

Nearly three decades after independence, Ghanaians finally accepted the hard truth: Kwame Nkrumah's elephant had been picked clean.

The lessons from Ghana depend on one's school of thought. At one extreme, it is argued that Ghana is proof that Africans cannot govern themselves. Westminster democracy died like the early white men, a victim of poisonous climes. A more generous variant is that African experiments have failed, and a new generation is returning to reality. Africans must fit into a wider world, embrace the free market, and reshape their societies to compete on equal terms with everyone else. The polite term for this is "pragmatism." Ask the U.S. State Department or the World Bank about positive signs in Africa. The invariable answer is: "There is a new pragmatism. . . ."

At the other extreme, the IMF measures are a pernicious form of international neocolonialism. The tidy macroeconomic figures mask the suffering of individuals who pay the price. Murky phrases of developmentspeak have a side that bankers miss on four-day parachute missions. "Trimming the public sector" means, for example, firing fathers whose paychecks each feed up to thirty people. In economies with no social security, that approaches a death sentence. That some entrepreneur might open a factory in the future is scant comfort to a mother with an empty food bowl—less so if she suspects her fortunate countryman's factory will be in Virginia.

Bitter critics refer to J. J. as Junior Jesus, and they say the Ghanaian Miracle is that someone can get along when food alone costs three times his salary.

But the lesson to draw from Ghana is the same one learned in Tanzania and Kenya, in Sudan and the Sahel, and everywhere else on the continent. Africa cannot work without functioning institutions, however they are designed and whoever designs them.

Western societies work because someone audits the books and enforces the laws. Does anyone seriously think that Englishmen or Americans would not exploit personal advantage if they had only their consciences to stop them? Many would likely seek to be honest. But what if presidents and prime ministers stole heavily and rewarded civil servants and military officers by sharing the loot? What if power, once obtained, was absolute? To survive, everyone in the society is forced to exploit what little advantage he has.

Take the Englishwoman at the airport. When ticket agents sell boarding passes to people with no seats, order is impossible. Whoever gets on board and stays there gets to go; everyone else is left behind.

It is an extreme case of nice-guys-finish-last. When you consider what last means in Africa, it is not hard to understand.

It is clear enough that Westminster democracy did not survive the climate. What is less clear is why. West African history offers some clues.

The first Europeans found similar structures among most African tribes. Chiefs were in charge, and they depended on trappings of power. With limited resources, a few more head of cattle, some extra wives, and a fancy stool were usually enough. Most tribal leaders knew they trod a thin line, and impeachment proceedings could be grisly. They balanced justice and brutality in the manner of medieval European kings.

But in the last few centuries, as Western societies found ways to curb tyranny at home, they fortified a new breed of tyrants in Africa. Suddenly, thanks to a steady stream of European ships, African despots had wherewithal. There was slavery, for example.

These days, it is as impossible as it is pointless to assess guilt. For nearly four centuries, slaves were shipped to America and to British and French colonies elsewhere around the world. Without European shippers and buyers, there would have been no sales. Without African slavers and wholesalers, there would have been no merchandise. Some argue that African leaders were forced into providing slaves. The Dahomeyan kings disproved that thesis, growing rich on human exports and then dropping out of the business. There is hardly cause for inherited guilt on any side. More important is the mark left on Africa.

A tribal chief who rounded up enemies could sell them for guns and irons which could be used to capture more prisoners to be sold for yet more guns and irons. Fragile empires grew into powerful states, and the quest for power became steadily more bloody.

At the same time, elite classes acquired literacy and then knowledge. As long as someone else had guns and irons, knowledge was only potential power. When colonial governments stamped out slavery, the whole balance was thrown into disarray. Warrior classes found themselves at the mercy of whoever could read law books and letters of credit. Bitter enmities smoldered, kept from flame only by omnipresent colonial police forces.

The first years of independence brought a chaotic reordering of political balance. Civilians found they could not govern with the army's guns. And military officers, whether generals or flight lieutenants, realized they needed more than power to run a country.

*R*awlings is at least a realist. In March 1987, Ghana celebrated its thirtieth anniversary, after fifteen coups d'état and eight changes of government since the heady days of independence. Rawlings told the nation: "Thirty years ago, you and I breathed in the sweet air of freedom. But did that sweet air of freedom ever give you the freedom of food or good health? We still face the humiliation of those dying in the hundreds of thousands today from famine."

*N*igeria is a harrowing example of these factors at their worst. One of every five Africans is a Nigerian, and an equal proportion of the continent's business is conducted in Nigeria.

In 1987, the sixth general to try his luck running the country announced a budget of draconian austerity. It was a new twist. In the fifteen years since Nigeria ended its civil war, writer Chinua Achebe estimated, the country "frittered away" $100 billion in oil money. That is more than all Western donors gave Africa during that period. And it is more than half the continent's foreign debt. If not all of it was wasted, Achebe was not far off.

But Nigeria is also a monument to Africans' adaptability and vitality. Nigerians have had trouble making a nation, but success stories abound among individuals, families, and clans. Some have thrived by honest labor. Others have amassed fortunes by smuggling and drug-running. But even illegal profits fuel an underground economy nearly as active as the official one.

By any standard but British convenience, the borders of Nigeria make no sense at all. Its national symbol is a rough circle sectioned by a giant Y, like an old New York subway token. It represents the

Niger and Benue rivers, which meet in the center and flow together to the Atlantic coast. Not intentionally, the three sections also symbolize the country's ethnic make-up. That was what the war was about.

Northern Nigeria is Islamic desert country, peopled by Hausa, Fulani, and other pastoralists. Kano is an ancient caravan terminus, the seat of a powerful emirate, with ways of life prescribed by the Koran and polished by custom. Northerners tend to regard with suspicion anyone who can bear Lagos.

The west is inhabited by Yoruba, a tightly knit tribe with a refined sense of magic, mystic religion, and social order. Nothing in the world exudes confident arrogance like a Yoruba chief, who believes himself privileged, moving belly and chin first among lesser beings. Yorubaland produces an array of variations on that theme, along with a counterweight of people with extraordinary humor and creativity. Soyinka and Fela are both from Abeokuta, the Yoruba heartland.

The east is Iboland, a loose amalgam of clans and clusters. Unlike the Hausa and the Yoruba, the Ibo had few societal taboos to prevent them from flourishing under colonialism. They pooled resources to send the smartest children to British schools. Their pay-off was jobs for the boys. In the early years of independence, Ibos controlled the railways and civil service. Ibo traders ranged the country, dominating commerce.

Nigeria started out wealthy and hopeful. But early tension drew blood, and politics were soon in chaos. Ibo officers led a coup d'état and seized power in 1966. They murdered Prime Minister Sir Abubakar Tafawa Balewa, a northerner loved by his people, and two regional premiers. Later that year, Hausa officers took over in Lagos. Lieutenant Colonel Yakubu Gowon, from a north-central minority tribe, was put in charge. And in the north, vicious pogroms killed Ibos by the thousands.

When the first waves of terrified Ibos reached the south, their fellow Ibos set upon northerners in revenge. Tens of thousands of Nigerians were put to death around the country for being from the wrong ethnic group in the wrong place. Shortly thereafter, an

Oxford-educated officer named Odumegwu Ojukwu took the Eastern Region out of Nigeria. He declared it the independent state of Biafra.

I went to live in Nigeria in 1968 to cover the war, and no one today believes that I liked the place. Corruption was already widespread, but in a leisurely and self-deprecating way. Gifts speeded along services that had been a long time in coming. But someone always fixed the electricity, and there were five flavors of ice cream in the supermarkets. People partied until dawn and told political jokes on television. There were as many artists as bandits.

The sandbags and dimmed lights at night suggested war. But except when I headed east to find the front lines, it was almost an abstraction in Lagos.

Each morning at 6:00 A.M. in Lagos, I tuned the radio until a familiar voice trilled: "The prrrice of liberrty is eternal vigilance. Biafrrra! Be vigilant!" For ten minutes, I heard exaggerated accounts of what the "Nigerian vandals" had perpetrated on the valiant freedom fighters.

At 7:00, I turned the dial 180 degrees. Radio Nigeria explained how patriotic forces had pushed back the secessionist rabble. Ojukwu, the criminal, was starving his people to elicit sympathy from a gullible world.

For all the rhetoric, there was a grudging admiration among the warring high commands. Neither side at first expected the other to hold out long. At the front, the temperature varied sharply. Some Hausa units bore down on Ibos with all the zeal of holy warriors. But often Nigerians and Biafrans played football on the no-man's-land between them, stopping to shoot at each other only when officers dropped by for inspection.

Nigeria's economy was doing surprisingly well. Its income came from cocoa, palm oil, and other cash crops. Farmers grew food and sold it at reasonable prices. There was no choice. Most of Nigeria's oil was in the east. Federal troops wrested away the oil fields near Port Harcourt and Calabar. But Biafrans had sabotaged installations that were not damaged in fighting. War was too close for production or exploration.

Periodically, reporters got into Biafra and described mass starvation. When it was impossible to see conditions firsthand, we relayed the urgent alarms of Red Cross and relief officials. We knew hundreds of thousands of children were dying, but Nigeria remained an abstraction. In the United States, the war went all but unnoticed. And then *Life* put on its cover a child stricken with kwashiorkor.

For the first time, people saw what later would turn into a numbing, unsalable cliché: spindly limbs and bulging belly; crinkly orange-tinted hair and large pleading eyes. Overnight, "Biafra" was a reality, the way "Ethiopia" was sixteen years later.

A rush of sympathy poured into the secessionist state. Rickety old aircraft sneaked in at night past the Nigerian MiG fighters. Relief workers could not use all the fruits of world generosity: electrical toys, mismatched high-heeled shoes, canned gourmet delicacies. But there was also food and medicine.

The fresh support prolonged Ojukwu's rebellion. Few people stopped to notice that plenty of food grown in Biafra was hoarded and sold for tremendous black-market profits. Or that the mercy pilots who risked their lives each night had to fork over huge landing fees to Ojukwu. As so often happens in Africa, there was a right side and a wrong one. The nuances in between fell away.

French arms did more than relief supplies. Charles de Gaulle was uneasy about a huge English-speaking nation in the midst of the French African Community. There was oil at stake and a huge market for everything from Peugeot trucks to Périgord goose liver. France supplied weapons as well as the legitimacy Ojukwu desperately needed. De Gaulle prevailed upon Gabon and the Ivory Coast to recognize Biafra.

Late one evening, in place of the usual "The price of liberty . . ," a calm voice said that the commander in chief would address the nation. Stay tuned. I waited all night. Just after 5:00 A.M., Ojukwu's polished voice announced that it was speaking from a tape recorder. "I have gone in search of peace," the voice said. Ojukwu had fled to Gabon, leaving Biafra to the wolves.

What followed amazed the cynics. Major Philip Effiong flew to Lagos to sign an armistice. He was received warmly, and there were remarkably few reprisals. Within a year or two, the east was thriving again. Scars remained, but the surface wounds healed quickly. Ojukwu settled unmolested in the Ivory Coast, from where he ran a transportation company in the United States. Within a decade, he was back in Nigeria running for office.

But the war brutalized Nigeria. Soldiers used to submachine guns and looted beer were not ready to go back to digging cassava roots. Politicians, put out of work by military rule, devoted themselves to amassing fortunes. Foreigners streamed in to build up the oil industry just as prices were soaring. Within a few years after the war ended, Nigeria had plenty to steal and no shortage of people to steal it.

Before I returned in 1981, I dismissed the unending string of travelers' warnings as fanciful exaggeration. I was wrong. By 1980, Nigeria was the world's sixth-largest oil producer, with rich offshore reserves. But it appeared to be made up of 90 million underfed poor people, a slim middle class, and a fringe of multimillionaires arrogant enough to make deified chiefs seem humble. Nearly everyone seemed to have found a way to milk the economy and direct their illicit earnings out of the country. Armed gangs took theirs in cash, on the spot. Periodic crackdowns on corruption and crime made little impact.

Bandits hijacked cars in broad daylight and smashed into heavily guarded homes. Police at roadblocks fleeced motorists who escaped less-official thieves. Trade deals and investments depended upon huge bribes. Lagos was such an awful city to visit that only a foreigner with something to gain would put up with it.

Holiday Inn ran a hotel on the crowded island of Victoria, which I had known as mostly weeds and sand. I got a room only because an official friend had a cousin on the desk. Like everyone else, I paid double the room rate as deposit for each day reserved. On the morning I was to check out, my room was double-locked. "You owe money," said a sour cashier, shoving a bill toward me. It was for the official equivalent of $1.80. I gave her two one-dollar bills, which she would likely change for five dollars' worth of naira on the black market. She threw them in a drawer and turned away. "Madame," I said, "may I have my change?" I was at least not going to leave a tip. She extracted a grimy, torn note, worth about fifteen cents. With a scowl, she flung it at me.

I had more nasty experiences in those ten days than in the two years I had lived in Nigeria. Taking pictures at Tinubu Square, in the filthy and traffic-choked center of Lagos, I felt, for the first time in Africa, racial hatred directed against me. I moved away quickly, careful not to show the fear that might have ignited the small crowd around me and left me in a puddle on the street.

An old friend, a Nigerian journalist, was despondent. "You can't go out at night, and you're even afraid in your own home. You can't even trust the police. Often they are in league with the bloody rogues."

But it was still Nigeria, and full of surprises. I lost a notebook, and I was desperate. I retraced my steps to the Federal Palace Hotel. At the desk, the clerk sneered when I asked if there was a Lost and Found. A security policeman laughed at me. As I got back in the cab, stricken, a little boy came up. "Did you lose this, sir?" he asked. He had seen me drop it in the parking lot and, knowing I would be back, waited an hour. He refused a reward until I wrapped his fingers around a bill and made him promise to give it to his mother.

Old pals fell on me with the sort of warmth and ebullience that Europeans seldom let themselves express. For better as well as worse, there are not many places like Nigeria.

As soon as oil revenue resumed after the war, the government abandoned agriculture. Plantations fell into ruin. Farmers came to town to work for service companies or hung out on the city streets. At the same time, the Nigerian naira operated in a private fantasy. It was so overvalued that the country could buy food abroad at a fraction of what it cost local farmers to produce. During the early 1980s, $2 billion a year was spent importing food to a country that once earned a comfortable living by agriculture alone.

Inevitably, the land suffered. Little thought was given to how trees were cut or where cattle grazed. Official attention was preoccupied with making money. Instead of plowing oil earnings back into the land, the government squandered billions. Work was started on a new capital at Abuja, but vast sums disappeared into needless services, overbilled invoices, and personal kickbacks.

Foreign exchanges paid for luxuries that slipped across Nigeria's porous borders. Colonial frontiers divided lands but not families; Nigerian Yorubas trade freely with Yorubas in neighboring Benin, and likewise among the northern tribes. Back roads skirt customs posts at every border. And business is business. If necessary, a reasonable bribe seldom fails to divert an inspector's eyes to a convenient wrong direction.

By the mid-1980s, the reverse shock had set in. Nigeria budgeted for 1986 by counting on twenty-five dollars a barrel for its oil. The price fell below nine. The new military head of state, General Ibrahim Babangida, decreed a war on corruption he clearly intended to win. He railed against inefficiency and needless luxury. All but essential imports were banned; Nigerians would eat cassava flour the way they used to.

New emphasis was put on agriculture. Farm prices rose sharply, and entrepreneurs realized there was money to be made. Jobless youths left Lagos for the farms. And Babangida sat down for the same grisly fiscal discussions as Rawlings in Ghana. Foreign exchange was auctioned off each week in a complex procedure to float the value of the naira. That amounted to a 30 percent devaluation and a steady slide. Prices went up, and some goods disappeared. The 1987 budget was the tightest in a decade. But stability seemed to be returning. If so, the World Bank and the IMF were there to help.

Like Ghanaians, Nigerians were peering over the brink. But so many Nigerians describe their countrymen as undisciplined, pushy, and greedy that many wonder if they will be able to pull back.

There were signs of hope. U.S. Ambassador Princeton Lyman, a tested hand at African affairs, told the Washington *Post*: "It has registered on a lot of people in the U.S. government that this is one of the most exciting reforms in Africa." Ishrat Husain of the World Bank put it, "If the government can sustain these changes, Nigeria could be the shining star of Africa."

Babangida found a way to reject the IMF and do the same thing the fund wanted, with a made-in-Nigeria label. Information Minister Tony Momoh explained why Nigeria might rescue itself in the same way it squandered its $100 billion oil windfall: "Nigerians are so self-centered that they don't make rational decisions when the choices are imposed on them from the outside. Nigerians believe there are things superior to reason. Things such as pride."

Authorities mounted a massive campaign in 1986 to convince the world that Nigeria was not all that bad. They reasoned that once people thought better of the place, its fortunes would improve. They had a lot to work with; Nigeria is not all that bad. But it is a challenge to the best of the public relations breed.

I asked for a visa to go look for myself; a consular officer, after high-level intervention, offered only a three-day tourist visa provided I swore not to write anything. Journalist visas can take a long time, if granted at all. As a result, I was stuck with outside sources.

The sober London-based weekly _West Africa_ carried a two-part article by Lindsay Barrett, an old Nigeria hand, which shed some light. "There can hardly be a single Nigerian who does not fear that the nation might not survive as a single entity to the end of the century," he wrote.

He noted that austerity brought no shortage of Mercedes-Benzes, BMWs, and Audis at prices starting above $50,000. Hostility and envy fuel the instability.

"In the last three months, fourteen of my friends have been attacked and wounded seriously by young night-time marauders; five died," Barrett wrote. And he detailed some cases:

—Bandits took a well-known commentator's new Peugeot 505. He was handicapped and did not get out fast enough. They pushed him out, at some speed, and then backed over him. He spent four months in the hospital.

—A gang stopped a bus on the Lagos-Benin road and approached a wealthy-looking passenger. He turned out to be broke, so they dashed his child's head against a rock.

—Thieves broke into a luxurious home and spent two hours ransacking it and brutalizing the young couple who owned it. They fired five bullets into the husband's groin and left with a crude joke about his future sexual abilities.

There were others: an inspector-general of police lost his car; author Naiwu Osahon, an outspoken advocate of the common man's rights, was attacked with clubs and a machete as he hailed a cab in full view of a police station in downtown Lagos.

Bendel State lives in near criminal anarchy, Barrett wrote. An armed gang seized one of their members from the courtroom during his trial. Authorities dismissed a high-court judge in Bendel and charged him with involvement in a ritual murder.

The Anambra state capital of Enugu, once the capital of Biafra, was under nightly siege for six months. Igwe Amobi, of Ogidi, an important traditional ruler, held off bandits in his barricaded home but was mortally wounded after police arrived to rescue him.

Barrett used this last incident to make a point with which many agree, in and out of Nigeria:

"The pervasive impression that he might have been the victim of indiscriminate police firepower remains difficult to remove from the public mind. What this type of mishap seems to indicate, however, is that the whole mismanagement of security and the imposition of violence on the nation are taking on the aspect of common fate in Nigeria."

The local press can be equally frank. But it is not easy on journalists. The weekly magazine *Newswatch* built a solid reputation for saying unpleasant truths. But late in 1986, the cover picture was of the mangled remains of the editor, Dele Giwa. He was murdered by a letter bomb not long after government secret-service officers took a distinct interest in his journalism. Later, the magazine was banned.

Another widely respected Nigerian editor, a friend, is not hopeful for the future. "It is the elites who have chosen their own narrow interests over everything else. Now the whole place is twisted because you cannot expect justice, and you cannot expect your fair share. They have robbed the country and ruined it."

The original idea was to build a single nation of disparate people working toward a single purpose. But, he said, no one gives anything to a nation that is incapable of giving them something back.

Early in 1987, information officials pressed their public relations campaign. One cornered a group of reporters who had come to cover a visit by U.S. Secretary of State George Shultz. Why, he demanded, had American reporters ignored Nigeria's reforms? Why didn't they write about improvements? The U.S. Embassy press officer beamed with pleasure. She was glad he brought that up, she said. She'd been trying for months to help two reporters get visas to visit Nigeria.

Nigeria will need more than public relations. In 1977, as head of state, General Olusegun Obasanjo described Nigeria as "a place where people are prepared to destroy anything, to cover up any crime, if doing so promotes their economic interest or might." In 1987, four young men shot and killed his wife while she was stuck in traffic. They wanted her new Peugeot 505.

Things may get better, and they seem headed in that direction. But a form of natural selection remains at work in Nigeria, for doing business as a foreigner or for living your daily life as a Nigerian. You might call it the law of the jungle.

Sierra Leone is the sort of place Joseph Conrad could love. It is a small bite out of the west coast next to Guinea, cheery and bustling and, at the same time, darkly sinister. The country started with promise. Smart-looking police in khaki shorts directed desultory traffic. Judges sweated in torrents under heavy white English wigs. The niceties of Westminster took solid root. More important, Sierre Leone had diamonds.

The mines of Sierre Leone produced quality gems. If no limitless fortune, they were enough to get a little nation of 2.5 million people off to a good start. But a lot of the stones ended up in the wrong pile.

Once, I was there during a spectacular diamond robbery at the airport. Couriers were bringing a valise of gems from the mines to Freetown for export through regular channels. Someone walked up to the man with the bag and blew black pepper into his eyes. When he sneezed, the mysterious robber fled with the rocks. Sure.

For much of its career as a country, a former labor leader named Siaka Stevens held power. He survived assassination attempts, coups d'état, and riots. But Sierra Leone's economy crumbled while Stevens struggled to keep dissidents in line. In 1985, he retired and designated

Below: Nax the Bushman with Doug Williamson in Kalahari.

Below: From the air, a Kalahari cattle post is an artificial oasis surrounded by desolation.

Above: In Mopti, Mali, Abdul Rahman Diku's son in his entire wardrobe - a scrounged shirt - takes his turn at a rare bowl of food.

Left: Abandoned wildebeest calf near Lake Xau.

Below: An old fishing canoe sits stranded on the dried bed of the Niger River.

Right: Tuareg children settled in Niamey.

Far right: An ancient Tuareg woman tries to adjust to a settled life along the Niger River.

Below right: Tuareg nomads-turned-farmers hold council at Tin Tellout near Timbuktu.

Above: Tuaregs carry scarce firewood from the Sahel desert by donkey caravan.

Right: A giant hole, terraced for depth, serves as a well outside Timbuktu.

Below: Sudanese women pound down dirt to build an irrigation dyke.

Above: Rusted USAID pumps sit useless at Diré, Mali. At rear is a new motor pump donated by the U. N. Children's fund.

Right: Refugees in western Somalia using piped water at a camp. The water levels drop often because nomad women, unaccustomed to taps, break them off and water escapes.

Below: With only a well and watering buckets, Sahelian farmers' vegetables bloom in the desert.

Above: A stricken mother and child at Timbuktu.

Right: West African children at play in a narrow alleyway.

Below: Women at work in the streets of Mopti, Mali.

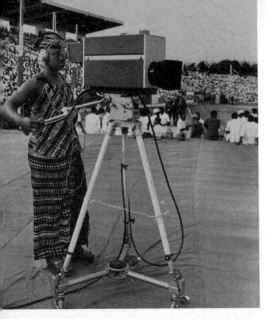

Above left: A Guinean woman operates a television camera in Conakry.

Above: Djibril Diallo, on a U. N. trip to Djenne, Mali, looks at terra cotta copies of gold jewellery women can no longer afford.

Left: A Sudanese harvesting rice.

Below: Kenyan bus.

General Joseph Momoh to run for president. Momoh won and set about trying to reorder the economy along IMF guidelines.

Tourists who seek only good beaches, relative security and friendly people have a good time in Sierra Leone. But agriculture, Sierra Leone's main activity, is badly organized despite World Bank investment. Europa's *Africa South of the Sahara 1987*, a standard reference, offers this bit of understatement:

"As with numerous other large-scale agricultural schemes in tropical Africa, the achievements of these projects have, so far, been more conspicuous in infrastructural expenditure than in any increase of marketed output."

Next to Sierra Leone is an English-speaking colony that Britain never owned. It is Liberia, established in 1822 by freed slaves from America and made independent in 1847; it remains the closest thing the United States has to a former colony in Africa. Firestone's huge rubber plantations accounted for 35.9 percent of Liberia's income in 1955. Until the 1950s, the only means of communication with the rest of the world was a shaky telephone line to Akron, Ohio.

The Liberian flag looks so much like Old Glory, in fact, that a visiting State Department official mistook the nine-story Executive Mansion for the U.S. Embassy. The mansion was built by William V. S. Tubman, president from 1944 until his death in 1971. He had the Temptations and the Impressions piped through the Muzak system. When the ornate fountain out front was turned on, people for blocks around did without water. Traffic was paralyzed for hours whenever Tubman's Cadillac was scheduled to roll by.

The diminutive president liked cigars, top hats, and order. Faithful aides provided all three. An elite stratum of "Americo-Liberians" held power over indigenous tribes. No opposition was tolerated. Tubman was succeeded by William Tolbert, his vice president for twenty-nine years. Tolbert lasted until he tried to encourage local rice production by raising the price to consumers. In the riots that followed, at least 100 people were killed. Tolbert rushed to apply a rice subsidy, but the damage was done.

On April 12, 1980, a group of soldiers under Master Sergeant

Samuel K. Doe shot their way into the Executive Mansion, assassinated Tolbert and overthrew the government. Then they invited Liberians to a public execution of thirteen leading officials of the former regime, including the chief justice. Doe had overthrown not only the government but also the old social order.

Throughout the following years of bloodshed, economic chaos, vote rigging, and corruption, U.S. aid poured steadily into Liberia: $463 million since 1980. President Reagan was otherwise preoccupied; when Doe visited Washington, Reagan welcomed Colonel Moe.

By 1987, the country was broke. Liberia's currency remained the U.S. dollar, but greenbacks in circulation were snatched up by traders concerned with the future. Instead, the government churned out five-dollar coins for which no one had change. Liberia could not even raise the $800,000 it needed to meet requirements for further U.S. aid.

On an African visit in 1987, Shultz told reporters that Liberia had a free press, an elected government, and no political prisoners. In human rights, he said, "there is genuine progress."

That raised eyebrows all over Liberia. One local reporter who asked not to be identified said he avoided the slightest criticism for fear of arrest. The publisher of *Footprints*, one of two papers recently closed down, wondered what Shultz was talking about.

And Ellen Johnson-Sirleaf was outraged. She should know. Mrs. Johnson-Sirleaf, a former finance minister, gave up her job in Nairobi as Citibank vice president for Africa when Doe would not let her leave the country. She formed an opposition party, but eventually fled Liberia in fear of her life.

Shultz's statements, she told the New York *Times*, were "either deliberate misinformation or ignorance."

*D*oe is an embarrassment to African leaders struggling hard to build their credibility. Not long after he took over, the New York *Times* reported a conversation between the new head of state and one of his financial advisers. Doe did not want to authorize a rise in gasoline prices. Exasperated, the adviser made it plain: "You don't sign this paper, country go blooey." Doe signed, but the country went blooey, anyway.

In 1987, Senator Edward M. Kennedy, quoting from a General Accounting Office report, said Liberia could not account for $16.5 million in U.S. commodity support assistance. There was more. "It is clear that General Doe has used his position to enrich himself and his associates at the expense of the American taxpayer," Kennedy said, urging an end to all U.S. aid.

Doe's spokesmen denied it. But then Liberia gave up all pretense of economic independence. Doe authorized a shadow cabinet of seventeen American financial experts to oversee all expenses and accounts. Proponents say that meant Doe was coming clean. Critics say his government had no choice.

The last little piece of former British West Africa is the Gambia, reaching into Senegal like—choose your simile—a dagger or a grafted vital organ. Independent since 1965, it is run by Sir Dawda Jawara, who is quietly becoming the dean of African statesmen.

A former veterinarian, Jawara once campaigned on a simple slogan: "Every cow knows me personally." He converted to Islam, but he is no prude. In the late 1960s, when the trend in tourism shifted to topless, he allowed naked Swedes to cavort outside the windows of his modest palace.

Respect for humans and protection of their rights were shown in the Gambia long after much of Africa abandoned such luxuries. Not by everyone, however. A coup d'état attempt nearly unseated Jawara in 1981. He was saved only by troops dispatched by his friend and neighbor President Abdou Diouf of Senegal.

Afterward, the two countries launched a promising experiment in postcolonial Africa: Senegambia. The two states melded into one, more or less, ignoring the deep differences in their colonial background.

"If it can work anywhere, it can work in the Gambia and Senegal," remarked Wally N'Dow, a former Gambian minister and now a senior U.N. official. But he was not yet sure that it would. There was motivation, he said. But only time would tell whether African roots would overcome the differences between the British and French ways of looking at things.

Whatever their colonial background, the states of West Africa seem unlikely to thrive unless they integrate their economies. Time and again, they have tried. The most energetic effort is the Economic Community of West African States, Ecowas, which has been trying to get started since the mid-1970s.

Nigeria, the natural cornerstone for any regional cooperation, has seldom been interested. In 1983, authorities abruptly sent home a million Ghanaians and other West Africans to free jobs for Nigerians. Immigrants who had been settled for years were offered neither compensation nor time to pack. Convoys of miserable refugees backed up at borders.

The next year, a new government sealed the country's land borders. That stopped neither smuggling nor currency fraud, but it paralyzed some of its neighbors' vital trade. Then another 700,000 people were expelled.

But Babangida was host to the 1986 Ecowas summit in the half-finished capital of Abuja. Nigeria announced with a flourish that Ecowas citizens needed no visas or work permits. Closer inspection revealed conditions. Only certain professionals, like doctors and architects, qualified. The riffraff, like lawyers and journalists, did not.

At each new summit, speakers insist on the natural affinity of the region, the common problems, the need to understand each other better. But, to outsiders, it seems that each year just as many delegates need simultaneous interpreters to hear their neighbors' points of view.

8 FRENCH AFRICA
Balkans on the Slave Coast

*T*he French, unlike the British, came to West Africa to stay. They had it carefully worked out. First, they would turn Africans into Frenchmen. Then, they would turn Africa into France. That they succeeded so well is a major reason why regional groupings seldom work. Senegalese, Ivorians, and the others often have more in common with the French than with Nigerians or Ghanaians.

But the French did not do as well as they expected. In their ritual reading of Descartes, the architects of France's African colonial empire found this in the *Discours de la Méthode*: If man correctly serves reason, "we can render ourselves the master and the possessor of nature."

French engineers converted forests to fields and bent the rivers. Nature, like the natives, was subject to Paris. The natives have since declared independence. Now it is nature's turn.

The elements are proving with grim finality that they take no orders. But Descartes left himself an out. He warned that man would have to serve reason if he was to conquer nature. In French Africa, and in the quarter-century since independence, reason has been little in evidence.

The French plan to shape Africa in their own image was part of a historic mission to radiate civilization into the heart of darkness. As teachers and missionaries shaped young minds, engineers worked on the land.

In 1919, a master builder named Belime put it clearly enough: "How do we justify our renown as a colonizing people if we allow, as in the time of the Negro kings, the waters of a great river [the Niger] to uselessly traverse our African domain?" He started work on a network of dams and canals to water a million acres of flood plain.

Across the colonies, trees were cleared to make room for great plantations: coffee, cocoa, groundnuts, oil palms, cotton. Minerals were tracked down and exploited. Railroads linked productive zones to the coast. Waterways were dredged and channeled into irrigation canals.

The empire builders had cause to puff out their chests. A growing class of black Frenchmen helped to run a thriving economic system from Senegal to Chad and south to the Congo River.

Few were concerned by the forced labor that broke down traditional systems to provide plantation workers, hewers, and haulers. Paying taxes, in kind or in labor, was simply a duty of Frenchmen. The empire could abandon reference to the Slave Coast; there were no more slaves. That the Ivory Coast was also a misnomer—the elephants were all but gone—bothered almost no one. Wildlife was hunted down for sport, killed off to protect cattle from disease, and simply crowded off the land.

Scarce game presented no problem. Workers could buy bits of beef. It was all part of the plan. Africa's old system of subsistence farming was *dépassé*. Cash crops paid wages to farmers, who could buy food they did not grow. As Governor-General Roume, of Senegal, noted at the turn of the century, "The alpha and omega of colonial policy was . . . produce and transport."

A French Overseas Army handbook rhapsodized on Roume's theme:

That formula happily sums up what is necessary to the modern equipment of a colony. Equip a colony: Those words ring in our ears, in the engineer corps, like the words, "equip a battlefront." Equip a colony: That is to provide the tools and means to develop to the maximum its economic value and its force for political expansion; it is to create tracks, roads, railways, telegraph and telephone lines . . . to install and maintain with a minimum of troops this French peace which has nothing to envy over the famous Pax Romana . . . this French peace that assures the moral conquest of our natives and makes of France an empire of 100 million inhabitants.

With Paris to organize supply lines, no colony needed to be self-sufficient. Food shortages brought misery but seldom for long. Telecommunications, transport aircraft, and bridges shrank the distances. Faceless planning officers fixed the imbalances.

Tribes bickered among themselves, but all of them answered to the same Ministry of the Colonies. Funds were often short, but there were no budget crises. Petty pilferage was harshly punished. The big profits, the monopolies and cartels and concessions, were all *l'affaire des blancs*, white man's business.

The British colonized the coasts of their territory and then worked through traditional rulers. The French settled the hinterlands and sent the Foreign Legion after recalcitrant desert war lords. Palm-fringed oases and *Beau Geste* forts displayed the Tricolor.

Regionalization was by decree. The empire fanned outward from the little island of Saint-Louis off the Senegalese coast. French stone-masons and ironworkers fashioned a European capital with elaborate care, fitting louvered shutters in deference to the tropics. Later, Dakar replaced Saint-Louis, and other cities grew along the coast. French buildings rose among the mud mosques in Bamako and Gao, Niamey and Agadès. But it was all French West Africa.

Farther south, French Equatorial Africa spread from Brazzaville, across from Léopoldville, on the Congo River. At the end of the last century, France tried hard to hold enough of Sudan to link their vast holdings in the west to the Red Sea of Djibouti.

Breezes of change ruffled the fringes of empire after World War II. Charles de Gaulle gathered colonial administrators in Brazzaville in 1944 to say that African blood spilled for France must be rewarded. No Africans were invited to hear him, and another fourteen years passed before he took up the matter again.

Into the 1950s, France was spread thickly throughout its African territory. Schoolchildren studied a text that began, in French: "Our ancestors the Gauls were blond and robust." They lived in dread of *le symbole*, a piece of wood that was passed around in class like the Old Maid card. When the kid with *le symbole* heard a classmate speak an African word, he passed it to him. And so on. The psychological pressure was devastating, and some children rejected their tribal languages. But any youngster so inclined could get himself educated and work toward a bright future.

In 1958, De Gaulle put a choice to each of the colonies. They could remain an integral part of France. They could go off totally on their own. Or they could be independent but still in "association" with France. As he had hoped, almost all chose the last. Gabon wanted to be part of France, but was nudged out of the nest. Guinea wanted a clean break, so the French stomped out, taking even the light bulbs and Government House dishes with them.

Thirteen new states chose association. They shared the same currency, backed by the Bank of France. When they ran short at the end of the year, a check materialized from the Elysée Palace. If there was an unauthorized coup d'état attempt, French planes scrambled from local military bases kept as part of the deal.

Today, there are 300,000 Frenchmen in Africa, twice as many as at independence.

To varying degrees, the new states followed similar patterns. Elites in power struck their deals with Paris to insure they kept control. So far, no party has been voted out of office against the wishes of the incumbents, or the French; some don't bother with elections. Coups d'état have been frequent. But whatever ideology a new leader espouses, his attention turns immediately to his Paris embassy.

Most people joined the system. Dissidents found opposition politics a lonely and dangerous business. Entrepreneurs were paralyzed without a sheaf of official permissions. Intellectuals took out party cards and worked for the state. And the schools fed the apparatus a stream of new black Frenchmen; Senegal even retained *le symbole*. The mark of success was a white shirt with French cuffs.

Farmwork was for ignorant peasants. Bright children were put through school and then sent off to try their luck at striking it rich and supporting their village. Food production slipped. Irrigation canals silted up, and pumps broke down. Fields were depleted and abandoned. Transportation systems collapsed.

No one noticed nature's warnings that the land was under pressure. Jobs were plentiful. Each new country had ministries to fill, state enterprises to run, and civil services to staff. They shared Air Afrique and research facilities. The new members of the club had their quotas for U.N. sinecures. French companies needed executives, some real ones and some as window dressing. With France barely out of sight in the wings, the old structures lumbered along.

The backbone of the Balkanized French African states was the CFA franc, a common currency backed by the Bank of France. For the price of letting Paris control the bulk of their foreign reserves, the young nations had fully convertible currency and substantial commercial credit. Goods moved among the former colonies and into France with relative ease.

But so did people. Rather than build separate nations, united by a common purpose, former French Africans went to where their opportunities were greatest. Ivorians and Senegalese sent their fortunes to France and then followed them. Mali and Upper Volta (now Burkina Faso) had no resources except willing, well-qualified workers, who migrated to the Ivory Coast. Togo and Dahomey (now Benin) were too small for the more ambitious, and brains drained away.

Few governments sought to stem the flow. Overachievers meant a political threat. Each time army officers seized power, they forced much of the previous ruling class into exile. Within a decade, nearly every country had at least one shadow cabinet plotting in Paris. Governments spent as much effort protecting themselves as helping their people prosper.

In such a climate, leaders and civil servants had to make their money before it was too late. And each had legions of dependents to support. Such long-range frivolities as conservation and careful land use were the subject of countless speeches. In practice, they were an obstacle to the practical business of getting rich fast.

Officials sold off vast, irreplaceable hardwood forests. Timber earned foreign exchange. More, logging concessions paid handsome dividends to those who granted them. European and Amerian contractors dangled attractive propositions. Ministers agreed that every modern state needed a steel mill and high-tech factories, especially when thank-you notes came in fat envelopes. Details such as lack of markets or managers could be sorted out later.

Before long, economies were distended. Debts rose along with unemployment. Cities bulged with hungry people. Food prices were kept artificially low. Agriculture, a natural resource needing only rain, would take care of itself. As farmers depleted their land, they simply set fire to the bush and chopped down trees to open new land.

Reality sank in only when nature had had enough. By then, for many teetering in a precarious balance, it was too late.

The cornerstone colony, Senegal, set out with high hopes. Like Ghana, it started as one of Africa's most prosperous states. President Léopold Sédar Senghor was a former French cabinet minister and an accomplished poet. He had a wide base of Senegalese technicians and intellectuals. He made generous use of the counselors and technicians France left behind. The only thing Senegal lacked was resources. It lived, literally, on peanuts.

Senegal's groundnut crop kept the economy climbing slowly upward. But drought in the mid-1980s devastated the groundnut crop, and the land along with it. Food supplies were desperately short. The economy dropped 4 percent in 1984 in real terms. In spite of stability under Senghor and his hand-picked successor, Abdou Diouf, the country is in crisis. Late in 1985, Diouf flew to Paris to ask for a check, so he could pay government salaries. Paris obliged, but the cash-flow problem remained.

Senegal spent heavily on oil and food. Deficits in freight and insurance payments skyrocketed. Interest payments climbed on a growing debt. The country was helped mainly by its major export: people. Senegalese workers in France remit large amounts. But pressure in France sent many Africans home and closed the door to others. A third of Senegal's people now live in cities at home, two-thirds in Dakar. The jobless are numerous—and bitter.

Investment in agriculture brought a surplus of rice. But it cost more to grow rice in Senegal than to buy it from Southeast Asia.

In some ways, Senegal is a rare success. Its university turns out thinkers who can speak their mind. Its president, tall and impressive in stylish but somber suits, is a voice of moderation on a continent short of leaders. Opposition parties point out his mistakes. But Senegal lives on a knife edge.

The Ivorian Miracle is one of those hoary staples of modern Africa. Under the circumstances, it is miraculous that Côte d'Ivoire—the Ivory Coast—has done so well. But spending the future to purchase a prosperous present is no miracle.

President Félix Houphouët-Boigny, a devoted capitalist, was not impressed with Frantz Fanon's *The Wretched of the Earth*. Critics say he sold his soul to the French. He did, but he got a pretty good deal. As a minister of the French government in the 1950s, he learned who he was dealing with. Then he watched Kwame Nkrumah mortgage Ghana to the Soviets and pay for it with his job. Houphouët-Boigny's ego was no smaller than Nkrumah's, but he wanted to reach a ripe old age and be remembered for greatness. He achieved the first goal; as to the second, only another decade will tell.

By the French tax collector's traditional guideline—external signs of wealth—the Ivory Coast is a smashing success. Abidjan, if you stand far back, gleams and glitters. A skyline of taste and style towers over cloverleaf freeway exchanges. Bridges soar across a thriving harbor. Discos, beach clubs, linen-and-crystal restaurants, and golf courses are full to bursting. Ivorian women cover their bosoms with Cacharel silks; French women sun theirs on the decks of swift white yachts.

The interior is laced together by a reliable airline, good roads, and telephone circuits. Up a four-lane superhighway is Yamoussoukro, a futuristic rural capital of grand esplanades, blazing lights, luxurious hotels, a sumptuous presidential palace, and hardly any visitors at all. Most nights, six-lane freeways and elaborate cloverleafs serve only the occasional bicycle. Yamoussoukro is, coincidentally, Houphouët-Boigny's home village.

In Abidjan, black couples dance long past midnight at a floating disco tied up off the Boulevard Charles de Gaulle. Their fashions are no farther behind Paris than the eight hours it takes to fly them down. Over the bridge in Treichville, friends gather around outdoor tables at backyard restaurants, called *maquis*, to consume peppery fish and beer by the liter.

Supermarkets burst with obscure French cheeses, freshly ground foie gras and fruits from around the world. There is even an American specialty shop for Aunt Jemima pancake mix, taco sauce, and chunky peanut butter.

And, visitors are told ceaselessly, the nation's wealth all grows on trees. The Ivory Coast produces coffee and cocoa, palm oil and bananas. Unlike neighboring Guinea, which has iron, bauxite, and manganese, the Ivory Coast has few minerals. The country's success is man-made, with only limited help from small oil reserves, which cover most local consumption. Hydroelectricity powers small industries and the blaze of city lights.

Up close, the glitter dims.

The Ivory Coast's luxuriant hardwood forests covered 70 percent of the country at the turn of the century. By 1986, the figure was 5 percent. Watersheds are so badly degraded that the hydroelectric turbines could not generate enough current for Abidjan during the last drought. Office workers trudged up twenty flights of stairs and sat by inert electric typewriters. Deprived of air conditioning, high-rise buildings with sealed windows were Turkish baths.

Fast-lane living for some has created bitterness among a huge sector of the unemployed. Corruption is rife at all levels. Petty thievery and serious crime are widespread. When I last left Abidjan, a friend rushed me along Boulevard François Mitterrand toward the airport. A motorcycle cop stopped us; he was immaculate in white patent leather and khaki. He pointed to my unfastened seat belt. I apologized and said we were late for a plane. A grin spread over his face. Before I realized it, I had doubled the price of the "fine" by revealing my desperation.

Later, a friend took the comfortable old Ouagadougou Choo Choo, the night train from Abidjan into Burkina Faso. Three times, robbers moved through the cars, cleaning out the passengers at gunpoint.

Houphouët-Boigny has hung onto power well into his eighties, moving aside efficient deputies who might present a challenge. Diplomats acknowledge that he has kept the country stable and relatively prosperous. He shuns the embarrassment of political prisoners, and castigates brash young colleagues who give Africa a bad name. But there is a single newspaper, and no dissent.

And the president's flights of fancy raise eyebrows, if not hackles. Hard-pressed in the 1980s and with one of Africa's highest per-capita debts, he pushed ahead with lavish construction projects. In Abidjan, he built a huge cathedral. And then, as bankers negotiated a rescue package to reschedule the towering debt, he announced plans for a basilica at Yamoussoukro. Its dome would dwarf that of St. Peter's in Rome. Its cost, not announced, was expected to run into hundreds of millions of dollars.

In 1987 the basilica's construction was already paying country club dues for many of the 150 Frenchmen hired to supervise it. One French executive was indignant when asked by an American visitor whether it was not folly to build one of the world's biggest churches in empty African bush. "Don't you think," he replied, "there were people starving and homeless when the cornerstone was laid for Notre Dame?"

The money would not come from the state, but, rather, from Houphouët-Boigny's personal fund for good works. Where a country doctor–turned–politician amassed that kind of wherewithal is no question to ask in the Ivory Coast.

Guinea is the alter ego of the Ivory Coast. When Houphouët-Boigny stuck closely to France, Ahmed Sékou Touré turned sharply to the left. He gave up Guinea's claim to French aid and advice; he argued that neither was necessary. Guinea's soil was as rich as its neighbors. Better, the land was marbled with valuable ore. But Guinea slipped steadily backward.

Soviet aid accomplished little. Sékou Touré's energetic socialism discouraged farmers and workers both. Secret police grew heavy-handed as economic failure brought unrest. Little thought was given to land management. Tall trees and underbrush were cleared from wide sections of the Fouta Djalon, the source of the Niger, causing serious damage to the lifeline of the Sahel.

Invasions, coup attempts, and general paranoia kept Guinea's notorious prisons full. The country's 6 million people, largely dispirited and frightened of the government, produced little.

Sékou Touré began inching back into the fold in 1979, inviting French President Valery Giscard d'Estaing down for an emotional welcome. When Guinea's founding father died five years later, generals seized power and turned the country sharply back toward France. The French, of course, were ready. Guinea received $88.6 million in aid for 1985. Investors and merchants poured in. French weaponry replaced the Soviet hand-me-downs. A scientific research center was set up. And whereas the Ivory Coast sent home unneeded French advisers, Guinea complained bitterly that it was not getting enough of them.

*T*wo former French colonies seized upon Karl Marx after a series of coups d'état sent each into a spin. Benin, a sliver of a state next to Nigeria, started out as Dahomey, the coup capital of Africa. I covered a few revolutions in Cotonou, the pleasant little palm-shaded urban center, but I missed most of them. In 1972, Major Mathieu Kerekou took power and kept it. He set up a Marxist-Leninist socialist state in 1974. He castigated France. He did not, however, give up the CFA franc. Fifteen years after the revolution, Kerekou had little to show for his ties with Moscow. Whatever the rhetoric, he still looked toward France.

By 1986, Benin's telecommunications department offered consumers a new service. On their home terminals, under "Enter Category Name," they could tap out a request for their horoscopes—or the latest quotations on the New York Stock Exchange.

The Congo, across from Zaire, has managed the same balancing act. The slogans are Marxist, but France still controls a third of the economy and sells two-thirds of the imports. President Denis Sassou-Nguesso, at the time a hard-line colonel, took power in 1979 not long after yet another assassination. But he switched to natty three-piece suits and opened the economy to the West. And he pushed hard for efficiency. In government offices, a popular slogan exhorts: "Seven hours of work, not seven hours at work." France still marks the Congo, down to its familiar yellow mailboxes. Brazzaville's train station, for example, is a replica of Deauville's.

Mali, Niger, and Mauritania each moved away from France. But none went far, and each came back when circumstances demanded.

Upper Volta floundered from coup to coup until Captain Thomas Sankara led a revolution in 1983. He changed the country's name to Burkina Faso and tried to change its way of life. He stamped down hard on corruption, not only at home but also in regional organizations, and imposed austerity. Mitterrand visited Ouagadougou in 1986 and sat stiffly while Sankara admonished him on French African policy. But both leaders, with little choice in any case, departed friends.

Thomas Sankara and his southern neighbor, Jerry Rawlings in Ghana, have worked to build a bridge over the colonial gulf. Tom and Jerry summits brim with African verve, ebullient bursts of camaraderie and new ideas. They joke together in English, share tastes in music and style and, above all, see themselves in similar revolutionary roles.

Rawlings, in an interview with *West Africa*, accused outsiders of categorizing Africans as a means of domination. "We will not make their work easier by picking up one of their labels and slapping it on ourselves," he said. "Maybe journalists should help this continent refuse the indignity of such demeaning labels in favor of finding our true character." Sankara says the same thing. "Development," he told me in 1986, "is what we do ourselves." France left behind its language in Africa, he said, but in French he could speak to oppressed peoples everywhere.

Cameroon bridged the colonial gap from independence. Most of Cameroon was French, but its western wing was British. As a bilingual state, it has done well playing on its strengths. Agricultural yields are high. Oil revenues have been meted out carefully to avoid the oil fever that crippled Cameroon's neighbors, Nigeria and Gabon.

Gleaming buildings went up in the capital, Yaounde, and the bustling port, Douala. A fast highway linked the two, and a growing middle class bought cars to drive along it. The Bamiléké, a western tribe of legendary business skills, infused entrepreneurial skills into the economy. In Douala, for example, a teenaged Bamiléké named Irene Pessonka slowly builds her fortune selling cigarettes. Talking to Richard Everett of the Associated Press, she glanced up toward a nearby 15-story building. "I want to get into real estate," she explained.

In northwest Cameroon, farmers are showing how well development might work in Africa. In seven years, a $44 million project designed for 200,000 people now reaches nearly a million. Food production grew by 50 percent; some yields have doubled. Maize surpluses, coffee and vegetables are sold for cash. A research facility developed fifteen varieties of maize. Newly trained extension agents —many of them women—work with the farmers. The Ministry of Agriculture sells fertilizer at low rates. The government project is helped by aid agencies, including the U.N. International Fund for Agricultural Development, which aids the world's poorest farmers.

President Ahmadou Ahidjo ran Cameroon with a firm hand, discouraging political challenges. At first, French troops and secret agents helped him quash the UPC. Félix Moumié, Ahidjo's UPC challenger at the time of independence, died of rat poison in a Geneva restaurant. Ahidjo retired in 1982 and tapped Paul Biya as his successor. Mild criticism can be uttered in public. But those with power do not expose themselves to the possibility of losing it.

*I*n Gabon, Cameroon's little neighbor to the south, there is no such ambiguity. Gabon remains faithful to France and to profit, mainly for President Omar Bongo and a handful of French interests. Shortly after independence, a coup d'état toppled President Léon M'Ba. France righted him again. When M'Ba fell sick, French strategists agreed upon Bongo, an ambitious postal worker, and helped him into office. Once in, he stayed.

During the oil boom, money fell on Gabon and accumulated in drifts. For a single three-day Organization of African Unity summit, Bongo spent $2 billion, counting the lavish hotel-village and circular freeway that went nowhere. Though a tropical state with agricultural potential, Gabon imported its food, down to tomatoes, onions and water bottled in France. Hard times brought a scramble back to the fields. After years of neglect, agriculture produced little for the agonizing country. But France was there to soften the blow.

Bongo pushed ahead on the Transgabonese Railway, one of the world's largest construction projects, although major foreign donors dropped out. It was inaugurated at the end of 1986 after thirteen years of labor: fifty bridges, a tunnel and 420 miles of track through dense hardwood forest. It has cost billions, leaving little for other development. To operate, the railroad needs a subsidy of $60 million a year. With only timber to sell, Gabon will have to cut down a lot of trees.

The railroad was supposed to reach iron deposits in the north at Belinga. The World Bank and others objected when the track was diverted south to a town called Franceville. There is no iron at Franceville. But it is Bongo's hometown.

*T*he Central African Republic also stayed close to France, sometimes closer than the French wanted. But air bases at Bangui and Bouar, among other strategic and commercial interests, outweighed a little passing embarrassment. It is a main staging point for France's 8,500 troops in Africa.

At independence, France supported David Dacko against a more radical candidate. To no one's surprise, Dacko won. After five years, however, the French grew tired of subsidizing Dacko's inefficiency. French agents stirred up trouble, expecting to maneuver into office the head of the gendarmes, Jean Izamo. Instead, they got Jean-Bedel Bokassa.

Bokassa had been a sergeant in the French army and a loyal subject. When Charles de Gaulle died, he sobbed, "I've lost my papa." De Gaulle was not so affectionate. When he learned that Bokassa, Dacko's cousin and chief of staff, had pulled off a coup d'état, de Gaulle roasted his own envoys. He thundered: "Who is that jerk we have in Bangui?"

Georges Pompidou tolerated Bokassa. But Valery Giscard d'Estaing, a big-game hunter, pursued his friendship. France paid perhaps $90 million so Bokassa could crown himself emperor like his hero, Napoleon I. A senior French minister defended the extravagance. It was racist, he observed, to criticize Bokassa's coronation and not the lavish festivities for the twenty-fifth anniversary of Queen Elizabeth's reign.

Despite a scandal over diamonds which Bokassa gave Giscard d'Estaing, relations held firm. But then Bokassa was linked to a massacre of schoolchildren who refused to wear uniforms manufactured by his family's factory. It was the last straw. When Bokassa took his next trip, France changed the locks on the country. French troops flew down from Paris with a new president: David Dacko. Alexandre de Marenches, who directed the French intelligence agency, recalled later in *Le Secret des Princes*: "In fact, we helped (Dacko) prepare his speech because he is quite deficient intellectually. We stressed the fact that we didn't want anything and, besides, that was true . . ."

When the French replaced Dacko later with André Kolingba, they took no more chances. A permanent "adviser," a French colonel, shadowed the president.

Bokassa was sentenced to death in absentia for murder, cannibalism and massive embezzlement. But no one tried to bring him back. Houphouët-Boigny was obliged to offer the exiled emperor hospitality for as long as he could stand it. Then Bokassa came to France. He lived on a French military pension in the only property authorities did not seize, a moderately grand chateau near Paris which he could not afford to heat. Each year his appeals grew more plaintive: He was an African who wanted to go home; France held him hostage. In 1986, he made a U-turn into the wrong lane of a freeway, slipped away from the French police and flew to Bangui from Brussels.

A new trial was ordered. The man Giscard d'Estaing once called France's best friend in Africa was charged with cannibalism, mutilation, sadism, massive embezzlement and thirty-eight murders. One witness said Bokassa ordered the execution of her aged mother because she had four breasts—"a monkey woman"—which endowed her with the magical powers to free her son from Bokassa's captivity; the son, General Martin Lingoupou, died in any case from lack of food and water. Another said the severed penis of a second general, Jean-Claude Mandala, was presented to Bokassa as proof that the man had been executed. Such testimony went on for hours.

Philippe Linguissa, a former chef to Bokassa, recounted how the emperor locked him in the kitchen with a human body. "Bokassa gave me a razor to clean the body," he testified. "I did it. I stuffed it with rice and bread and carefully sewed it together and put it in the oven . . . I flambéed the body with gin, while Bokassa drank. I set the table and he sat down, alone. He began with the hands, and then the feet."

Most Africans would have just as soon forgotten the whole episode which, along with the depredations of Idi Amin Dada in Uganda and Francisco Macias Nguema in Equatorial Guinea, did little for their image. The French were uneasy that Bokassa might expound on the contents of secret papers they carted off to Paris after the coup d'état. But Kolingba wanted Bokassa to have his chance. He had not executed anyone since seizing power in 1981. The past, he said, should be buried.

*T*he French also settled Madagascar, the world's fourth largest island, which lies 200 miles east of Mozambique. It won independence in 1960 but, unlike other French territories, its colonial history was bitter and bloody. For much of Madagascar's independence, a left-leaning government has kept its distance from Paris. In 1975, a civilian government, dominated by revolutionaries, promised to achieve "a socialist paradise under divine protection by the year 2000." More than a decade later, it was behind schedule.

In Madagascar, the political revolution made a full turn. President Didier Ratsiraka retained Marxism. But at a summit in Paris to celebrate the speaking of French, in 1986, he told France: "Know that, whatever you may think, in the four corners of the planet there are people who speak your language, who love your country and who are your friends. The people of Madagascar are among them, despite the ups and downs of history and the vicissitudes of events."

It is the natural revolution that is threatening Madagascar.

Portuguese explorers declared the island was Eden. In 1771, French naturalist Philibert Commerson reported: "May I announce to you that Madagascar is the naturalists' promised land? Nature seems to have retreated there into a private sanctuary, where she could work on different models from any she has used elsewhere. There, you meet bizarre and marvelous forms at every step."

More recently, however, the World Bank said Madagascar was perhaps the most eroded place on earth. Commerson had found rich hardwood forests over the whole island; today only 15 percent is forested, in a ragged ring around the island's edges. Unique species of animals and plants are disappearing along with their habitats.

Madagascar was home to the great Aepyornis, the largest bird that ever lived, likely the inspiration for the "roc" in *Sinbad the Sailor*. It is extinct; only a ten-foot-high skeleton in the museum remains. There are still little lemurs, the world's most ancient surviving primate, but lemurs the size of female gorillas have died out.

Four-fifths of Madagascar is barren, burned off by subsistence farmers or herders. Late in 1985, attending a conservation meeting, Prince Philip, Duke of Edinburgh and president of the World Wildlife Fund, watched a farmer burn towering baobab trees to clear a cornfield. He told one leader, "Your country is committing suicide." He was not exaggerating. Scientists who know the island well worry that little will remain by the turn of the century.

France set up a series of parks and reserves more than a half century ago. Thirty-six of them remain on the books. But in 1986, the *New Scientist* reported on government efforts to stop the squandering. Conservation, along with reversal of past damage, is in the hands of Madagascar's Waters and Forest Administration. Its entire annual operating budget, after salaries, comes to $900.

Chad was the last African territory that French troops tamed late last century. And some would argue that France has yet to tame Chad. The country extends a half-million square miles from the rich cotton country along the Chari River to the sandy wastes of southern Libya. Most of its 5 million inhabitants are Sara and other Bantus; they farm the better-watered south. The north is peopled sparsely by the Toubou and other Moslem nomads. At any given moment, groups of these people are likely to be at war with one another.

Independent Chad started off in 1960 with the optimism shared by neighbors. François Tombalbaye, a southern Protestant, was elected prime minister, and had a Moslem-dominated legislature. Later, as president, he banned all parties but his own. By 1968, rebellion percolated in the extremities, and the French Air Force lent a hand. In 1969, 1,600 French troops were sent in to battle the Chad National Liberation Front, FROLINAT. France lost but declared a victory, setting a handy precedent for dealing with Chad.

From the time FROLINAT dug in, in the unassailable northern mountains, French strategists quietly concentrated on *le Tchad utile*, the useful part. In theory, France would fight to keep Chad united within its original borders. But in fact, there was the productive south, defensible with limited ground troops and air strikes. And there was the north, a quagmire best left to rebels and Libyans.

Tombalbaye was assassinated, touching off a chain of shifting alliances and acronyms among Chadian political forces. Hissène Habré and Goukouni Oueddei were brothers-in-arms, then bitter foes, and then allies again. Libya occupied the Aozou strip in the far north and probed deeply as opportunities arose. Leaders in the capital, N'Djamena, exhorted farmers to grow more cotton and food in spite of the turmoil. But periodically government troops massacred peasants suspected of rebel loyalties. The main constant was France.

French leaders since De Gaulle found the unruly stretch of desert to be key to their African policy. Chad offered little reward. With military bases in the Central African Republic and Gabon, France did not need the place. But Chad was a symbol. France had taken up the role of gendarme on most of the continent. But African leaders were nervous that the French might not answer the whistle.

The situation remains essentially the same. France has to defend Chad. Or, at least, French diplomats have to convince everyone— Chadians, Libyans, other Africans, Americans, and Frenchmen— that France is defending Chad.

But in early 1987, Habré and Oueddei added a new element to the balance. A Chadian force routed 14,500 Libyan soldiers, killing or capturing a third of them, to take back most of northern Chad. They overran Wadi Doum and Faya Largeau, seizing a half-billion dollars' worth of Libyan arms, including Czech-made L-29 jet fighters, SAM missile batteries, and T-55 tanks. Colonel Halifi Belkacem, one of Qaddafi's best officers, led his men in ignominious retreat. Officials in N'Djamena and Paris insisted the Chadians did it on their own; French troops stayed in the south.

As is usual in such cases, they neglected to mention the substantial team of French intelligence officers camped discreetly a few dunes away from the reporters who came up to look over the fields of victory.

In each of its former territories, the imprint of France is indelible. For a lot of Africans, this is a problem. Ayi Kwei Armah, writing in the magazine *West Africa*, decried the fact that, in the absence of their own lingua franca, Africans depend on French. This, of course, suits the French push for *la francophonie*. Two directions have been taken: *l'enracinement*, using a local language going back to one's roots, and *l'ouverture*, using a language for speaking to the world. Armah wrote:

> So African politicos, bureaucrats and businesspeople who
> spend weekends in their ancestral villages, wear amulets to

protect them from discovery of the fact that they have embezzled rural aid funds, chat with the old folks in indigenous languages, wear down home clothes and drink palm wine are practicing *l'enracinement*. When, come Monday, these same dignitaries fly to Paris or Rome to cadge loans and grants (for our starving people), stop over in Geneva to deposit some in safe accounts, or jet to New York to abolish apartheid with resolutions, they are into *l'ouverture*. Now the Francophone line is that the language most suitable for *l'ouverture* is French. For *l'enracinement*, you're welcome to use your own African mother tongue.

The damage, Armah wrote, is that Africans are ordaining a hierarchy that maximizes foreign values and minimizes national values. Knowledge and experience are not shared across the generations. To change this presupposes a new generation of African leaders "no longer willing to have the continent's resources perennially pillaged and devalued, no longer willing to have the continent's people, languages and culture serve as cannon fodder in war between the imperialists."

He concluded: "The remaining question . . . is whether, in picking on the African people as headporter of their cultural dreams of grandeur, the French are not simply getting set to repeat a history of failure. Time—not alone but together with African behavior over the coming decades—will tell."

For decades, these questions hardly arose. France was not only the cultural grandmotherland, but also the pot of gold for adventuresome young Africans seeking to make their fortune. In 1986, however, the wind shifted. French authorities cracking down on illegal immigrants loaded 101 Malians onto a chartered aircraft overnight, with no hearing, and sent them home. Some objected that their papers were in order. To calm their protests, police shackled some of the passengers to their seats.

The more rhetorical noticed one of those bitter African ironies. People were brought out of Africa in chains; now, their descendants were being sent back the same way.

*F*or many in French Africa and France, the symbiosis is evident. African leaders listen politely to the occasional moral lecture from France but lose little sleep afterward. During 1986, a scandal broke in Paris that blunted French credibility. Several million dollars disappeared from an association known as Carrefour du Développement, funded by the Ministry of Cooperation. French officials were prosecuted for embezzling money meant for developing Africa.

Some of the missing money paid for extras—prostitutes and party gear, among other things—at the 1984 Franco-African summit in Burundi. Each year, France spends heavily for the summit, which is essentially a celebration of its role in the Third World. At the 1986 meeting, the presidents of such unlikely places as Liberia and Sierra Leone were among the nineteen heads of state. The official family of states numbers twenty-five full members. Counting guests from as far away as Haiti, there were thirty-nine delegations.

The host was Togo, a dynamic little former French colony next to Benin. Togo has done fairly well by opening its doors. Foreigners put money into small industries and tourists flock down despite the dangerous undertow on Togo's beaches. People are friendly, and the nights are lively.

The interesting part of the Togo meeting was its timing. A month earlier, a small band of invaders crossed into Togo from Ghana and tried to overthrow President Gnassingbé Eyadema. The general ordered troops out to meet them. Then he called the Elysée Palace. French paratroopers scurried into Transall aircraft and dissuaded any potential opponents from unruliness.

On December 19, thirteen people were sentenced to death for, as the president put it, subverting "peaceful democracy." Among eleven others, convicted in absentia was a son of Sylvanus Olympio, who was shot by Eyadema in 1963, thus vacating the office of president. A few days before the trial, Eyadema was reelected president. He was the only candidate, and his margin was 99.95 percent. With the direct help of France, Togo was assured seven more years of peaceful democracy.

9 PORTUGUESE AFRICA
First In, Last Out

*P*ortuguese explorers reached the western coast in 1443, the first Europeans in Africa. And embattled Portuguese troops clung to shrinking territory until 1975. After more than 500 years, Portugal ended up with few riches and even less glory. Throughout its days of empire, it remained among the most backward countries of Europe. And its colonies were the most miserable in Africa.

By the time the last Portuguese flags were hauled down in Angola, Mozambique, and Guinea-Bissau, the three mainland colonies seemed headed for trouble. The expectations were correct.

Portugal's ignominious end in Africa contrasted sharply with its heroic beginning. In seventy-foot caravels, shorter than modern racing yachts, Vasco da Gama and Bartolomeu Dias went farther than Columbus at much greater risk. Portuguese sea captains mastered the qualities usual in their day: cruelty, rapacity, and greed. Looking for the Orient, they charted the coasts of Africa and India, took Africans back to Europe, and set up trading posts.

As the centuries rolled by, however, Portugal hardly moved beyond its trading-post approach. A hearty appetite for slaves kept the sea lanes busy. Stone forts loomed over key ports and islands in the south Atlantic. But the abolition of slavery threw colonial economies into turmoil.

The state, with little money to spend, granted mining rights and plantation land to private entrepreneurs. In exchange, concessionaires were to provide government and local development. Few did. Instead, most found ways to appropriate peasants' farm surpluses and exploit their labor.

Portugal built a few lovely coastal cities—Luanda was one of Africa's jewels—but kept only a token force in the interior. In 1958, a European traveler spent nineteen days in northern Mozambique, driving from Lake Malawi along the Tanzania border to the coast, without seeing a white face or a motor vehicle. In 1970, only 3 percent of Angola was occupied by Portuguese settlers.

But the Portuguese, more than the British or the French, figured out how to play on tribal politics. The slave trade had left deep scars among tribes, and colonial administrators exploited them with skill. Rival chieftains were pitted against one another. When one emerged triumphant, he was suppressed as a threat to the state. Black troops collected taxes, recruited forced-labor gangs, and ran roughshod over recalcitrant regions.

Education and health care were left largely to missionaries.

In the 1950s and 1960s, Portugal began investing heavily in dams, irrigation, roads, and public services. Lisbon encouraged whites to emigrate to Africa. Oil boomed in Angola; from 1961 to 1968, income doubled from oil, diamonds, iron, and coffee. In the same period, Mozambique's exports increased by 50 percent. But by then it was too late.

The harsh years had sent dissidents into the bush and over the borders. Portuguese Africans, sniffing the winds, wanted independence.

While the French, British, and Belgians headed north, Portuguese transports carried reinforcements southward. Antonio de Oliveira Salazar, the aging and ailing dictator in Lisbon, was determined to spend the state's dwindling resources on shoring up former glory. In all three territories, colonial wars floundered on for more than a decade.

Each Portuguese foot soldier was given a single pair of canvas boots for his two-year tour of duty. When they wore out, it was his problem. Much of Portugal's colonial army, if shod at all, wore clapped-out sneakers, leather scraps, or Japanese rubber shower shoes.

A geologist friend who prospected for years in Mozambique was once in a convoy ambushed by rebels. The trucks stopped, and everyone scrambled for the bushes. Firing stopped after a few minutes, followed by a long, agonizing silence. Finally, one soldier decided it was over and set out alone to investigate. He was masked by thick bush, but, as he reached the lead vehicle, a rebel shot him neatly through the head. The loud slap of his flip-flops on the hard roadbed gave him away.

During one long stretch in Angola, no food reached bush outposts. The army survived by grubbing for roots and berries. Troops had Unimog patrol vehicles. But often the gasoline ration was only enough to allow for a single round trip a month to collect supplies. Morale sagged further when troops from the bush found officers in Luanda racing their sports cars around, with unlimited fuel.

Ridgway Knight, who was U.S. ambassador to Portugal at the time, toured the colonies. He estimated that Portuguese casualties were twenty times greater than American losses in Vietnam, on a proportional basis. Guerrillas' land mines and booby traps took a heavy toll. "The country was poor, and soldiers were not fitted properly with artificial limbs," he recalled. "That was what finally got to the morale, all those young men limping around Lisbon on crutches."

Salazar died, and a military coup in April 1974 broke the lingering stalemate. The army revolted over pay and promotion. In Africa, morale plummeted. Nationalist guerrillas pressed on all sides. Within six months, a new government in Lisbon threw in the towel. During 1975, Portuguese soldiers, civil servants, and settlers scrambled out of the colonies, taking as much of their wealth as they could carry. New African governments, free at last, pushed them along with vigor.

Just before the wars ended, Doug spent months in Angola assessing the ecological effects of prospecting operations. He traveled in Mozambique frequently over the years. Both colonies, beautiful and rich in places, exuded potential.

The atmosphere was a sharp contrast to French and English colonies, even with war. Portuguese settlers had happily taken Africans to bed from the beginning, and the racial mix was a subtle graduation of hues. Many immigrants had been poor and ignorant; they had worked as domestic servants and farm laborers, jobs no Briton or Frenchman would consider for a moment. Lourenço Marques (now Maputo) and Luanda blended Latin sights and smells with those of Africa, and their charm suggested harmony.

Once, Doug walked at dawn in Lourenço Marques. Pastel houses loomed suddenly and then disappeared in the mist. Every door was closed; the streets were empty. The heavy sea air was tinged with the perfume of frangipanis. Footsteps on polished stones and tiles rang out in the silence. At the ocher-colored fort, soldiers on guard seemed less like oppressing tyrants than just a few extras in yet another remake of *Beau Geste*.

Later, he watched young men imported from Portugal perform feats he had seen before only on vases from ancient Crete. In the Lourenço Marques arena, each stood unarmed before his bull. He taunted it with whistles and shouts, strutting in comical arrogance. When the bull charged, he grasped the horns and somersaulted over its head—in theory, at least. Often, someone missed and ended up tangled among the bull's pounding hooves. The crowd loved it. Black, white, and every shade in between, they shouted their enthusiasm in Portuguese.

Doug was struck hardest by the Iona National Park, in Angola, which stretches north from the Namibia border at the edge of the Namib desert. It is stunning, mountainous and arid, with vistas across the forbidding cliffs near the coast, gentle hills of golden grass, and plains of pastel-pink sand. Farther away, the cliffs are so rich in the past life that fossils can be gouged out with a fingernail. But the once abundant wildlife had been nearly annihilated.

The last oryx, springbok, dik-dik, mountain zebra, and black rhino are disappearing fast. Poachers shot a zebra while Doug was there. He found its remains carefully skinned; not an ounce of meat had been taken.

At least no one poached the Welwitchia mirabilis, one of the world's weirdest plants. It is a primitive sort of conifer, with two huge green straps for leaves, up to nine feet long and tattered at the ends. A short circular stem barely protrudes out of the ground. All the moisture it needs comes from fog off the coast. Each mature Welwitchia has lived up to two thousand years on arid ground, kept alive only by its periodic hit of morning mist.

The people are as engaging as the land. The prospectors had hired Ovahimba, pastoralists who followed their cattle from the stark Kaokaveld, in Namibia, to southern Angola with little regard for lines on the map. Many have magnificent, statuesque bodies, like the Masai, but powerfully muscled. They preen with ocher and animal grease.

The Ovahimba were amazingly friendly at the time, given the war raging around them. They earned extra money by selling goats to the prospectors, cheerfully dispatching the animals in a practiced manner that suggested they had come to terms with life and death.

Independence might have given the Iona and its endangered life forms a new chance of survival. When one war was over, however, others started. Soon the remaining wildlife, and the herders who had lived among it for a thousand years, were again caught in the crossfire. And so was most of the rest of Portuguese Africa.

Postindependence upheaval surprised no one. Like France, Portugal had adopted a policy of assimilation, allowing educated Africans to become black Portuguese. Toward the end, to counter international pressure, Salazar made Angola and Mozambique overseas provinces of Portugal. Juridically, Africans had equal rights. But, particularly after the influx from Europe after 1950, whites held all key jobs. With scarce funds going to the army, little money was left for education.

At independence, few Africans were trained in simple administration, let alone the technical specialties of developing remote stretches of African bush. Worse, fierce rivalries encouraged by the Portuguese left all three mainland states fragmented by tribal and ideological hatred.

Young governments leaned heavily toward the friend who armed them against Portugal: the Soviet Union. With little thought to the recent history of peasants in Russia, leaders embraced Marxism.

In Angola, ideology was largely the landscape of a bitter fight for power. Agostinho Neto's Movement for the Liberation of the Angolan People (MPLA) came out on top; he was Moscow's candidate. Holden Roberto, of the National Front for the Liberation of Angola (FNLA), was close to the Central Intelligence Agency and President Mobutu of neighboring Zaire. Roberto fought hard, but his forces slipped away. Meanwhile, Jonas Savimbi, then a distant third, marshaled his Unita forces from Zambia, to the east.

With help from South Africa and the United States, among others, Savimbi has emerged as a serious contender to the MPLA. His wide swath of territory changes in shape, and his fortunes still rise and fall. Neto has died, but Jose Eduardo dos Santos is now president in Luanda, and the MPLA, with the biggest piece of the country, speaks for Angola. But little governing is going on, and international experts charged with development are happy enough just to get food relief into pockets of famine.

Late in 1986, I spoke with a United Nations expert who knew Angola well. Every conservation problem known to Africa was virulent in Angola, he said. Forests were being cut too fast in the wrong places. Land was eroding. Wild animals were disappearing fast from wide areas. Not much is being done to stop it, or even measure it. He added, with a helpless shrug: "Do you think, with all that's going on, that anyone is worried about trees and animals?"

During 1986, Associated Press reporter James Smith spent three days and nights clattering across parts of Central Angola held by Savimbi's Unita forces. It was classic African game country. But there was no game. A rinderpest epidemic had wiped out the animals decades earlier, and bush soldiers have been killing them ever since.

War is a full-time and constant occupation there. When a reporter offered to buy one soldier's hat, the man replied: "What would I do with the money?"

Savimbi knows what to do with money. He collected at least $15 million in U.S. aid during 1986, apparently including Soviet-made heat-seeking missiles captured elsewhere. British investigators suspect that that is what hit a civilian airliner flown for Angola by a British crew.

Apart from their internal conflicts, Angolan forces fight a running war with South African forces along the southern border. Namibian guerrillas of the South West African People's Organization seek refuge in Angola, and the South Africans go after them.

No one can calculate how many billions of dollars Angola has lost in a decade of war, nor how many tens of thousands of civilians have died. But the effect is clear. The country has returned to the same sort of barter economy the Portuguese found centuries ago. Instead of slaves for trinkets, it is coffee for food. Since so many roads are cut, and so few airplanes fly, communication with the interior is hardly better than it was before colonialism.

Marxist litany prevails, and the Soviet Union watches over its investment. Cuban troops fortify the MPLA. But Angola's income derives largely from oil produced and refined by Americans in the enclave of Cabinda. Ideology is one thing; survival is another. The Cubans stand guard over U.S. oil installations.

*M*ozambique's troubles were of a different nature. The first fight against the Portuguese was led by Eduardo Mondlane and his broad-based Mozambican Liberation Front, Frelimo. But Mondlane was assassinated in 1969, and Frelimo took a sharp Marxist-Leninist turn. In 1974, Joaquim Chissano led a transitional government. The following year, Mozambique was independent, under President Samora Machel.

Almost immediately, the Portuguese fled. Race riots went on for weeks. Machel seized property, and individuals exacted revenge for the past. Of 250,000 Portuguese in Mozambique, from top officials to grocers in the bush, perhaps 20,000 remained. With no one trained to run a government or an economy, the young nation slipped into chaos.

Machel put Mozambique squarely into the mainstream of African politics. Zimbabwean guerrillas sought refuge behind his borders, which brought vicious hot pursuit from Rhodesia. South Africa was no friendlier as a neighbor, and Western governments distrusted Machel's politics.

Soon after taking power, Machel flew to Ndola, in the copper belt of northern Zambia. He declaimed in stirring Portuguese: "The revolution of the people of Ndola is an integral part of the revolution of the people of Mozambique." When his words were translated, the conservative aldermen nodded politely. They had turned up in the black robes and white wigs left behind by the British a decade earlier.

Machel struggled hard to reshape his colonial economy into a socialist state. He had little help. The Mozambique National Resistance, Renamo, used South African arms to weaken further the floundering country. They were officially dismissed as "armed bandits," but they cut vital roads and rail lines. Without fertilizer, tools, or transportation, food production plunged. Intermittent drought and floods starved to death hundreds of thousands who were managing to scrape by

Within five years, Machel quietly began dismantling his socialist structure. He invited back the Portuguese and opened up to the West. U.S. aid started to trickle slowly in, but conservative legislators objected. Machel made grudging peace with the South Africans, accepting a reality that his people needed jobs over the border and income from South African businessmen and tourists. He needed help to exploit three deep-water ports, hydroelectric power, and mineral deposits. "Two things you cannot choose," he once remarked, "are brothers and neighbors. We cannot move our country."

Machel's stature rose after he convinced his friend Robert Mugabe and other Zimbabwean leaders to accept terms offered by the British. He urged Mugabe not to make the mistake he had in scaring off the whites.

But Renamo kept Mozambique in turmoil. Guerrillas closed the highway from South Africa and roads across most of the country. Transportation was safe only by air, but planes and fuel were in desperately short supply. So was everything else. Visitors found stores with row after row of bare shelves.

Renamo, like the ruling Frelimo, operated on a shoestring. An English journalist reported how strapped they were by 1986: Guerrillas once stopped a bus to rob its passengers. They were going to burn it, but neither they nor any of the passengers had a match. Nonetheless, they found enough bullets to kill teachers, administrators, and medical workers. Villagers, meanwhile, were terrorized by both sides.

Machel held on, spellbinding African audiences with his oratory. He urged front-line states to press for revolution in South Africa while dealing pragmatically with Pretoria. He refused Soviet bases and Cuban advisers. He waited patiently for help from Washington, but right-wing legislators there complained about the $40 million in humanitarian relief aid given to Mozambique in 1985. They likened Renamo to the Nicaraguan contras and Unita in Angola.

Late in 1986, Machel and other front-line presidents prevailed on Hastings Kamuzu Banda, of Malawi, to stop sheltering Renamo. Banda, the only African leader to have recognized South Africa, was not a neighborhood favorite. Threatened with sealed access to the sea, he agreed. But instead of handing 12,000 guerrillas over to Machel, he sent them back into Mozambique. They captured five towns.

South Africa, meanwhile, reacted bitterly to a land mine on the Mozambican border that injured five white soldiers. Labor accords going back to colonial days were threatened. About 70,000 legal workers were to be expelled, and no more Mozambicans would be recruited. Counting the illegals, worker remittances of about $90 million made up a third of the country's foreign earnings. Gradually, the matter was dropped.

Machel went to a front-line summit in Zambia in October 1986. On the way home, his Soviet Tupolev aircraft hit a bare hilltop in South Africa, killing him and thirty-three others.

Joaquim Chissano, named president, vowed to follow Machel's course. He agreed that the crash might well have been an accident or the pilot's fault, but he would blame South Africa if he could. In the meantime, he had enough troubles.

In 1987, Mozambique was again facing catastrophe. Tony Vaux, director of Oxfam's Disaster Emergency Unit, spent three weeks assessing the refugee situation. Of Mozambique's 14 million inhabitants, he estimated, 4 million were on the run from the war. Families clustered near towns and cities, which were running out of food. Farmers left their fields, so there were few crops. And food trucks could not move down the roads.

Only coastal areas could be supplied, Vaux said, and only when boats were available to do it. Oxfam pleaded for an airlift before it was too late.

But in Africa, too late is a relative concept. Tens of thousands had already died, or were marked for life, in the latest round of Mozambican calamity. Rebels destroyed hundreds of clinics and schools. Much of the country was paralyzed. Until there is enough stability to head off such disasters, or at least to respond to them as they occur, it will always be too late.

*I*n late April 1987, Michael Buerk was back on BBC television with more bad news. He stood on the grounds of a long-departed Portuguese landowner's home and began: "In colonial times, they called the house among the coconut groves Villa Paradise. Now it is a refuge for 10,000 desperate people." In 1984, he noted, it was in Ethiopia that a natural disaster was exacerbated by man. This time, it was in Mozambique that a man-made disaster—war—was worsened by nature. A child was dying every six minutes. It would surely get worse before it got better.

Buerk, like other reporters in Mozambique, found little cause for hope in the short or long term. Farmers had no incentives to grow, even when the war did not stop them. They could not get crops to market, and there was nothing to buy in case they earned anything. Some tried anyway. But it was not easy. On one large state farm, for instance, he counted fifty combine harvesters. Forty-nine of them were broken.

*S*pain had a single colony in Black Africa, Equatorial Guinea, which linked the mainland enclave of Rio Muni and the island of Fernando

Poo. In 1979, Francisco Macias Nguema, who ruled since 1968, was executed for genocide, treason, and massive theft. No one knows how many tens of thousands he put to death on his pestilential little island, renamed Bioko, where Fangs from the mainland crushed the traditional power of Bubis. An estimated third of the inhabitants fled the country.

I had gone there in the late 1960s, before Spain hauled down its flag. On the peaceful old street, fronted with pastel-painted stone buildings and graceful palms, Spanish settlers ran the plantations, the economy, and the law. Africans worked and stayed out of the way. It seemed as if tranquility would last forever.

*T*imes were also turbulent for Guinea-Bissau, Portugal's little bite out of the West African coast. The colony was set free at the same time as the others, after a long bitter fight. Amilcar Cabral, the independence hero, was assassinated. His half-brother, Luis Cabral, took over and turned the place into what critics called "the Albania of West Africa." With only peanuts to export, and a chaotic Marxist-Leninist economy, the country was a shambles.

Joao Bernardo Vieira took charge in 1980. Up against the wall, like so many other African leaders, he reached for the IMF surgical kit. Slowly, and without changing the rhetoric, he moved the country to the right. Most commerce was opened to the private sector.

Vieira did not go overboard on democracy. In July 1986, he executed his number two, Paulo Correa, and five other officials. Asked by a reporter if Luis Cabral could return to the country from exile, he replied that he could. "But," he added, "you never know what might happen to him."

The C in the name of Guinea-Bissau's only political party, the PAIGC, stands for Cape Verde. But the little cluster of islands 240 miles west of Dakar is a different kind of country. President Aristide Pereira infused revolutionary dialectics from Bissau with some hard-minded pragmatism.

Cape Verde includes 1,557 square miles of craggy mountain and eroded flatlands, badly ravaged by drought. "If you put all of our statistics in a computer, it would probably tell you Cape Verde doesn't exist," observed one minister. Only international aid saved the population of 300,000 in the worst years, but donors seem happy that development aid has been well spent. Failing other resources, Pereira made use of his geography in a controversial manner. He allows South African Airways to refuel at Praia on flights to Europe.

São Tomé and Principe, Portugal's other former colony, is smaller and poorer. The islands lie south of Equatorial Guinea, which was the only Spanish colony in Black Africa. Its 100,000 people export cocoa, but not very much. During 1986, the leftist government sought to improve relations with Western Europe. France, not surprisingly, was interested.

Not a lot is reported from Portuguese Africa. Few journalists manage visas to Angola, and when they do, they go where they are taken. Mozambique is more hospitable, but reporters, like everyone else, have few means to travel beyond Maputo. But plenty of people are watching.

The two huge states that flank central-southern Africa are potential lifelines for Malawi, Zimbabwe, Zambia, and Zaire. They offer an access to the sea that does not cross South Africa. If Mozambique's ports and railroads have lost a billion dollars in direct or indirect business since 1980, South Africa has earned most of that income.

Africans have long since stopped looking at the former Portuguese states as a model of success. Now, most would be happy just to see them stable enough to maintain a dependable railroad.

10 SOUTHERN AFRICA
On the Front Line

"You can't really kick, you know," observed Mike, a white farmer friend in northern Zimbabwe. He patted a spreading stomach, grinned, and added: "We're all right." His cows were fat, and his tobacco prime. Crimson bougainvillaea crawled up wire netting that had protected his terrace from hand grenades during the independence war. Mike looked around the rambling home he had built over a generation, and his grin faded. "We're all right for now," he revised his assessment. "And as long as we don't leave."

Prime Minister Robert Mugabe made his position plain from the start. Whites were welcome to stay, as Zimbabweans. They kept their property and most of their rights. But if they leave, they can take only the equivalent of $500 dollars and a few belongings.

Mugabe learned his lesson from Samora Machel during the years he had his guerrillas from bases in Mozambique. A Zimbabwean official told me later, "Samora warned us again and again. Don't drive out the whites. Use them."

Many whites now say Zimbabwe is functioning smoothly as a multiracial state. And others vociferously argue the reverse. Zimbabwe is like that; it proves and disproves almost anything anyone wants to say about Africa.

Zimbabwe started late as an independent state, twenty years after most of Africa. It was part of territory pioneered a century ago by Cecil Rhodes, the English mining mogul who wanted a railroad from the Cape to Cairo. As prime minister of Cape Colony, he sought to tuck all of southern Africa under the British crown. His interests ran to crushing Boers, consolidating the De Beers diamond mines, and pushing a railroad beyond South Africa's northern border, the Limpopo River, toward copper in the north.

Britain exploited the mines in Northern Rhodesia, where a few settlers established farms. Most whites moved into Southern Rhodesia. In 1953, the two Rhodesias and Nyasaland were linked as the Central African Federation. Africans in Northern Rhodesia and Nyasaland objected, fearing domination by the whites in the south. Eleven years later, Britain freed Northern Rhodesia as Zambia and Nyasaland as Malawi.

In Southern Rhodesia, white settlers refused to compromise. In 1965, they issued a unilateral declaration of independence, UDI, and set off on their own. Independent Rhodesia was recognized officially by almost no one but the 225,000 whites determined to fight to the end, and South Africa. Unofficially, sanction busters flocked in. France supplied helicopters, weapons, and fuel.

With access to South African ports, Rhodesia thrived. Its farms produced rich tobacco and food surpluses. Factories turned out everything from heavy machinery to a half-dozen kinds of canned spaghetti. A tough regular army and a militia, with black troops and clandestine French military aid, battled two separate guerrilla armies.

Finally, with the handwriting appearing ever more clearly on the wall, South Africa cut loose its northern neighbor. Whites who had vowed their rule would last a thousand years negotiated peace in London. In 1980, Mugabe's majority party took Zimbabwe to independence. Blacks were in charge, but a carefully worded constitution protected whites' rights. And policy was to build the state on the functioning structures of Rhodesia.

How well it worked, naturally enough, depended on one's point of view. On my first visit, in 1981, I had a flash of the half-full or half-empty dichotomy. I left a notebook on board the Air Zimbabwe plane that brought me. A half-hour later, I called the airport. Frantic, I started to explain the problem. "Relax," a friendly voice said. "It is sitting on my desk." A functioning Lost and Found was nothing I had seen in Africa. When I went to get it, an elderly white woman was pacing in exasperation, because the Lost and Found lady was on a tea break. The woman grumbled, "You would have never seen this before."

Today in Zimbabwe, *before* remains a loaded word. If many blacks have forgiven, few have forgotten. A quarter-million whites held absolute sway over 7 million blacks, often with harsh racist attitudes.

Education and health services have lost some quality, the whites say. Some send their children abroad to school, and they go themselves for major medical care. But, argue the blacks, services now extend to more than just a fraction of the people.

The economy falters in some years, and prices are edging up faster than most people would want. In South Africa, unreconstructed white Rhodies assured me the whole country was sliding fast down the chute. That, however, has not stopped a reverse exodus of whites, who are going home after trying to make it in troubled South Africa.

In fact, more objective white Zimbabweans say it is amazing that so much has held together; that races coexist, if not mix, so comfortably; that old hatred has slowly cooled.

Soon after Mugabe's election, his tone began to harden. The government would not destroy what it had inherited, he said, but the long-term goal should be Marxism. A two-party system was a luxury ill suited to a struggling young state, he added; everyone should join his party. His ministers used far less tact in delivering the message.

But the lovely little capital of Harare, formerly Salisbury, displays no telltale signs that the east was red. When the jacarandas flower, falling blossoms swirl like flurries of purple snow against the parked Mercedes-Benzes and Range Rovers. Sun-burned blondes in jodhpurs trot their thoroughbred horses across vast suburban lawns, which are trimmed by black servants.

There are still 100,000 whites in the country. During the 1986

Non-Aligned Movement summit in Harare, leaders rode to meetings in sedans lent by white executives. Capitalists' secretaries typed their fiery speeches.

"You've got to learn to ignore the rhetoric, all that Marxist claptrap that Mugabe spouts for the masses," one of Mike's friends said. "That's what the local [black] party officials advise us, and I think they're right. Watch what he does, don't listen to what he says."

But it was not all rhetoric. Whites and blacks alike watch carefully as Mugabe charts his course.

When Zimbabwe first hoisted its flag, the United States pledged heavy assistance, the bulk of the package put together by Western donors. It gave $370 million over a decade. For the United States, the emergent nation symbolized hope for a continent that had rushed off in too many wrong directions. Within five years, U.S. aid had dwindled to a trickle. The 1983 level was slashed from $75 million to $40 million after Zimbabwe refused to condemn the Soviet Union for shooting down Korean Airlines' flight 007.

Mugabe's standing rose within the Non-Aligned Movement, but he squandered the good will Western donors had for him. His continual Marxist rhetoric sounded like fingernails on a pane of glass to Reagan Administration strategists.

The prime minister went to Washington and lectured Reagan on the Third World. "On a scale of one to ten, that visit was a minus two," a U.S. diplomat told me. Although AID officials insisted that each dollar spent in Zimbabwe achieved more than it would almost anywhere in Africa, politics got in the way. During 1986, former President Jimmy Carter stalked out of a banquet in Harare after a cabinet minister castigated American policy. Mugabe would not apologize. The last $13.5 million in aid was finally stopped.

Whatever Washington's wishes, multiparty democracy seems unlikely in Zimbabwe. Mugabe's Shona tribe makes up 80 percent of the population. Too many Shona militants use their advantage to avenge what they consider to be past depredations by the minority Ndebele.

As always in Africa, the country's current political situation dates far back before independence. The Ndebele, offshoots of the

Zulus, refined warfare to an art. Forced north from what is now South Africa, they muscled in on Shona territory. The Ndebele shunned Britain's colonial structures; the Shona read law and studied business. It was a classic African situation. A subjugated majority rounded on former masters.

Both tribes fought together against white Rhodesia. But their bitter rivalry erupted immediately after independence. Ndebele dissidents raided farms. Whites clustered in Bulawayo; some visited their farms under escort. Shona troops responded with vicious raids, raping, torturing, and killing Ndebele suspected of aiding the dissidents.

By 1986, Joshua Nkomo, the portly politico who spoke for most of the province of Matabeleland, agreed to link his Zimbabwe African Peoples' Union with Mugabe's Zimbabwe African National Union. Ian Smith, the diehard former prime minister, tacitly accepted a gradual diminishing of whites' constitutional guarantees. Neither had a choice. Smith remained in Parliament, where he apologized from time to time for saying things like most of Zimbabwe's blacks are illiterate and ignorant of politics. But in 1987, Mugabe's talks with Nkomo broke down. And Smith was finally suspended from Parliament.

*I*n the context of Black Africa, Zimbabwe has been a ringing success. Once landless peasants now add to a corn crop that, in a normal year, surpasses domestic needs by a million and a half tons. Black farmers are growing tobacco, once an exclusive reserve of the whites. They are raising cattle on commercial farms and using their profits to invest in businesses.

Black Africa's best agricultural extension service offers advice; banks provide credit. With fair prices, farmers can afford fertilizer and pesticides. Their crops get to market, and surpluses are stored safely for years.

When I called Mike, he was out in the fields and did not answer the phone. Instead, I sent a telegram. An answer came back in hours. For much of Africa, that borders on the miraculous.

Zimbabwe is not, however, as enlightened as its champions present it. Journalists are expelled capriciously, and other foreigners walk a careful line. The violent fight for independence left deep scars, and leaders can be touchy. Mugabe himself spent a decade in prison and years in the bush. Enos Nkala, the senior Ndebele in the ZANU–Patriotic Front, was with him most of the time. As home affairs minister, Nkala runs a tough police force. When Amnesty International documented torture in Matabeleland, authorities reacted angrily. The government, Nkala said, will listen to the courts when it feels like it.

A heavy official hand often stifles what might otherwise be development.

Matt Franjola, an American friend who put aside journalism to run a gold mine in Zimbabwe, finally gave up and left. Handsome and hearty, in a Denys Finch-Hatton sort of way, he was sorry to go. His mine was in the hills east of Harare. He had slopped around in the mud, taken his old dog hunting for the pot, and bounced into town in a truck.

He had, he said, an ankle-level view of Zimbabwe: Whoever had Wherewithal rose as quickly as possible at the expense of others. One local entrepreneur had a truck in which he drove sick people to the hospital at usurious rates. He was unhappy with Franjola, who did not charge. But Franjola was someone to be courted assiduously. He had Wherewithal.

Security was a problem. Occasionally police would report to Franjola that "dis'dents" were lurking in the region. As an outsider, he did not want to get caught in the middle. But that wasn't what beat him. He mined enough to turn a profit, and pay substantial taxes, at world market prices. But gold miners had to sell to the government at fixed rates in Zimbabwe dollars. Politics overshadowed the economics; Franjola went home, and Zimbabwe lost that much production.

In 1987, Zimbabwe was headed for hard times. Jan Raath took a close look for the London *Times* and concluded: "Economists fear that unless drastic reforms are implemented, the long slide into intractable poverty may begin." The government spent heavily on education and defense, cutting deeply into foreign exchange. Not enough was left for spare parts and raw materials, so factories closed. That triggered a cycle downward.

Most of Zimbabwe's $2.7 billion debt was contracted just after independence. Since then, revenue was lost in subsidizing cumbersome state enterprises. By 1990, the country's schools will have turned out a million graduates. But its economy may produce no more than 140,000 jobs for them.

Mugabe's repeated pledges to impose sanctions against South Africa, and to build up the strength to resist South African incursions, enhances his standing as a leader in the Third World. But it scares the daylights out of prospective foreign investors, and creditors.

*E*ven with all its problems, Zimbabwe preserves its parks and wildlife better than any country on the continent but South Africa. The last sizable herd of black rhinos lives along the Zambezi. Elephants are so numerous they must be culled. An energetic wildlife department enforces laws, studies threats, and plans for the future.

Scientists are looking for ways to fit development into conservation. Experiments suggest that buffalo and other wildlife can be restocked by transplanting embryos to domestic livestock.

Ecologists push hard to reduce the abuse of long-lasting pesticides, which threaten wildlife networks. Glyn Vale has discovered that tsetse are attracted to a substance in ox breath; baiting traps with that is far safer than the repeated spraying of poisons.

But the wildlife department is fighting uphill. Pressure for land is pushing at the edges of national parks. Tsetse-fly eradication opens new areas to cattle. Funds grow scarcer with each new economic problem.

Along the Zambezi, rhino poaching is out of Zimbabwe's control. Poachers come across from Zambia, where rangers are convinced that local authorities are involved. The war intensifies but the poachers keep coming. The herd that a few years earlier numbered more than 700 has fallen below 400.

*I*n Zambia, rhinos are not a top priority. More urgent is the question of the country's survival. Zambia is larger than Zimbabwe, with richer land, more water, and fewer mouths to feed. In addition, its northern hills have produced high-grade copper ore for generations. And, at the end of 1986, there were food riots in Zambia.

Zambia started out with a per-capita income of $267, far higher than much of Africa. President Kenneth Kaunda, a Presbyterian minister and man of the people, set out to give every Zambian a piece of the wealth.

Most white-owned farms were shifted to state control or broken up into small holdings. Production plummeted, but no one worried. Copper spun wealth that subsidized scores of state enterprises: auto-assembly plants, match factories, insurance companies, an airline. Most of these enterprises were paralyzed by inefficiency and reported steadily growing losses, but they provided jobs. As in Nigeria and Gabon during the oil boom, agriculture fell steadily into neglect.

By 1975, copper was producing 90 percent of Zambia's foreign exchange, and it was squandered to prop up a hopelessly inefficient public sector. Then the world price dropped. For years, international lenders continued to pour in loans. The price kept dropping.

Zambia forged ahead with disastrous state enterprises, leaving its few hard-pressed farmers to their own devices. By 1985, the price of copper was 60 percent of what it had been during the heyday. And soon it would not matter anyway. Reserves were expected to run out within two decades.

Like most African leaders, Kaunda had a problem balancing the needs of the urban dwellers and the rural peasants. City people and miners had to buy food with what little they earned. The farmers who grew the food needed to buy tools, fuel, pesticides, and fertilizer. Unlike those in Zimbabwe, urban people generally looked down on farmers. In the cities, in shirts and shoes, they had escaped the drudgery of the past.

Zambia's foreign debt of $4 billion was the seventh largest in the world, per capita. Interest payments would take up forty cents of every dollar—if Zambia paid interest. Of all new loans, 82 percent go to service the existing debt. Zambia reached the catastrophe point: even with IMF shock treatment, it could not borrow or produce itself to solvency.

Toward the end of 1985, Kaunda tried his last weapon. He declared a week of prayer for economic salvation. The country staggers forward on artificial life support, kept going by nations and bankers who cannot afford to let it die.

Finally, Kaunda gave the nation the bitter dose prescribed by the IMF. He agreed to weekly currency auctions, so the kwacha would find its real worth outside Zambia. In a year, its value against the dollar fell from 2.2 to 15. Jobs were eliminated, and prices were held down. Then Kaunda faced up to the African leader's nightmare. He slashed food subsidies. The farmers needed a better deal; city dwellers would have to understand.

At the end of 1986, the price doubled for breakfast mealies, a popular corn staple. Young mobs rampaged through copper-belt towns. Riots spread to the capital, Lusaka, where since independence the urban population had counted on subsidized food. Cars were smashed and stores were looted. At least fifteen rioters were killed in the worst threat to order since 1964. Grey Zulu, secretary-general of the ruling party, observed that the IMF "has brought about untold misery and suffering in many a developing country, Zambia included." Kaunda appeared on television, tears streaming from his eyes. He was sorry. Subsidies would be restored. Milling companies would be national-ized. The IMF could take its pebble-grain briefcases and miracle cures back to Washington. New subsidies would collapse the teetering budget. But otherwise, Kaunda and his party might be ignominiously hounded out of the nation they had founded and run for a quarter of a century.

*F*rom a distance, Lusaka's skyline reflects the glow of copper opti-mism. Up close, it symbolizes the hard realities of a quarter-century of misguided development. The tallest building rises twenty-three stories, a futuristic creation of separated layers balanced on a narrow column. All day long, office workers line up to use the single working elevator. When its doors eventually open, they jam themselves inside and ignore the unlit panel of buttons. Instead, they bellow floor numbers to a man perched on the roof of the car. He operates a jerry-built manual rig to raise and lower the elevator.

The country is like that, a blend of fanciful hope and desperate reality.

To hear Kaunda speak, he is a kindly and frugal grandfather who has shaped his life around his philosophy for Zambia: humanism. But he heaps praise on Colonel Mengistu for enriching the lives of Ethiopians. And his own police abuse Zambians and foreigners alike.

At the end of 1986, John Edlin, a Harare-based reporter from New Zealand, was arrested, apparently mistakenly. During his five days in prison, he said he saw hundreds of people who had been detained for up to four years without charge. Boys as young as seven, jailed for petty offenses, were smuggled into adult cells as prostitutes. Prisoners ate corn meal and beans contaminated by cockroaches. Guards stole the meat ration. More than 500 prisoners shared three small cells, which were infested with lice and bedbugs.

"There is very little evidence in the prison life of humanism as a philosophy that President Kaunda preaches," he told the *Sunday Times* of London. "Zambia, as chairman of the front-line states, is one of the major critics of the policies of South Africa, and yet one sees the same sort of thing in Zambia, only worse in regard to detention of children as young as seven years old."

Earlier, some Swiss travelers had been arrested, beaten, and imprisoned by police, who accused them of being South African agents. Western embassies warned their citizens to beware of Zambia.

South Africa is a touchy subject in Zambia. Kaunda has paid a heavy price as a front-line leader, and he is firm on the subject. In 1986, he startled the visiting British foreign secretary, Sir Geoffrey Howe, with a diatribe: "You and President Reagan are kissing apartheid. I see some kind of conspiracy between the Thatcher Administration and the Reagan Administration. Sir Geoffrey, you people will not be forgiven by history."

But Zambia does most of its business with, or through, South Africa. Its copper is mined with South African machinery, and ore goes out on South African rolling stock. A mining executive told me, "We would love to get our equipment somewhere else, but what can we do? If something breaks, it would take three weeks to get it from Melbourne. I can get it overnight from Durban."

On state visits, when leaders assemble in Lusaka to denounce apartheid, they walk up to Kaunda's official headquarters on a red carpet made in South Africa.

South Africa is one of the few things the two former Rhodesias have in common. Eighty-five percent of Zimbabwe's imports and exports come through South Africa. Most of them start and stop there. Nearly 70 percent of Zambian trade also moves through Cape Town or Durban.

Immediately after Zambia and Zimbabwe demanded sanctions against South Africa at the 1986 OAU summit, Pretoria imposed its own, against them. Surcharges were slipped on goods from the north. Import licenses were required, and there were delays at the border. The message, expensive and direct, was received. More often, the pressure is less subtle. Occasionally, for example, fuel tankers arrive in Zimbabwe nearly empty. South African dispatchers leave the stopcocks slightly open to make their point.

Zambia could export directly to Tanzania on the Chinese-built railway. But it is mainly paralyzed. The Tanzanians say Zambia does not pay its bills, so there is no money to run the docks. Zambia says Tanzanians steal everything anyway, so there is no point in paying.

Outlets through Mozambique appear more promising. But Zimbabwe has had to maintain 12,000 troops in Mozambique to defend the Beira Corridor from Renamo guerrillas. Even then, using the railroad or the pipeline is risky business.

States in the region have formed the Southern African Development Coordination Conference to find ways out of their bind. Edward G. Cross, a white executive of SADCC, calculated it would cost $3 billion over four years to replace South African transport routes.

The 142-mile Beira Corridor is crucial. But there are also two other railroads to Mozambique and the line to Dar es Salaam. In the north, the Benguela Railroad runs from eastern Angola to the Atlantic Ocean. But rebel activity has stalled it for a decade. It does not seem about to open any time soon, and the South Africans know it.

Botswana is more pragmatic about its dependency on South Africa. It relies on its giant neighbor for 90 percent of its transport, all of its oil, 40 percent of its electricity, and 150,000 tons of food a year. A fifth of Botswana's labor force works in South African mines.

But more than this dependence is behind Botswana's pragmatism. It is that sort of country, sober, practical, and prepared to take things at face value. Gaborone is a no-frills little capital just over the line from the Transvaal. At the border post, South Africans check names on a long list and scrutinize cars. When finally waved through, it is like being absolved from suspicion of some unnamed crime. You can feel the tension release when you cross over.

Botswana has managed its affairs carefully. At independence in 1966, per-capita income was sixty dollars a year. Now it is near $1,000. Most people are Tswana, or Botswana, relieving the country of ethnic strife. Parliamentary democracy has survived intact.

But there are problems. Income distribution is badly skewed, and a handful of people profit from beef exports. According to Morag Bell, in *Contemporary Africa*, only 7 percent of rural households had no cattle in 1943. By 1975, 45 percent had no cattle. In 1943, 11 percent of cattle owners had fewer than ten. In 1975, 66 percent had fewer than ten. Development has been hard on the environment. Land and water have been exploited as commodities for commercial ranching. And there is the diamond mining.

Botswana's main resource are mines owned jointly with De Beers of South Africa. They provide substantial income, but jobs within the country have not kept up with demand. Many Botswanans still migrate across the border to work.

South Africa looms over the future in other ways. Twice, invasion forces ignored the border to look—without success—for African National Congress bases. Bloodshed was especially bitter to the peaceful little population.

"You can't imagine the change," a diplomat friend warned at the end of 1986. "Whites used to be able to go anywhere unnoticed. They were welcome. Now if you drive into a strange neighborhood, five people will call the police. They think everyone is a South African agent. It is brutalizing the Botswanans."

The "front-line" states of Lesotho and Swaziland are not on the line at all. They are each smack in the belly of the beast. Lesotho is a dramatic mountaintop kingdom totally at the mercy of South Africa. Its trade is linked intimately with its giant neighbor. And so are its politics.

During 1985, young activists, trained in North Korea, showed signs of warming to the East. And then Chief Leabua Jonathan, the prime minister, refused to sign a security agreement with South Africa or expel African National Congress militants. Pretoria closed the border. Jonathan threatened to seek help from the Soviet Union and Cuba; he was promptly overthrown.

Lesotho's people drain regularly out to South Africa. Two of every three households depend on at least one migrant worker over the border, Morag Bell noted. But the people come and go. The land itself is carried off steadily to South Africa, and it is gone forever.

Water is practically Lesotho's only natural resource. But with a new system of tunnels and canals, that, too, is going to South Africa. A project was designed to dam the upper Orange River and divert water into the Vaal system to the north. Lesotho would receive fixed royalties for the water. Chief Jonathan had refused the final condition—he insisted that Lesotho control the sluice gate—but his successor did not. However badly Lesotho might need water during a drought, South Africa would get its fixed ration. Royalties were to go not only to Lesotho but also to the World Bank. The bank was lending $48 million to the project.

Engineers working on the system were sure of one thing: Water leaving Lesotho would be chocolate brown.

I once met an Englishman who had been in charge of conservation in Lesotho. Every year, he said, 6 percent of the country's topsoil is washed away. That figure might be disputed—it is too hard to measure or define. But the loss is enormous. Nearly all of the trees have been cut from steep mountain slopes that make up much of the country. Deep erosion gulleys scar land once used for crops and cattle.

Whatever the figures, the effect is plain. With each rain and gust of wind, more of Lesotho vanishes.

Swaziland, by contrast, is flatter, a stretch of low and high veld beyond the Transvaal. It is only 6,704 square miles, but is rich in minerals and well watered. It is a handy little safety valve for South Africa, particularly well suited to breaking sanctions. When South African mercenaries flew off to attack the Seychelles in 1981, they caught a scheduled Royal Swazi flight. In 1986, Swaziland exported twice as much fruit as it grew.

King Sobhuza II, the old lion of Swaziland, reigned for sixty-one years, until his death in 1982. Years of vicious infighting followed, but with only figurative backstabbing. Mswati III took the throne in April 1986. The new king, a teen-ager, took a break from studies in England to attend his coronation. Prince Bhekimpi Alpheus Dlamini was made prime minister. But Swazi affairs are shaped in Pretoria.

Malawi's president for life, Hastings Kamuzu Banda, long ago made his peace with the devil. He is the only African leader to recognize South Africa, just as he refused to declare sanctions against Rhodesia. For years, he profited from it. South Africa was generous with development aid.

Up to now, Malawi has had some economic success. Its agriculture is diversified, and hydroelectric power runs small industries. Farmers are free to make decisions and to earn heavy profits as a result. But that is one of the few freedoms in Malawi.

Banda runs the country like a private farm where no one dares speak up to the boss. People work hard and mind their own business. It is, the wags say, a one-man Banda. The main question is what will happen when Banda's president-for-life term comes to an end. He is in his eighties and has not delegated power.

Even before then, a crisis looms. Malawi's lifeline is the railroad to Nacala and Beira in Mozambique. But traffic is hit often by Renamo rebels. They are financed, naturally enough, by Banda's friends, the South Africans.

11 SOUTH AFRICA
Beyond the Politics

From Doug, an insider:

"SEX KILLER RAPES NUN UNDER HOLY TREE" was not the sort of headline you could ignore. That and others like it spiced my daily trudge home in Johannesburg in the late 1960s. The *Post*, an exuberantly sensational black newspaper, reflected the cultural ferment that was all around. It did not occur to me to notice that those headlines were never political.

I worked for a law firm, about to be a lawyer. Each morning and evening, I threaded through crowds of people hurrying in and out of the train station reserved for blacks. Zulu women in elaborate head ties, beads, and embroidered skirts jostled natty Sotho men in slick Western suits. Shops that displayed dried bits of skin for medicine men stood next to haberdasheries and fast-food joints offering corn meal and gravy.

To me, it seemed amazingly unpoliticized. I remember no unpleasant incidents; nobody showed any interest in me at all. The question of safety never arose. Given the disparity in incomes and political rights, the tolerance between blacks and whites was incredible. Like everyone else in South Africa, I found it hard to situate the reality of black and white coexistence. Despite my volunteer work for the Progressive Party, I was not political. It was clear that life should be better, but I was suspicious of glib answers from the left and the right. Mainly, I was confused and frustrated.

Growing up, I had looked forward to being an adult in a country where people's rights were balanced. My father was a senior judge; he had spent his life upholding the rule of law. Two of my brothers had gone into law, and I was doing the same. But South Africa was letting me down.

Even for a privileged paleface, South Africa was troubled and unhappy. I spent my first years in the complacent and comfortable suburbs of northern Johannesburg. Whites did not then discuss their worth in relation to blacks; such things were understood.

I went to an English boarding school in Johannesburg started by an Anglican order, the Community of the Resurrection. The priests also ran a mission in Sophiatown, a little community north of town where blacks were allowed to own land. Suddenly, authorities changed their minds. They ran off the blacks and created a suburb for poor whites. It was called Triomf. Triumph, in Afrikaans. I learned this later. Such events passed unnoticed by white schoolkids.

The Sharpeville massacre was harder to ignore. The tension from it gripped our little world at school. A friend's parents witnessed it, but somehow could not get it across. I was simply not equipped to imagine it. It was only later, at the University of Witwatersrand, that I began to realize how apartheid intruded directly into my life.

Wits was liberal, English-speaking, and committed to academic freedom. But the government was muscling in. The Afrikaner-dominated Nationalist Party restricted the entry of nonwhite students, and the government hired informers to spy on left-leaning campus organizations. Police made sure no one objected.

Once, students joined with the Black Sash, a civil-rights organization run by women, to protest new repressive security measures. The women stood in silent vigil around a symbolic flame of freedom on the steps of Johannesburg City Hall. Suddenly, a rowdy mob pushed them aside and tried to knock over the flame. The leader was a giant, rough and toothless, who turned out to be an off-duty policeman. I saw him knock an old lady to the ground, hitting her with, of all things, a huge slab of raw fish.

At Wits, we dug deeply into the country's problems. In constitutional law, we traced how the government had destroyed mixed-race voting rights in the Cape. Rights could be withdrawn only by a two-thirds majority in both houses of Parliament. Lacking the votes, the government tried to cheat. When an independent appeals court stood in the way, the government replied with fraud. The Nationalist Party simply appointed senators, enough to carry the vote. For good measure, it also packed the Appellate Division, thus destroying the nation's legal safeguard.

As a lawyer, I watched authorities manipulate the law. Flawed court proceedings drastically curtailed justice. A white's word prevailed over a black's. For equal crimes, blacks paid far more heavily. I managed some successes for black clients charged with minor offenses. But many apartheid laws were enforced by bureaucrats, bypassing the courts.

I helped to defend two people charged under the Immorality Act, which banned interracial sex. They were well-educated professionals who cared deeply for one another; their relationship would not have rated a second thought anywhere else in the world. State's evidence came from upright young Calvinist policemen employed as Peeping Toms. Police had searched the scene of the crime with excruciating zeal. A crude, dour officer recounted intimate details of what had been seen and found. It was a monstrous, humiliating invasion of privacy, a striking example of Joseph Conrad's "somber imbecility of political fanatacism."

The man was a critic of the government, and the trial was an attempt to smear him. For some Nationalists, prosecution under the Immorality Act was a crushing stigma. The main result was wide condemnation of ruthless methods and a contemptible law.

I was also part of the defense team in a show trial against the editor and a senior reporter of the *Rand Daily Mail*. They were accused of distorting facts about South African prisons, after a series written by a political prisoner. The writer had detailed barbaric and unsanitary conditions. He was punished, but the state wanted also to scare journalists off a touchy subject. Convicts, all subject to police pressure, swore to the felicity and salubricity of prison life. I picked out enough contradictions, inconsistencies, and absurdities for any remotely objective judge to throw the case out of court. But this was South Africa. The judge, carefully chosen beforehand, found them guilty.

That brushed away my last shreds of respect for legality in South Africa. No citizen, not even an influential white one, could rely on the law to protect him from the state. We had gifted and principled judges. But many laws they had to implement were grossly unjust. At any time, the government could maneuver them aside with its own lackeys.

At the same time, the government was systematically eroding the few nonracial institutions in the country. Fort Hare, for example, was founded by the Presbyterian church as a private college in 1916. It was one of the first places on the continent to provide higher education for Africans. Its graduates included Robert Mugabe and Oliver Tambo. But the Nationalists made it over into an apartheid-style tribal college, complete with heavy-handed Afrikaner administrators.

Corruption undermined the state. Nationalist politicians, learning in advance where homelands would be proclaimed, bought land cheaply and sold it back handsomely to the government. Afrikaners had preference in the civil service and Defense Force, in the awarding of contracts and premiums. It was African tribalism. White officials' control over blacks' lives offered leverage for bribes at every level.

Although corruption was often worse elsewhere in Africa, the impression was of a South Africa run for the benefit of the Afrikaners at the expense of everyone else. Other factors reinforced the impression. Bullying and abuse were a daily feature of life.

One peaceful Sunday, I stopped with some friends at a little town in the northern Transvaal. A musclebound youth punched one of my friends through the car window. I hurried up, and the young thug slugged me hard enough to send me skidding up the sidewalk on my back. His pals cheered encouragement. The problem, we could only guess, was my friend's long hair.

My friend was white, but the incident reflected the tense mood that demoralized black South Africans. Bullying racism would explode into the violent reaction now racking the country; then, it was the dull ache of impotence.

Once, my brother and I went hiking in the Magaliesberg Mountains on a glorious winter day. It was early, crisp and clear, the sort of day that makes the world seem at its best. We came to a small hut, with a black man sitting out front by a small fire. He was ill at ease as we approached, and he looked away as he returned our greeting. I asked his name, and he replied with shattering servility: "Ek is Koos Barnard se kaffir." That means, essentially, I am Koos Barnard's nigger.

I began to detest the smugness that masked signs of what was coming. Afrikaners have always liked to tell outsiders, "We know the kaffirs. You people don't understand them at all." Yet what they have always seen were not real people, but, rather, a flawed stereotype implanted in their minds by their history and their culture. Their insistence on that image perpetuates it. And their overriding interests prevent them from allowing black people to prove them wrong.

More and more, I resented the government's arrogant assumption that it could tell me the circles I could frequent. I had no close friendships with Africans or Asians, just cordial, good-humored relationships on an equal footing. The rationale of apartheid seemed perverse, because I couldn't picture myself as superior to anyone else. Colleagues, meanwhile, were slipping into the golden trap of South African opulence, with enough servants and swimming pools to dull troubled consciences. Living rich and empty in Johannesburg's lush suburbs had no lure for me. I was happiest away from the society's pressures, on the land itself.

*I*t is easy enough to get the African bush in your blood. The father of my friend Chris McBride owned a game farm at the edge of Kruger National Park, where we spent hours walking through unspoiled bushveld, rich in wildlife.

Our best times were with a local tracker, Jack Mathebula. He was so good at tracking invisible spoor that we would end up on top of the lions we followed. Once we tracked a lioness with cubs all morning long. We reached a dry stream bed and were about to climb the steep bush-covered bank when Jack signaled a halt. The lioness was crouched in the bush, as if she was waiting for us.

We slunk back sixty yards and tried changing directions for a clear view. She remained out of sight. Chris suggested tossing a pebble to flush her out. The first two landed wide. The third hit her with a dull thump, and the bush exploded in feline fury. She charged straight at us, and I ran. Two things saved my life: The bush screened me from her view; and Chris and Jack stood fast.

It was a weird feeling. Instinct said, Go, and I was running full tilt before I got around to fear. But bushcraft commands, Stay put. Lions, unless wounded, often only feign a charge and pull up short if you stand your ground. (If you try this and get eaten, do not complain to the publisher; lions are like that.)

That sort of experience converts you to an Africa that transcends the stupidities and cruelties of some of the people who occupy it. The richness of plant and animal life, the purity of places unspoiled by man, the pungent smells, and the solitude exude an atmosphere of uneasy tranquillity. There is always the promise of beauty and danger.

Once, some bush junkie friends and I drove a thousand miles, round trip, to spend a single moonlit night by a pool in the otherwise dry Nuanetsi River of Zimbabwe, then Rhodesia. It was worth it. The scene was from Kipling's *Jungle Book*. Thousands of elephant and buffalo streamed past us for a drink at the pool; we sat watching from the bank. That pageant of pristine Africa has never left me.

We hiked often in Drakensberg, the Bushmen's ancient stronghold, in the mountains of the Cape, and on beaches of northern Zululand that were then remote and unspoiled.

And once we walked into the magic valley of the Witels. The trail climbs hard and steep to a small stone hut, the first night's camp. A thin stream emerged from a pool at the top of the ridge, near Worcester, in the Cape mountains. We followed the stream at a precarious angle to the bottom of the valley. From there, the little river meandered for miles among vast gardens of wild flowers in pastel colors.

Occasionally the banks were fringed with disa, an exquisitely simple crimson orchid. The stream was thick with trout. The magic of the Witels is that the valley gets narrower and narrower and the river gets wider and wider. Eventually, there is only water rushing between steep rocky cliffs. That's where the fun starts. We inflated air mattresses to float our backpacks. And we bobbed along behind, swimming with the current.

In the summer heat, it was bliss to float down a crystal stream with trout leaping up around us. At times, the cliffs closed overhead, and we swam through cool, stone cathedral vaults that echoed the gently lapping water.

The contrast between this and Johannesburg was too strong. Eventually I could no longer practice law among authorities with so little respect for legality. I was excited at the idea of a life spent working for the conservation of wild Africa and studying natural history. The time and money it would cost to reeducate myself was a small price.

I wanted to get far enough into the rest of the world to understand my own and to come to terms with it in my own way. I went to Humboldt State University in Arcata, California, for a master's degree in wildlife management. Then I spent a decade in Botswana. My work was ecological research and conservation. But I was in the next country over from South Africa, often with weeks to myself in secluded places. It gave me the chance to reflect on South Africa and the forces that were tearing apart a country I loved.

Apartheid was plainly a stupid policy that could only worsen problems it was meant to avert. It was a bizarre fantasy for whites to imagine they could exploit black labor in perpetuity while maintaining a monopoly on wealth and power. Black South Africans were in desperate need of immediate change. From a distance, I could analyze the formulas that outsiders offered.

To start with, I could not manage to feel moral superiority over Afrikaners. Had I been born into a narrow, authoritarian Calvinist community; had I seen from birth my parents and other adults humiliating and despising black people; had my education been thoroughly racist, would I be a racist? Most likely. The prejudice produced by this sort of conditioning is a disability, like illiteracy, to be cured rather than punished.

It seemed hard to expect ordinary people to transcend their upbringing when the most intelligent had trouble doing it. Jan Smuts, who helped shape South Africa early this century, started school at the age of twelve, but immediately passed his classmates. The great English jurist, Professor Maitland, called Smuts the most brilliant student he had ever taught. But Smuts' son wrote: "My father had complete confidence in the intellectual and administrative superiority of the white man. He was convinced that, come what will, these . . . would enable him to live indefinitely in a state of semioverlordship over the blacks."

I could not blame the oppressive system totally on Nationalists in power. The imperial British government handed the county over to a white minority in spite of early and accurate warnings of what would emerge. New generations perpetuated colonial racism and brought it to new excesses. The Western world, not wholly innocent of racism, took its time to object in forceful terms.

As a people, Afrikaners are neither uniquely evil nor brutal. Nor are they backward. An Afrikaner performed the world's first heart transplant; others produce sensitive literature and moving art. Many decent, humane, and compassionate people are blocked from view in the shadow of official Afrikanerdom.

Glib comparisons to Nazi Germany shed little light on a complex portrait. The domination and humiliation of one ethnic group by another is wrong, but it is not simple.

The struggle has as much to do with political and economic power as it does with race. Discrimination is not a program of genocide, but, rather, an absolute refusal to cede political control. It is understandable that Afrikaners worry about being crushed under a one-man-one-vote system: no natural justice decrees that majorities have the right to dominate minorities.

But, even less, minorities cannot dominate majorities. The government's deliberate denial of not only political power but also human achievement suggests malice and contempt. So does their callous and brutal social engineering.

I've heard no convincing answers for South Africa. But there is no shortage of people who are willing to suggest some. And those with the simplest answers tend to be those who do not understand the questions.

Many want to destroy South Africa to save it. They forget that the country was built by generations of black labor, under the harshest of conditions. Their reward was meager. But their children and grandchildren, when given access to their political rights, might prosper from that sacrifice.

A blind call to violence ignores the fact that South Africa has seen only a trickle of the potential bloodshed. Who would gain from an all-out race war?

At the other extreme, some argue that if the Afrikaners are left alone, pushed gently in the right direction, they will change. But frustrated black communities will no longer accept a piecemeal dismantling of the surface apparatus at a pace that suits the overprivileged whites.

It has been well over a decade since I last lived or worked in South Africa. And I am no clairvoyant. But it is obvious there is need for radical change. And no such change is likely to be peaceful. Diehard whites believe they can dictate the nature and pace of change. Militant blacks feel they have the right to demand immediate and unconditional surrender of white self-determination. There is little room for compromise.

If negotiations are to stand a chance, each side must make major—and improbable—concessions. Meanwhile, people die every day because of apartheid, and tens of billions of dollars have been wasted on it. There may be less personal corruption in the South African government than in some other African governments, but there is scarcely less waste.

The onus for breaking the impasse is mainly on the government. But it is hard to foresee what the government will do. My country seems to have gotten itself into the kind of situation, like those in the Middle East, that defies solution by human reason. It is a deeply discouraging thought.

*F*or me, the split ends of my schizophrenic background come involuntarily closer together every time I look again at South Africa. As a lawyer, my concern was for social justice. As an ecologist, I sought to protect the land. Now, one is inextricably linked to the other. The politics of apartheid is destroying the land itself.

To segregate tribal groups and keep control of the best land, white authorities created a patchwork of nine Bantustans, the homelands. Four of them maintain the fiction of being independent countries. Some are made up of unconnected pieces; KwaZulu is a plethora of odd-shaped fragments of Natal Province. And nearly every homeland is desperately overgrazed, stripped of trees, and eroding at a rate that greatly exceeds the capacity of renewal. Each year, along with the high birth rate, more people are moved to homelands.

People will learn too late that man's relationship to the land that sustains him is as fundamental as the politics. Failing to deal with the problems of human impact on the environment may prove to be an even greater folly than apartheid.

More than a decade ago, I drove back from the Drakensberg as a violent summer storm swept down from the mountains. At first, driving through a nature reserve, water coursing down the hillsides was crystal clear. The stream we crossed was so clean we could see every stone on its bed. Then we left the reserve and entered KwaZulu. The stream immediately turned into an opaque torrent. Great rivers of red mud swept across the road from the denuded and eroded hillside.

It was as if the earth were bleeding.

*F*rom Mort, an outsider:

By the time I first saw South Africa, in 1981, a lot of Doug's land had bled to death. The world has since learned a little Afrikaans and Zulu. It knows *sjambok*, the short nasty whip used for thrashing rioters. It knows *laagers*, the Afrikaners' forts of encircled wagons, and *impis*, the Zulu phalanxes that attack them. It does not know *donga*, a gaping eroded canyon that scars earth that has died.

In 1985, I drove down the road Doug described; those same KwaZulu slopes were rocky wasteland, gashed deeply by *dongas* that stretched far into the flat plain.

Color plays tricks on the outsider visiting South Africa. Politically, Zululand is black. But on satellite photographs, it is largely white, its once rich hillsides eroded down to bare shale. You do not need satellites to see it: Great raw caverns of collapsing earth are not easy to miss.

It is not only so in KwaZulu. In the little homeland of QwaQwa, on the back slopes of the mountains of Lesotho, runoff water looks like molten chocolate. Periodically, great slices of land tumble into the widening *dongas*, sometimes taking a hut or two along with them. Other homelands are the same.

There is no lack of scientists to sound the alarm. But instead of combating erosion, each year authorities push more people into the reserves. New families crowd into the valleys and up the slopes, bringing yet more cattle to tear out the last roots of vegetation. The newcomers, like everyone else, cut down the dwindling trees for fuel and heat.

"Yes, erosion is a terribly important problem, and we spend half of the agriculture budget on combating it," an Afrikaner adviser to the QwaQwa government told me. I asked what percentage the agriculture budget was of the total? He smiled weakly. "Two percent."

South Africans are among the world's most skilled managers of land and wildlife when they choose to be. The Natal Parks Board, for example, is staffed by earnest men and women in forest green who know exactly what is happening, and why. I spoke to Ian Colvin, a specialist whose job it was to measure land deterioration.

He unrolled photo after photo, showing by color shifts how rich forestland had been reduced by 90 percent, not only in KwaZulu, but also in Natal Province, white South Africa. He pinpointed degraded rangeland and eroded hill country. He explained how terracing, reforestation, and range management could at least halt the damage, if not restore the land.

I asked why the government wasn't doing something. He looked hard at me for a second, making sure I was as dumb as I seemed. "All they can think about is politics," he answered. "That overshadows everything."

Politics, of course, does overshadow everything in South Africa. Logically, one might expect the homeland governments to devote more money to conservation, perhaps squeezing more out of Pretoria for such a clearly pressing problem. Few of them do.

Sometimes, the problem is greed. In Transkei, the Xhosa homeland that calls itself an independent nation, authorities hired a South African ecologist to supervise conservation. When he tried to prevent white South Africans from building summer homes on Transkei's unspoiled Wild Coast, he was chastized. Black officials punished a white man for trying to keep South Africans from ruining Transkei's most valuable tourism asset.

More often, the problem is power. I went into KwaZulu hoping to talk about conservation with Mangosuthu Buthelezi, political leader of the bulk of 6 million Zulus. He was busy that day.

Just outside Durban, thousands of Zulus had crowded into a football stadium for an *indaba*, a political and cultural pep rally, rooted deep in Zulu tradition. It has been generations since Zulu warriors have been in a position to work themselves up to a real battle of the sort that made them famous. But many have not given up hope.

Warriors wore polyester jogging suits, serge slacks, or bathing trunks under leopard-skin cloaks and moth-eaten headdresses. Lion-hair ankle ruffs spilled over Adidas sneakers and imitation Guccis. The wrists that flexed over heirloom spears were adorned with Seikos or, occasionally, gold Rolexes.

But when the Zulu warriors formed into *impis*, their traditional platoons, with blind discipline and precision movement, they were a chilling sight. A drill sergeant bellowed orders. In a single motion, each *impi* surged forward with a coughing growl, like a lion who had missed lunch.

Buthelezi harangued his people. Toward the whites, he was moderate. He wanted a solution that respected all interests. South

Africa was big enough for everyone. He saved his vitriol for black leaders who preached the sort of violence that would end in bloody repression. Watching him up close, I could see a reality that escaped many of the deluded long-distance analysts who see South Africa in black and white and who ignore the racial and political nuances that smolder toward explosion.

The militia of Buthelezi's Inkatha Party, and a range of opposing groups, fight murderous vendettas. A hundred Inkatha officials were killed from 1983 to 1986, the chief says; survivors have exacted revenge. Buthelezi has a huge following. But millions of black South Africans—Xhosas, Sothos, Tswana, and not a few Zulus—fear domination by Inkatha nearly as much as by the white Nationalists. As I watched him speak, plowing through the churning political currents, he did not look like a man concerned with land erosion.

I have no more answers for South Africa than anyone else. There is no compromise that will take into account everyone's interests. It is not only rights that are at stake. Nor is the racial conflict anything an outsider can understand without a look at what is involved.

From birth, South Africans distinguish a person's color and make judgments—or make a judgment to try not to make a judgment—based on it.

A black friend named Chris More, a reporter for the Johannesburg *Star*, loves flying. He wants to be a pilot, and he can do it. The Johannesburg Flying Club is "open." But he laughs about it. "There is no way I am ever going to fly for South African Airways. I can just hear me over the loudspeaker: 'Good morning, this is Captain More.' The only people still in their seats will be dead of a heart attack."

There will be a black pilot for South African Airways during somebody's lifetime. And each passenger will either say, "My God, get me out of here" or "Isn't that wonderful, a black pilot." But he or she will not go unnoticed.

The logical assumption is that when rights are given to blacks, the problem will be solved. But what about power. Neither Chris More nor any other South African black sees his color as a political definition. Most want to be regarded as full human beings. But they also want to choose leaders who will not persecute them for being of the wrong ideology or the wrong tribe. At the same time, even those whites who are prepared to accept blacks as full human beings tend to draw a line at one man one vote.

And there is the upbringing Doug mentioned. People's minds are twisted from birth. Chris and I went to KwaNdebele, a homeland near Pretoria about to be given independence and a casino license. The Afrikaner attached to the local government's economic department was explaining to us the facts of life: "Yes, blacks have to get up at four o'clock in the morning to catch the bus to work. But they enjoy that. It's part of their life, travel, movement." Chris was in movement behind me. I could hear his chair scraping, and I could only think, Man, I wouldn't blame you. But don't do it.

As a result, race and racism mean something entirely different from what they did during the civil-rights struggle in the United States. It is one thing to fear that an inferior person will ruin your lunch or even lower your real estate values. It is another to fear that an overpowering number of people will take over your life and land, dispossess you, or, worse, turn the beloved country of your great-great-grandfather into a savage jungle of corruption, chaos, and Communism.

The only sensible thing an outsider can learn about South Africa is that there is no easy answer, for blacks or whites. Later, in New York, a young American cornered me in a bar. He knew I had been in the belly of the beast. "If anything is fucking clear, it is South Africa. It is so simple. Why don't we just go in and—"

And what?

Violence may end up being the answer by default, but it does not seem like the best way. It is easy to understand why some people think it is. But those outsiders who urge blacks to stand up to Afrikaner guns might at least inform themselves of the stakes. And the odds.

On the other side of Durban, I visited Alan Paton, who has spent a lot of time thinking about the land and the politics. He was eighty-three, stooped and white, and still stalking his beloved country, the Valley of a Thousand Hills.

"Each morning I read the papers and feel like shooting myself," Paton told me. He looked like he meant it. "I'm fed up with talking about South Africa's troubles, you know." Then he spent two hours doing exactly that. He proposed what he called a "fairyland scenario" for a federal structure, with blacks and whites sharing separate and common power in federated regions. But he described his persistent hope as thin: "A new generation will bring solutions—if we have a generation to wait. I don't know that we do."

Paton is no proponent of sanctions. "To destroy an economy to bring about some noble end is absolute rubbish." In the end, he said, he had faith in the black's ability to persevere. "I think the Americans broke the Red Indians' heart. We have never been able to break the heart of the blacks. We haven't come close to it."

Paton's last book, *Ah, but Your Land Is Beautiful*, could hardly have been better named. Having looked around 145 countries on every continent, I have never seen anything as beautiful as South Africa. That was what Paton meant by his title. Whenever political discussions reached that inevitable impasse, his visitors never failed to say, "Ah, but your land is beautiful."

From the sweeping majesty of the northern Transvaal, across the rich farms of the Orange Free State, and down across the dramatic southern coast, South Africa eludes description. Driving south in the wine country from Paarl to Stellenbosch, the mountains and flowers and Cape Dutch farms—the overwhelming beauty—brought moisture to my eyes.

Stellenbosch is a university town of flowering trees and stately streets of whitewashed stucco houses. A gentle river meanders through it, its banks lush with blossoms that scent the air. In a little stone house with heavy wood beams, a handsome Afrikaner woman sells herbs, honey, and deep-red tomatoes the size of softballs.

"No, we don't really feel the tension here," she told me. "We hear about the trouble in Crossroads, around Capetown, and it is just down the road. But it is another world."

Still, she acknowledged, it was not exactly the same. Her friends had eliminated evening drives to Cape Town, not far away on a four-lane freeway. They were afraid that disgruntled blacks might drop rocks on their cars from the pedestrian walkways over the highway.

Above Stellenbosch, I pulled into a vineyard and farm owned by an old friend from Kenya.

We climbed into his jeep and drove up the steep hill at the edge of his property. To the west, you could see Table Mountain rising over Cape Town in the distance. Down the slope, teams of Xhosa pickers worked among the ripened grapes. We sipped a chilled glass of his latest success.

"This is paradise," he said, "and it is surrounded by hell."

He did not know what to do. All his life, he had dreamed of making wine. He had a reputation and a life he loved. But he sympathized with the revolution he knew was coming. He was no racist; he hated racism. His South African wife wanted to move to England. He was already paying his workers so much over the going rate that his neighbors were furious.

"At night, I work things out and decide it is all right," he said. "And in the morning I listen to BBC and my conscience is pricked all over again."

Consciences are pricked all over the country, including the parts that are not so beautiful. KwaThema is a black township in the East Rand, as ugly a spot as I have ever seen. It is built in standard township style. A wide road runs around it, suitable for tanks should they ever be needed. Tall poles support the arc lighting that eliminates the dark corners where thieves—or troublemakers—might hide. People live crammed into homes; a few are two-story and comfortable, but most are thin-walled shacks.

Although suburban Johannesburg has some of the fanciest and best-stocked supermarkets in the world, KwaThema's commerce is limited to a few scruffy shops with broken barred windows. Shopkeepers are shielded behind thick wire grids, and they deliver purchases to customers item by item. A rank-smelling bar and snack shop sells greasy meat pies.

The undertaker had been busy the week I visited him. He had buried fourteen people, all but one of them shot in vital organs by police bullets. But, yes, he said, sometimes he buried people who had been murdered by other blacks. Suspected police informers—and many black policemen—were likely targets. Some were neck-laced. That is another of those peculiarly South African terms. Young toughs put a tire filled with gasoline around their victim's neck and set it alight. It is quickly but painfully fatal.

In their fearful social engineering, the Afrikaners outfoxed themselves. They can control who goes in and out of the townships but not what happens inside. As soon as the police in armored cars roll past, the "comrades" take over. Young militants watch the three or four access arteries. When they decide no one will go to work, no one does. They burn buses meant to carry workers. If anyone defies them, they burn his house when he is gone—or when he is home. Rent boycotts are easy to enforce. A torch is persuasive enough.

When there is a boycott against white stores, the comrades check parcels of people coming home. Groceries are smashed. Sometimes housewives are forced to drink their purchases, even cooking oil and bleach. The system is run by kids, fifteen to twenty years old. Many of them hate the United States and are getting more radically Marxist by the season.

The government has worked hard at dividing to conquer, exploiting old tribal hatreds. Now, blacks seem to be uniting against a common enemy. I met one young man in KwaThema—I'll call him Jackson—who explained why.

Jackson did not mess around with politics; he had a wife and a young son. He hated the system but was prepared to live with it. He finished work one day and, as always, took the bus. A patrol of white and black policemen stopped him as he walked to his house. Some kids had thrown rocks at a police car, and they were looking for suspects. Jackson explained who he was and where he was going. Abruptly, a black cop ordered him to pick up two stones lying on the ground. Jackson was no fool; he refused. And the officer shot him.

A religious leader asked me to give him a lift to the doctor in Johannesburg for yet another spinal treatment. Jackson told me his story on the way. He was fired for tangling with the police, and no one else would give him a job. That meant he would have to return to his homeland, where there was no chance of finding work. He had other plans, in any case. He was going underground to help the African National Congress kill whites and black collaborators.

*F*or a detached outsider, it is this force of circumstance that is so tragic. Also in KwaThema, I met Bishop Simeon Nkoane. He is an Anglican, the East Johannesburg counterpart of Bishop Desmond Tutu. Nkoane uses a gentle humor to bridge the gap between the comrades and white officials. It is not easy. Police fire-bombed his home one night while he was out; his eighty-year-old mother huddled alone until morning in the smoldering ruin of his living room. Once, he persuaded some young toughs not to burn a car and the people inside. Walking home afterward, he was arrested by police for disturbing the peace.

"If you had told me two years earlier that I would be standing up, speaking out at funerals, I would have said you were crazy," he told me. Now, he says, he has little choice.

Eventually, the simple logistics of it all, and the enormous cost, will pressure South African whites toward some change. Whites, blacks, coloreds, and Indians are all separate on the books; public services in quadruplicate are expensive. The Defense Force and the National Intelligence Service, along with local police departments, are a growing expense. War is not only hell; it is also damned costly.

The homeland policy has distorted the economy. Artificial governments compete for scarce industry with tax concessions. They must subsidize transportation and services, an economic sacrifice for the social goal of breaking up population densities. Because people are dispersed, and separated from productive land, authorities must run feeding centers. No Western donor offers food aid; so funds must be spent to buy it.

With so much money going into security and services, little is left for conservation. But 70 percent of South Africa's population is crowded onto 8.5 percent of its land. And it is the worst land, hillside catchment areas. Whites have kept the plateaus and coastal plains. They need water for the farms and mines, and it is growing scarce. During dry months, cattle and goats strip off the grasses needed to hold the soil. Rains then wash the bare earth away. Rivers silt up, and topsoil is carried far into the estuaries, smothering the once rich marine life.

The whites' main complaint is that the government has no long-term plan. There is talk of reform, but little is done. That is not enough for the liberals; it is too much for the far right. And public relations is not a South African strong point.

Conservative Afrikaners work hard to convince the world they are right. They point to trouble elsewhere in Africa; they dig into history and current affairs. What they miss is that the concept of apartheid negates it all. The more they argue, the less ground they gain. And the greater their frustration.

As Western governments screw up the courage to impose strong sanctions, Pretoria fights back bitterly. South Africa can paralyze Lesotho, Swaziland, and Botswana, and it can squeeze the life out of Zimbabwe, Zambia, and Mozambique. But by bullying its neighbors in spite, it is simply adding to the animosity against it.

Late in 1986, the South African government gave up all pretense of being a democratic government in the Western sense. With press-censorship measures that might have done credit to Stalin, authorities banned references to unpleasant subjects and expelled a range of correspondents. As they hoped, less was said about depredations in black areas. But they were, in effect, simply pushing harder against a spring.

"I don't know many whites who aren't at least thinking about where they could go," a white South African friend told me. "Ninety percent have either left or are getting organized." To leave South Africa is to "do the ducks." It is yet another addition to the colorful lexicon. Whatever else happens in Alan Paton's beloved country, doing the ducks will get to be a common term.

*I*n early 1987, Denis Worrall, the South African ambassador to London, did the ducks in reverse. "Ambassador Defects," American papers announced, as they had reported the repeated defections of senior Ethiopian diplomats. But Worrall did not flee to Boston and apply for a green card. In South Africa, the Orwellian nuances of opposition are much too complicated. Worrall returned to South Africa from London to run against the National Party, joining a mounting tide of surprise defectors.

Wimpie De Klerk, editor of the rockbound Afrikaner newspaper, *Rapport*, quit his job. He was followed later by David DeVilliers, director of the Nasionale Pers chain which publishes *Die Burger* in Cape Town, virtually the government's voice. A broad spectrum of academics bolted at the University of Stellenbosch, Afrikanerdom's intellectual heartland. There were others, and there would be more.

South Africa, caught between democracy and tyranny, was paralyzed with confusion. At the height of press control, Ken Owens was free enough to write in *Business Day*: "Not since the 1890s has any government led us into such grave danger as the belligerent and short-tempered President Botha has done." Foreign Minister Botha, he added, "suffers intellectual bankruptcy."

Police raided the Johannesburg *Star* to seize copies of the paper carrying an advertisement urging the release of people detained without trial. But editor Harvey Tyson stopped them with a court order. "How can any fair-minded person, even in a state of emergency— even in a state of war—support the idea that no one can call for the release of detainees?" the paper editorialized. "To what depths have some so-called representatives of nationalism sunk?"

As the whites' parliamentary elections approached in May 1985, blacks increased the pressure. Winnie Mandela, wife of the imprisoned African National Congress leader, Nelson Mandela, told the BBC that whites "are drifting away in droves from narrow-minded nationalism." With a general strike, blacks protested elections open to only one in six South Africans. But Botha's National Party held a wide majority. The more extreme right won nearly a third of the vote; white anti-apartheid activists were routed.

Authorities squeeze and squeeze. But at the Market Street Theater, multiracial casts in plays like "Born in the RSA" excoriate in bitter terms. Life in the RSA—the Republic of South Africa—spins along in its unique world of fantasy. Black surfers can take their chances along with whites against the odd shark at Durban's Bay of Plenty. But few of them do. At downtown cinemas, only the whites stand in line for Eddie Murphy and Richard Pryor. On Sunday afternoons in the suburbs, white weight-watchers suspend their vows and fall upon trays of rich creamcakes in glitzy cafés.

American and European corporations sold off interests in South Africa with great fanfare. A message was delivered, and some companies suffered losses as a result. Often, however, South Africans bought up the properties cheaply and tossed aside the benefits that foreigners had insisted upon for black workers. Most multinationals still collected their substantial licensing fees, royalties, and other payments.

Alan Cowell of the New York *Times*, among the correspondents who were expelled, captured the mood in his swan-song dispatch: "Washington has succeeded only in accelerating the demise of moderation and the narrowing of the few options that ever existed in this society. Whites, like blacks, know now that the status quo cannot continue. . . . But for now, there are no answers beyond the maintenance, by detention and emergency rule, of an untenable status quo."

Anyone who expects Afrikaners simply to pack up and leave is best advised to visit the Voortrekker Monument. You can see the monument from the hilltops of Pretoria, a squat square mass sitting back off the freeway to Johannesburg. It commemorates the great trek that brought the Afrikaners inland, over the Orange and Vaal Rivers, to flee British persecution. Their conquest of the natives, their church teaches, was an act of God. That such rich land was there, waiting for hard work to turn it into a motherland, was Providence. The gold and rare metals were icing on the celestial cake. South Africa was the Promised Land; the Afrikaners were the Chosen.

The Voortrekker Monument enshrines this in stone. Inside its soaring granite walls, panels in relief show white mothers protecting their babies from howling savages. Other panels show the natural order of things: dark faces toiling under the benevolent gaze of whites.

The physics are such that at certain times of year, God sends his approval with light beams through the roof.

It is beautiful and ugly at once. But, above all, it is massive. The monument is so heavy, so deeply entrenched, so squarely placed, that it seems to the outsider that the people who built it could not demolish it if they wanted to. It would take, one fears, a very large explosion.

12 THE LAND
Finding a Balance

Disparate as they are, every country in Africa faces the same question: What balance must be struck between nature's patterns and man's? Imported species of animals and plants, dams and canals can contribute to Africa's prosperity—and to its devastation.

Cattle, for example, pose a dilemma to much of the continent. Domestic herds moved in late to Africa. Nature was organized without them. They eat too much, and they drink too often. They are vulnerable to disease. Few Africans slaughter them.

But whole tribes live on their milk and blood. Domestic animals pull plows and produce fertilizer. They are at the heart of social, economic, and political systems in every part of Africa. And they have been in Africa for 2,000 years. For cattle, yes or no is not the issue. The question is balance.

A century ago, cattle brought calamity to Africa. Rinderpest struck animals like the Black Death. The animal pandemic differed from the plague only in that it was more virulent. It killed up to 90 percent of livestock and wildlife populations. In four years, it spread from the Somali coast to the Cape. South Africa and the British protectorates alone lost 4.5 million head of cattle.

People who depended on livestock suffered along with the animals. An estimated two-thirds of the Masai tribe died in the rinderpest famine. They were not alone. Across Africa, the pandemic brought political upheaval and the equivalent of a monumental stock-market crash.

"The Great Rinderpest of the 1890s . . . most likely represents the dividing line between initiative and apathy on the part of a large number of African peoples, particularly in the eastern and southern parts of the continent," observed Helge Kjekshus, a Norwegian political economist. "It broke the economic backbone of many of the most prosperous and advanced communities, undermined the established authority and status structures and altered political contacts between peoples. It initiated the breakdown of a long-established ecological balance and placed nature again at the advantage."

Surviving herders restocked quickly in fear of a recurrence. Because they use cattle as bank accounts and insurance policies, they wanted high numbers, not maximum quality.

The African system made sense as long as mortality corrected the balance. Excess cattle starved or died of disease. But vaccines, medicine, and supplementary food and water have changed the picture. Africans are now combining old values with new technology, and there are too many cattle.

The FAO estimated cattle in Africa at 170 million in 1986, and, at current trends, the total would reach 200 million by 2010. In its comprehensive report, *African Agriculture: The Next 25 Years*, the FAO calculated that herds were overstocked by 50 to 100 percent.

Drought decimates herds, but populations are quickly recovered. The hardiest females survive. Nomads lend breeding stock to stricken neighbors. When rains return, a herd can double in seven years.

Controversy swirls around the subject of cattle, and their impact on the land. By the mid-1980s, the World Resource Institute in Washington estimated that overgrazing had created desert patches on 90 percent of Sahel-Sudan rangelands. In southern Africa, the figure was near 80 percent and rising fast. Huge tracts of Central Africa are eroded seriously by overgrazing.

But Stephen Sandford, an authority on pastoralism, argues that no one has proven an increase in livestock numbers. As for the incidence of desertization, he wrote, "The evidence and arguments are so weak that no substantial reliance should be put on them." Nonetheless, he acknowledges, "Domestic livestock populations have an inherent tendency to expand in numbers."

The trends are clear.

Tanzania had an estimated 4.5 million cattle before the Great Rinderpest. Now there are more than 15 million. In Botswana, the national herd increased by two and a half times from 1965 to 1976, to 3 million. The area occupied by cattle has increased by the same proportion.

During prolonged drought, cattle are a plague on fragile land. Ecologists A. R. E. Sinclair and J. M. Fryxel showed this with satellite images of a famine zone in the Sahel. A large green polygon seemed to leap off the photo. It was a five-year-old ranch, carefully managed, with a rotational grazing system. It received no more rain than the surrounding rangeland, but its vegetation was intact. Elsewhere, cattle created moonscape.

Doug has seen a similar phenomenon in Botswana. In the Sahel, researchers showed me test patches they had fenced off from cattle and goats. Inside, the vegetation was green and abundant. Outside, livestock had stripped the ground bare.

In semiarid areas, plants and animals both depend on rainfall. But boreholes alter the balance. They supply water to cattle but not to the surrounding vegetation, and grazing pressure increases dramatically. A denuded circle, known coyly as a "sacrifice area," spreads from the water source. By Sandford's conservative estimate, the sacrifice area has a radius of eight kilometers in times of acute drought. He notes that 1,000 water points were constructed between 1957 and 1968 in the Sudan alone. In droughts since, those sources alone would have stripped 200,000 square kilometers by his figures.

Boreholes or not, animals are inhibiting regeneration of arid land. Most specialists agree that the most effective way to restore desert vegetation is to leave it alone. Rather than disturb the ecology with exotic species, they say, authorities should keep off goats and cattle, to protect natural seedlings.

Goats are hardier than cattle. They survive longer, roam farther, and, in desperation, climb trees to eat the last green branches of a dying region. And they will eat almost anything.

There is controversy over whether land degradation is permanent. Noel Cossins, of the International Livestock Center for Africa, maintains that in the long term it is often not. But land could take generations or even centuries to come back, he allows. That leaves a lot of suffering in the meantime. Others argue that much of the devastated landscape is lost forever.

A World Bank study in 1985 put the Sahel-Sudan desertization crisis sharply into focus. Damage was serious. Whether it was caused more by weather or by man was beside the point; only man's activities could be altered. A conflict between long-term public use of resources and private short-term abuse wreaked havoc on the land. The Sahel already had 50 percent more people than fuel wood to sustain them, and the ratios were changing by the week.

*T*he pattern in Africa is simple enough. Growing herds are pushed into deteriorating rangeland. As land loses productivity, farmers clear away more forests. Eventually, the new land is overgrazed. Wide belts of tsetse fly, which once protected forests, are shrinking under massive doses of pesticides.

Other factors come into play. Wood is cut for fuel and building; 90 percent of energy in Africa comes from wood. Hardwood forests are logged out, and brush is cleared away. Slash-and-burn fires run wild, ravaging huge areas of vegetation. Rain races down cleared slopes, carrying off topsoil and clogging watersheds. In coastal regions, silt is carried far into estuaries, smothering marine life.

Damage to the land could be affecting the climate itself. Scientists are recording more frequent dust storms in the Sahel; increased dust is believed to interfere with the production of rain by convectional systems.

At the same time, vanishing vegetation is increasing the earth's albedo. Bare earth, lighter in color, reflects more sunlight. Heat is not retained, and the soil cools down. Since rain is caused by warm moist air rising, rainfall diminishes.

Ray Harris, a geographer at Durham University in England who specializes in African climate, says it is plain that human factors are worsening natural change. But meteorologists disagree over how much impact land degradation has on weather patterns. In fact, scientists of every sort argue about Africa. The reason is simple: Very little scientific research is being done to determine what exactly is causing damage, or even the extent of the damage already caused.

"Frankly, we don't know much about the climate," observed Michael Gwynne. As head of the African monitoring unit of the U.N. Environment Program, he knows as much as anyone. And he is worried.

"There will be no tropical forests by the year 2000 in virtually all of West Africa," he said in 1986. "The Niger River will be very seasonal. . . . The forests of East Africa which grow at high altitudes, important for water catchment areas, they are going."

And the World Bank vice president for eastern and southern Africa, Edward V. K. Jaycox, was blunt in a speech made at the same time:

> The physical environment is being degraded at an unprec-
> edented rate. We are facing ecological deterioration which
> is severely undermining Africa's economic future. . . . For-
> ests have been cut in half during this century and the rate
> of destruction is accelerating. The simple fact is that the
> stable and life-sustaining relationship between the people
> of Africa and their environmental support system is break-
> ing down—and will certainly break down under tomorrow's
> population densities unless the causes are recognized and
> dealt with right away.

A forestry official in Niger put it simply enough: "The Sahara is not moving south; we are pulling it south."

Lack of historical data makes it difficult to assess change. Hippo bones and fossils suggest that the Sahara began drying 5,000 years ago in a steady process. But the recent pace seems to have been rapid. Yellowed journals of African travelers drive home the point. French officers in Chad in the last century, for example, reported that marauding sultans sent slaves on ahead to clear the dense bush so their warriors could get through. Today, a war lord can race his jeep overland without a tree or a bush in the way.

No one can miss it, scientist or not. In dry regions, the slightest breeze stirs dust that was rangeland. Elsewhere, deep jagged gulleys run down the slopes. When rain does fall, runoff water speeds along in thick chocolate-brown torrents.

Gwynne says that proper research and monitoring costs more than governments are willing to spend, and it requires international agreements on political issues. "When you're talking about clouds and gases and things that float around, it's very easy to draft conventions," he said. "When you talk about people and livestock and crops, then these are the essentials, and it gets difficult."

Without a firm scientific base, remedies are often left to technical tourists who make brief visits and act on their experiences from somewhere else. They must work from questionable data, partisan lobbying, and experts' reports laced with personal prejudices.

Spared discouraging evidence, a number of technical tourists pushed hard for commercial cattle ranching in Africa. Everything was tried. Fragile rangeland was carved up into Texas-style ranges. Elaborate systems were devised, with feed lots and slaughterhouses.

The FAO report looks back harshly, saying that one billion dollars was wasted since 1960 on cattle projects. In Washington, a senior World Bank official rolled his eyes when pressed on the issue. "We have not had much luck with cattle projects in Africa."

The problem, as a World Bank expert put it in an internal report in 1983, is that outsiders can bring the technology but not the politics. Almost invariably, the wrong people seize control of the credits and the herds. Despite good intentions, stocking limits and range boundaries are ignored. The rich earn more, and the poor are left with plundered land.

The Bank's 1985 study concluded that the best way to protect fragile land was to step back and let it protect itself. Like ORSTROM, it recommended protecting young acacias and other indigenous trees. Where land is tilled, farmers can plant simple windbreaks, rows of trees to protect the soil and provide wood. Small networks of terraces and catchment dams, built simply with village labor, can conserve runoff water. Most of all, the report said, respect must be paid to the natural carrying capacity.

Gwynne, an African rangeland specialist, keeps returning to the question of balance. Cattle are essential, but not to the exclusion of all else. He says too much emphasis is placed on fat lazy cows.

"We need a proper understanding of pastoral systems and how they work," he says. "The tendency in the United States is to look down on them because they're different. Americans are meat eaters, and they like nothing better than to cut up an animal. But Africans' animals don't have to be muscle machines; skins and bones will produce just as much milk and blood."

Gwynne's belief is shared by David Western, a widely respected Kenyan ecologist with the New York Zoological Society who studies pastoral systems and their impact on the land. His approach is the same as Noumou Diakete's, the Malian expert in Mopti: Keep the farmers off fragile rangeland. Let pastoralists find their own balance with nature. And help them benefit from each other.

Apart from the environmental aspects, this ought to be a major concern. It has the added advantage of allowing a threatened fundamental indigenous African system to survive. Pastoralist herders, like the vanishing Bushmen, have a lot to teach the world.

But herders suffered from the classic African dichotomy. During the colonial period, it was the farmers, not the herders, who took to education. Sedentary tribesmen had a sense of location and boundaries. And they formed the governments. Leaders today are seldom sympathetic to pastoralists. They prefer quick profits from cattle, if possible with support from outside aid.

Sahelian governments, for instance, have done almost nothing to develop export markets for pastoralists' cattle. Abidjan, down the road from Mali, eats French and Argentine beef. Worse, in Bamako, the capital of Mali, 95 percent of the beef and dairy products consumed are imported from abroad. Even when nomads' cattle were dying in the drought, no way was found to get them to Bamako.

Gwynne recalled an international meeting on cattle policy during which someone argued that indigenous pastoralists should be assisted;

what they were doing was good for their kind of terrain. "A whole lot of the meat-eating rednecks got up and walked out," he said, with a rueful chuckle. "One of the worst things you can do is destroy something and replace it with nothing."

Neither Abdul Rahman Diku nor Nax the Bushman is on the World Bank mailing list. They are spared the stream of reports, with charts and summaries, that never seem to reveal that the subject at hand is human lives. To understand what is happening in Africa, it helps to know the numbers. But it helps just as much to read someone like Wilfred Thesinger. The great English traveler was not writing about African nomads in *Arabian Sands*. But he might have been.

> They were no ignorant savages [he wrote of the Bedu]. On the contrary, they were the lineal heirs of a very ancient civilization, who found within the framework of their society the personal freedom and self-discipline for which they craved. Now they were being driven out of the desert into towns where the qualities which once gave them mastery are no longer sufficient. Forces as uncontrollable as the droughts which so often killed them in the past have destroyed the economy of their lives. Now it is not death but degradation which faces them.

In the mid-1980s, a recurrence of the Great Rinderpest threatened to devastate Africa. Stricken cattle from Mauritania were herded south into Mali. The disease spread quickly across the continent, through the Horn and all the way south to Mozambique. It killed some cattle but never caught hold. Enough animals were vaccinated to keep it under control. But it was close. Then Andrew Dodson, a parasitologist at Princeton University, warned in late 1985 that conditions were ripe for a second pandemic, on the centenary of the first.

Wildlife zoologists had their fingers crossed. If the disease had spread to wildlife, specialists said, it could have killed 90 percent of the Serengeti wildebeest, more than a million animals.

Few issues raise more heat than tsetse-fly spraying. The tough little insect carries trypanosomiasis, or African sleeping sickness. It is fatal to cattle. The International Livestock Center for Africa estimates that 70 percent of the infested 10 million square kilometers could sustain livestock and mixed agriculture were it not for trypanosomiasis. That means, ILCA says, another 140 million cattle and an equivalent amount of sheep and goats.

Such a thought provokes nightmares among proponents of wildlife. Convincing evidence suggests that wild game can produce more revenue than livestock on marginal land. Along with what it might attract in tourism and safari hunting, it can be harvested for meat with little of the expense of livestock production. Conservationists tend to cheer for the tsetse as a last natural defense of ecosystems.

But government officials, often cattle owners themselves, seldom see it that way. Nor do some ecologists. "If we can control tsetse, we can get to the 60 percent of Tanzania that is unused, no good to anyone," Mike Norton-Griffiths maintains. "I'm all for it, because I think people are more important than animals."

When livestock and wildlife conflict, the cows almost always win. South Africa led the way.

In 1894, David Bruce, an army surgeon-major in Natal, discovered that tsetse flies transmitted trypanosomiasis to healthy livestock and that wild animals provided the reservoir for the parasite. He prepared for mass slaughter. But Bruce was transferred, and before anyone else could act, rinderpest wiped out 80 percent of the cattle. The tsetse fly went with them. Soon the flies were back. By 1917, hunters flocked to Natal for a free-for-all. No records were kept, but officials estimated that 25,000 wildebeest were exterminated in a single campaign.

Eventually someone figured out it would be wiser to kill the flies, not the animals. But their methods failed. In 1929, the massacres began again. A wave of hunters killed 15,130 zebra. Other species followed. New fly traps were tried without success. In the early 1940s, game was shot in the tens of thousands. In a few years, the toll was 138,529 wild animals. Only in the 1950s did chemicals, traps, and biological tinkering wipe out the South African tsetses.

Pesticides brought new problems, and no one knows the extent of them. Orchids in the Makitini flats are disappearing, perhaps because their insect pollinators were exterminated along with the tsetse fly.

Animals were hunted to the brink of extinction from the moment Europeans settled at the Cape. The world's last quagga, a sickly female, lay down and died in an Amsterdam zoo cage on August 12, 1883. It was only in that year, by coincidence, that the first wildlife conservation body was formed in South Africa.

The last wild quagga on the veld had been shot in 1867. Zoos seeking replacements were astonished to learn there were no more. Not long before, there had been huge numbers. The quagga was like a zebra whose stripes, more golden than black, trailed off halfway down its body. One early traveler described its "gay glittering coat." Unfortunately for the quagga, its hide made handsome shoes and grain sacks.

The first visitors to the vast Karoo wrote of wild herds of antelope and zebra stretching black over the horizon. Within a few generations, they were gone, replaced by sheep. And the rich grass of the Karoo was overgrazed, leaving an ecologically altered dwarf shrubland, with a fraction of its former carrying capacity.

Conservation came hard. In 1934, one group tried to persuade Minister of Lands Jan Kemp to set aside a reserve for the last few mountain zebra. Finally, Kemp had heard enough. "No!" he sputtered. "They're just a lot of donkeys in football jerseys."

But a reserve was started three years later for five stallions and a mare. Today, they are thriving. The southern white rhinoceros has been protected so successfully that rangers have to cull some to maintain ecological balance in the parks. Careful management has developed parks that earn substantial incomes, attracting tourists to see animals in a country widely despised for its treatment of humans.

South African ranchers have supplemented their own earnings by harvesting wildlife on their land, shooting and selling just enough game to keep the numbers steady. By innoculating their cattle and managing their range, few find problems with peaceful co-existence. Fifty thousand antelopes are sold a year, largely to restock private land. A single eland buck can bring $3,000 at an auction.

After giving over most of the country to domestic livestock, South African authorities have demonstrated that wild animals can also thrive. As long as they know their place.

*E*lsewhere in Africa, wildlife fight a losing battle. Botswana devotes 17 percent of its land to reserves. But animals do not carry maps. Once they are off protected land, they are fair game. For less than the price of a six-pack of beer, a Botswanan can buy a buffalo license. In practice, he can kill a dozen animals with the same piece of paper. Wardens are few, and they are desperately short of vehicles and fuel. Commercial companies outfit local hunters and buy their kills.

Even in Zimbabwe, where the government spends twenty-five times more per unit of land to protect its wildlife, poaching is a problem. In zones of Zimbabwe where cattle may be exposed to foot-and-mouth disease, the buffalo are exterminated.

It is easy enough to pass judgment from a distance. But the problem must be seen as Africans see it. In his ten years in Botswana, Doug saw every sign that, although foreigners found wildlife more esthetically pleasing, most Africans preferred to look at cows. Building up herds meant they were improving their standard of living. At best, they saw wildlife as irrelevant to this priority. At worst, the game was in the way.

Whatever anyone outside Africa decides, neither wild animals nor land will be conserved unless Africans decide it is in their interest to do it—that is, the people as well as the government. Animals will never be treated well if humans are treated badly.

The idea that wildlife is an international resource might take hold provided it is also an international responsibility. Desperately poor countries find little justice in demands from wealthy foreigners that they foot the bill with their scarce resources. They need help. Costs must include compensation for lost opportunity—what reserves might earn if used for something else. And individuals need indemnities for crop and pasture loss to herbivores, or stock losses to carnivores.

Such a plan is unlikely. Problems of sovereignty and equitability would arise. Western contributors would want to look closely at the books. But it could work. And failing something similar, outsiders have little ground for complaint as wildlife dwindles away.

More likely is an effort to demonstrate to each government, and each individual, the direct value of wildlife. Kenya, a prime tourist destination, needs no such proof. But Kenyan farmers who lose their corn to elephants are not convinced. Under the system in Kenya, every animal down to the field mice belongs to the state. Conservation works much better in Zimbabwe, where landowners can use the animals who wander across the premises. They can organize tourist camps or safaris, or they can harvest the game.

In each case, decision lies in the hands of the governments in power. If authorities take seriously the problem, a great deal can be done. If they follow narrow interests according to patterns already established, Africa will shift steadily farther away from Eden. Once again, it is a matter of balance.

*B*alance is equally the issue with major development projects in Africa. For all their majestic grandeur, African environments are much less forgiving than those in Europe and the Americas. Soils are generally poorer, and rainfall is erratic. A nudge to nature here and there is essential for food production, energy, and communications—even a big nudge, if properly conceived. But Africa, unwillingly or unwittingly, has provided the backdrop for some of history's greatest displays of human folly. It is too tempting for writers to pass up the irony of elephants: in Africa, white elephants threaten to survive the gray ones.

Among the worst failures were those conceived by colonial powers. After World War II, Britain sank huge amounts of scarce development funds into producing peanuts in central Tanganyika. Engineers put in a railroad, heavy equipment, and vast crews of laborers. They overlooked one detail: rain. The project was abandoned.

The French Office du Niger in Mali was nearly as bad, but no one had the good sense to stop it. It produced expensive cotton and rice only because once-flourishing regions to the south were stripped of able-bodied workers. The forced cooperation system threw Mali's village societies into turmoil.

Europe shaped tropical agricultural systems to produce cheap cash crops. That was why colonies existed. Food could be grown elsewhere and shipped in. African governments harp on this point, with reason. But few have reshaped their agriculture into something else despite a quarter-century of free choice. In many instances, they were following outside advice.

Robert Ndaw, a former Malian minister who directs the U.N. Environment Program's Desertification Center, told a BBC interviewer in 1986: "Many mistakes have been made, many times they have thought that something which was good for them is good for us, so kindly they came and helped us to develop what was good for them." The "something" he referred to was cash crops. "But, here in Africa it has destroyed land, it has destroyed people, it has destroyed the future for very short-term and long-term benefits."

Ndaw had an example in mind: "You can take Senegal, the groundnut basin. We call it the *désert arachide*, the groundnut desert, created by *arachide* production for export, for oil factories outside the continent. It is a misery."

Critics of cash-crop economies often forget that African countries need more than food and that export agriculture earns foreign exchange. But too much dependence on crops, especially when there is only one crop, leaves a country vulnerable to fluctuations in the world market. The terms of trade have plummeted sharply for many commodities. By 1975, Julius Nyerere once noted, the tractor that cost the equivalent of thirty-four bags of sisal in 1960 had gone up to 138 bags.

Again the answer is balance. Authorities must support revenue-earning agriculture. They also should help rural farmers to grow food, but they seldom do. After the 1973–74 Sahel famine, outsiders vowed to help the stricken countries attain food self-sufficiency. But of the $11 billion spent in the Sahel until the next major drought a decade later, 4 percent went into rain-fed food crops. Only 1.4 percent was spent on soil and water conservation or ecological stabilization.

Donors prefer visible, preferably large, projects, on which they can hang a flag. Aid officers design proposals with timetables in mind. Ideally, glory can be harvested before the end of a two-year tour of duty. Local governments often agree. Improvements such as seed, fertilizers, and farm credit can produce more food. But for much of the year, their investment is buried in the ground, out of sight.

Lloyd Timberlake, author of *Crisis in Africa*, notes that among the technical tourists, there are few anthropologists. They tend to look at socio-political realities, he says, and spoil everyone's fun by showing why a project will not work. Increasingly, there are ecologists, thanks in part to dust raised by specialists like Timberlake. But their warnings are frequently filed away and forgotten.

Anthropologists and ecologists howled in unison over a mammoth plan to dredge the Jonglei Canal, along the edge of the Sudd, on the upper White Nile. Early travelers competed hotly to find damning adjectives worthy of the region. Navigators poled yard by yard through the thick reeds and papyrus. Insects strafed and swarmed. Crocodiles, snakes, and hunting predators waited on the banks. It was the sort of place only nature would love.

Professional developers had a better idea. Since a lot of water evaporated in the vast swamp, why not bypass it? The Nile flow would be augmented, and Sudanese farmers could irrigate more crops. Objections were raised. The Aswan High Dam, which was supposed to regulate the Nile farther down, caused more problems than it solved. Irrigation at Gezira, south of Khartoum, the world's biggest farm, was operating well below potential. And diverting the water would dry out much of the Sudd.

Environmental impact studies were made. But when construction began, wildlife died in large numbers. Animals trying to cross the canal found it was too steep; they could not get out of it.

But it was a monumental project, evidence of development. The potential for making money was huge, not the least for the European engineers and contractors who would undertake it. There was heavy French involvement, and I talked about it in 1986 with Jacques-Yves Cousteau. The Cousteau team had made a survey of the Nile, and he knew the Sudd.

"It is a disaster," he said. "An absolute disaster. It will kill this unique ecosystem and cause great damage down the river. It is a simple case of people looking for short-term profit at the expense of the future."

With all the controversy, plans for the Jonglei Canal went ahead. But not much more than plans. War in the region supplied the balance that nature could not.

Most African successes have been small, undramatic ones, but they add up to a body of progress. A drought-resistant strain of sorghum is showing promise in the Sudan. Zimbabwean farmers are growing better maize with a hybrid. Researchers in Ethiopia have found a better shape for the traditional plow, and it can be pulled with a single ox instead of two.

Nyle Brady, former director of the International Rice Research Institute, in the Philippines, which engendered Asia's green revolution, has a different idea about Africa. "The job is going to take some time, but you just know it's going to unfold," he said. "I don't think there is any question the potential is there." But it is hard going. In West Africa, the French have found no breakthrough in millet and sorghum after fifty years of trying.

In the final assessment of Africa's environment, the optimists and pessimists are both right. There is a lot of uncultivated, forested land left in Africa. Much of the continent is still underpopulated. But in places, the calamity is widespread. Unless serious change takes place, it is simply a matter of time for the rest. And yet few people, in Africa and elsewhere, seem prepared to do anything about it.

Late in 1986, the New York Zoological Society assembled world authorities in every field to look at conservation through the twenty-first century. David Western was chairman, and the predominant theme was Africa.

Perez Olindo, who was the first African to head Kenya's national parks, argued that it was fruitless to try to impose parks on local people without including them in the picture. "If people can see what we are trying to achieve, they will respond," he said. "It may be necessary to negotiate the future with the people the parks affect."

He cautioned outsiders to consider reality. "These countries are overcrowded. If we tell Rwandans who left the country, you are our brothers but you cannot come back to your home because there is no land for you, how can you convince them that mountain gorillas have greater rights than they do?"

George Schaller had flown to New York from Tibet for the meeting. Over cold Sichuan noodles, he pondered the future with his old friend Richard Estes, a leading authority on African antelopes. Schaller agreed with Olindo: "I have come to the conclusion that there is no possible way of preserving the wildlife unless you convince local people it is in their interest to do it."

And so did Estes: "To expect these people below the poverty line to respect national parks forever is beyond human nature."

No one at the meeting seemed to feel African wildlife had much of a future outside reserves. And even then, there was pessimism. Norman Myers, an expert on species survival, put it: "Given their [wildlife's] talent for conflict with man, I don't see how they can survive long outside of parks. And in the longer term, how the parks themselves can survive."

Some species had already disappeared before anyone realized that they were going, scientists reported. They urged a reversal of the burden of proof: Governments and private companies should fund research to prove that vulnerable species are not in danger of extinction before encroaching further on their habitats.

The clear feeling was that a calamity was approaching, however vague the signs may be now. Jared Diamond, a University of California professor who specializes in conservation ethics, warned the group: "This is like the guy who is falling from the Empire State Building who reassures his friend on the twentieth floor: 'Cool it,

man. No crisis yet.' We have already pushed Africa off the Empire
State Building. But it hasn't hit the pavement yet."

After the meeting, I had a chilling reminder of how close the pavement was. I stopped to talk to a young man who had followed the
speakers attentively. He had just come from the Central African
Republic, where he was a researcher and a warden. I asked him
about the antipoaching patrols mounted in 1985 after someone shot
at President André Kolingba, who was visiting by helicopter.

"He was on the ground, and poachers opened fire," the young
man said. I'll call him Roger. "That clip of AK-47 did more for
conservation than anything we've done in years. But poaching is still
rampant."

His region typified much of Central Africa. Ivory moves to Khartoum in seven-ton Nissan trucks. When food aid is paralyzed, the
ivory gets through. The poachers are mostly herders from a Fulani
subtribe. They stock far too many cattle, Roger said, savaging the
environment. None are vaccinated against rinderpest. Cattle stamp
down the soil and bush. The men leave their families with the
herds and take off on horseback to hunt with Chinese AK-51s, Soviet
AK-47s, Belgian FALs.

"They go after antelope, ivory, rhino horn, leopard skin, pythons,
ostriches, cheetah claws. Anything. They are wiping out the hippos,
which is killing ponds." Hippos dig out mud bottoms of waterways.
Without them, the ponds evaporate. Without their dung in the water,
fish life dies. "There were 500 crocs in the area in 1969," Roger
said. "Now, zero. The waterways are critical for migrating birds in
the Sahel. This is a tremendous problem."

I mentioned that rangers in Zimbabwe had killed their twentieth
rhino poacher in a year. Roger snorted. That was nothing.

"What we are doing there as conservation is war," he said.
Soldiers and hired French settlers murdered poachers whenever they
caught them. "People have died as a result of what I have done."
Roger said he was high on a poachers' death list but felt he had no
choice. "I was sick-scared at first, and then sick-sorry later. But

we've got to do it. I have had too many nights of smelling burnt elephant flesh."

Roger shrugged. "Unless you have a short-term solution, there won't be a long-term," he concluded. "And the short term is a rifle."

But there is surely a better way than destroying Africans to save Africa. The continent's only hope is balance.

13 PEOPLE
Women and Children First

Some counsel calm in the face of Africa's population growth rate of more than 3 percent. If it is the world's highest, Africa also has the lowest population density. According to FAO figures, a lot of land is left. But that misses the point. Rwandans looking for land do not settle in northern Mali. Population is not a critical problem everywhere in Africa, but it will be.

The question, once again, is balance.

A World Bank study released in 1986 began, "The population of sub-Saharan Africa, currently about 470 million, will exceed 700 million by 2000. At no time in history has any group of nations faced the challenge of development in a situation of such rapid population growth."

That is on top of everything else. At a time when food production per capita continues to fall, when most Africans' real buying power is less now than it was at independence, population growth rates are climbing. In the 1970s, it was 2.8 percent. In 1985, it was 3.1 percent. And trends suggest it is going up. Everywhere else in the world, rates are dropping.

Ethiopia is struggling to feed its 42 million people on fast disappearing land. By the turn of the century, if famine can be staved off, there will be 65 million. If an Ethiopian infant saved in 1984 lives to age sixty-five, he may have to share his land with 170 million people.

Nigeria has 100 million inhabitants, in a country the size of Texas and New Mexico. By 2050, according to World Bank projections, there could be twice as many Nigerians in the world as there are Americans today.

Overall, the bank projects a sub-Saharan African population of 730 million for 2000. At a constant rate, that will grow to nearly 1.8 billion in 2050. If fertility is slowed, the figure might be 1.3 billion. But if it follows an upward trend, it could reach 2.2 billion. That is twice the current population of China.

In human terms, it is good news. In the past in Africa, nature arranged what a scientist friend coolly refers to as "massive mammal die-offs." Famine and disease wiped out populations whenever they got too large. If Africans survived their childhood, a hit-or-miss prospect, they were middle-aged in their teens.

Now we can alleviate famine and head off pandemics, just as we can fight disease and help mothers rear healthier children. What we have not done is to show mothers they need no longer be constantly pregnant, playing child roulette in hopes of ending up with enough surviving sons.

The problem is not too many people. It is too little economic growth to sustain them. In theory, there should be no reason to declare Africa more overpopulated than, say, Japan. Tokyo can afford not to grow its own food; in fact, grain producers around the world are anxious for Tokyo's business. But unless sudden massive strides are made in development, burgeoning populations in Africa translate to human misery—and disaster for the land, which will be called upon to be increasingly more productive.

Today, Africa is desperately short of jobs. Underemployment may be as high as 60 percent. Within thirty years, there are likely to be three times as many people in the labor force. By the same projections, Africa's cities will grow five times larger.

Birth-control programs might win some time. But more important is basic education. Educated women decide for themselves how many children to have. And they work out how best to teach their families old values and new methods.

In Kenya, every study on Africa reports, the average mother has 8.5 children. Kenya's population growth rate, over 4 percent, is perhaps the highest in the world.

Evelyn Muindi is a Kenyan mother. "I have two kids, and I don't want any more," she told me. "These days we don't want too many, maybe two or three." Mrs. Muindi, if one stretches it, is a rural Kenyan yuppie. She is twenty-eight, married, and has a modest job operating the radio on a sprawling farm near Thika. Her family has 10 acres of maize, beans, pumpkins, seven cows, twenty-two goats.

She finished a girls' high school and then studied typing and shorthand. She learned a little French. In short, she decided she could use her head for more than just a balancing pad for water pots and bales of firewood. That was her decision, not a family planner's.

But she is still in the minority. Kenyan President Daniel arap Moi presses hard to control the birthrate, against tremendous resistance. When he had free milk delivered to schools, some children scrambled out of windows rather than drink it. Their parents had warned them against being poisoned by antifertility drugs. A Kenyan brewery had to destroy 10,000 bottles after someone spread a rumor that the beer would cause impotency.

At the London School of Hygiene and Tropical Medicine, William Brass is working with Kenyan demographers to assess the situation. "We see no evidence of any significant drop," he reported. Later, I questioned a senior Kenyan cabinet minister about birth control. He was not fond of the subject. Finally, he dismissed further talk with a hearty guffaw: "Well, we're not going to sterilize the men."

African leaders on occasion express suspicion of Western efforts to curb their population. France, for example, pays Frenchwomen to produce children and urges Africans to use contraception. Western societies argue that their populations are dropping, while Africa's increases twentyfold in a century. A reasonable reply might be that this is a racist argument.

Rural farmers resist efforts to limit families. They cannot control their markets or their weather. All they control is their labor supply.

But rapid population growth is a serious concern. Africa is stretching its resources far too thinly, in too many places.

One notion often applied to African demography is flatly wrong. European populations once grew as fast as contemporary Africa, it is believed; they stabilized by emigration and education. In fact, between 1751 and 1939, the population of England and Wales seldom grew faster than just over one percent a year, with a doubling time of sixty-five years. At its highest levels, emigration did not reduce the population growth by more than 10 percent. Kenya's population doubling time is seventeen years, and emigration is no option. The United States, despite all of its immigrants, has grown at an average of 2 percent a year since independence.

Most of Europe showed similar patterns, still irrelevant to Africa's condition. But consider an analysis of Ireland by British demographer N. L. Tranter. From 1753 to 1845, it grew at rates up to 2.1 percent per year. The result was catastrophic destitution, leading to famine. Causes cited were lack of natural resources, no investment, absentee landlordism, tariffs, competition from foreign manufacturers, religious divisiveness, vast inequality between rich and poor, the communal nature of Irish agriculture, and a preference for leisure over working to accumulate material wealth.

Africa suffers from each of those problems, with dwindling resources at the head of the list. Economist Julian Simon argues that human ingenuity makes resources infinitely expandable. Such reasoning may refute Malthus on a grander scale, but it does little for an African herder out of grass. Technically, it is possible to restore much of the Sahel the way engineers can make a golf course of southern Arizona desert. But not even the tiniest fraction of the funds needed are available to do it.

Alternative fuel and building supplies could reduce the pressure on Africa's shrinking forests. Unless those alternatives are available, however, Africans will not stop cutting wood.

Unspoiled ecosystems and wildlife are disappearing fast under the spread of human populations. Some economists argue that such concerns are needless. One remarked to Doug that the concept of respect for the earth was "utterly inane." Anyone who sees the world in such purely economic terms has a tragically narrow view of its potential. Deprived of an ability to appreciate natural wealth, such a man is hardly in a position to call an African poor. Cold, mechanical calculation of profit and loss has already squandered far too much of Africa.

But some economists cling tightly to a one-dimensional view of the world. Simon writes, "Some people even impute feelings to trees or to animals, and they aim to prevent pain to these feelings." We have some wildebeest we would like to introduce to him. His human ingenuity may increase yields on depleted rangeland. But it will never replace a Bushman out after spring hare in the Kalahari sunrise.

To convince the bloodless, the argument goes beyond the question of natural resource.

African states now struggle to offer the most basic of education and health services to their current populations. How will they deal with greater numbers? It is clear that Africa must develop management skills, communications, civil services, industries, and practical sciences. While literacy stagnates in Africa, Japan turns out 71,000 new engineers a year.

Frederick T. Sai, a Ghanaian doctor and senior population adviser to the World Bank, remarked dryly: "We haven't got time on our side."

The point of development is to improve individuals' lives and equip their societies to compete in a modern world. Africa is falling behind on both counts.

Doug's friend Sam Modisane illustrates, as clearly as anyone, the loss to Africa's potential. Doug hired Sam to do some building on a farm he managed in Botswana. Sam soon revealed himself as an expert at everything: thatching, fixing motors, shoeing horses, welding gates, and playing the guitar. He was an African Zorba the Greek, down to the taste for working four days and getting blind drunk for three. Sam was paid by the job. Doug got his money's worth, and they became good friends.

Sam had spent two years at a mission school learning to read and write, but his father yanked him out to come back to work. He herded cattle and goats for a while and then ran away to the northern Transvaal. An Afrikaner family paid him fifty cents a month, plus food and lodging, to look after the kids. He loved the children but decided he had to move on.

After rough jobs with hard men, Sam found work with a kindly building contractor. The man broke South African law to train him in skills reserved then for whites. After a few years, Sam got into a drunken brawl and returned to Botswana, a step ahead of the police. At home, where his skills were badly needed, he had more work than he could handle.

His gifts were remarkable. "You know, Douglas," he said once, with no hint of a boast, "I understand things very quickly." He knew four-wheel drives intimately but preferred his donkey cart. "When I get drunk," he explained, "I fall into the back of the cart, and the donkeys take me home, no matter where I am."

Sam read perfectly in spite of his brief schooling. Given the education and the chance, he could have accomplished just about anything Botswana needed done. Africa cannot afford to waste its Sam Modisanes.

As much as its children, Africa wastes its women. "In our society, the woman is a beast of burden," Captain Thomas Sankara, of Burkina Faso, once remarked. "She is exploited like a cow which produces offspring, gives milk and has the force to work and offer pleasure. When she is old and tired, she is replaced by another cow."

Hotel employees in Gaborone once ejected a Ugandan guest for bringing too many women to his room. The man was indignant. "How can they prevent me from having women?" he demanded. "I must have a random sampling wherever I go."

African men, by and large, are cool to the idea of their women getting uppity. With the exception of some cabinet ministers—often tokens—there have been no women leaders of African governments. Far fewer women than men can read or write. But they carry 90 percent of the water and firewood, and they plant 80 percent of the food. An average woman's workday runs to eighteen hours—rearing children, pounding grain, cooking, farming, and hauling produce to market.

Because of a crippling lack of draft animals, it is the women who haul and pull. René Dumont calculated that to carry thirty tons of fertilizer to fields two miles away, women must carry fifty pounds for 4,000 miles.

Women, often illiterate, dominate West African markets and much of the commerce. Elsewhere in Africa, they run small businesses and amass substantial fortunes. When wronged, they face police and soldiers with surprising courage. But few stand up to their husbands.

Women live in fear that their husbands will throw them out. If they scrape together any cash, they buy jewelry and gold. It is their only security. Baule women in the Ivory Coast have a little ditty they sometimes sing on the job: "If I'd have known how hard it is to be a woman, I'd have been a man."

In neighboring Mali, Monique Munz of CARE told me, "The men have the power, and they won't give it up. Everything waits until the men gather. By the age of eight, a girl's thumbs are deformed from pounding millets. By womanhood, she has large splayed hands. Her clitoris is removed. In villages, you see only boys hanging around, or studying. The girls are working. Is that going to change? Come on, you're a man. How is that going to change?"

A new generation is showing some change. Desiré Ecaré, an Ivorian filmmaker, expressed an evolving attitude: "We must fix it so we don't have a twentieth-century man living with a woman of the Middle Ages."

Women are offering examples in every field. In Liberia, President Samuel Doe's greatest threat is from Ellen Johnson-Sirleaf, a former finance minister, who formed an opposition party when he would not let her leave the country. In exile, she directs international attention to Doe's excesses.

The problem is critical in rural areas where most Africans live, and where Sankara's description is distressingly apt. Men clear the land, tend cash crops and animals. If there is game, they hunt. But mainly they are in charge of customs and wisdom, and of spending the family money. Women do the rest.

Because of skewed divisions of labor, women run short of time for planting food. Often, crops are limited not by available land and seed, but, rather, by the efforts village women can muster. When there are surpluses, it is women who haul them to the nearest cross-roads and sell them in the market. Despite their leading role, women seldom receive the training, tools, or credits provided to men. They rarely share in the decisions on subsistence farms.

That especially peeves Josephine Ouedraogo, Sankara's minister for family development. "Agricultural modernization always passes through the hands of men while it is the women who form the pillar of family food production," she told a visiting reporter. "When a farmer decides to devote two-thirds of his land to cash crops, he is counting mainly on feminine labor, but the women never take part in the decision that creates a terrible load on their work schedule."

But Minister Ouedraogo, thirty-six and energetic, has few illusions about how much she can change. "The means of my ministry?" she reflected. "Zero, or almost. I've got the smallest budget in the government."

In every country of Africa, women have shown they can increase productivity, run flourishing enterprises, and devise new ways to increase the family income. But first they must break free of traditional constraints.

"Look, it is easy," said Fanta Babacissé Diallo, with a merry laugh. She waved her arm toward a legion of liberated housewives happily beavering away on an irrigation project in the ancient city of Djenné, in Mali. She is president and head motivator of a cooperative of several hundred Djenné women. Most are married and have children and a full range of wifely duties to perform, but they have broken their bonds.

Mrs. Diallo was showing off a self-help cooperative to grow rice and vegetables along the Bani River. The government supplied a gasoline-powered pump. Men and women, working together, did the rest. Later she took her visitors downtown. To drums and chanting, women performed Songhai and Bambara dances that, for lack of time to dance them, had been slipping toward oblivion.

Then we went to the craft shop. In the good old days, women on the river wore their riches above the shoulders: great gold earrings, necklaces of golden spheres the size of softballs, chunks of amber. Too poor for that any more, the women found a way to save their traditional dress. They carve gourds in the shape of the old jewelry and paint them in brilliant yellow. Only a banker or a killjoy would note the difference.

But Mrs. Diallo's real joy is the oven campaign. She worked out a pattern for a one-burner mud dome that consumes a fraction of the wood of an open fire. She knows to the oven how many are in service around Djenné, and there are more than a thousand.

Mrs. Diallo is thirty-three. Her first husband died, leaving her with three children. She married a lawyer who lives in Bamako, the Malian capital, but she preferred to stay and work with the women of Djenné. She will likely go far. But she is happy enough to be the mother of the improved mud oven.

If you can believe Professor Allan Wilson, of the University of California at Berkeley, all of us descended from a single Eve who lived in Eden, somewhere in Africa, 140,000 to 280,000 years ago. Wilson, a biochemist, bases his theory on the estimated rate of mutation of DNA in human cells. He concludes that preceding species in Indonesia, China, or Greece may have died out or been swept aside by the progeny of the African mother.

Maybe. But it is beyond dispute that African women form a class apart. Harvard physiologist Norman C. Heglund has determined that a 130-pound African woman can walk with a twenty-six-pound weight on her head and burn up no more energy than if she were carrying nothing. She can carry seventy-five pounds on her head with far less strain than an army recruit can hump a backpack.

That comes as no surprise to anyone who has visited Africa. I have seen a Nigerian woman glide smoothly through crowded streets with two king-size mattresses balanced on her head, and, in Zaire, a village woman similarly carrying a stack of folded textiles nearly as tall as she was. Heglund speculates that African women start carrying loads early enough so their bodies make the necessary adjustments. They learn balance and a smooth gait. My own theory is that they have no choice: How else would they get their work done?

*I*mproving women's lot must start with health and nutrition. In much of Africa, a woman is forty-five times more likely to die during child-birth than a woman her age in Sweden or Denmark. Her children are fifteen times more likely to die before age five.

From the outside, it would seem that Africa lives in mass terror of the acquired immune deficiency syndrome that seems to have spread from the continent's tropical center. But concern over AIDS is growing slowly. Africans have more immediate killers to worry about—like the common cold. A million children a year die of whoop-ing cough, measles, and tetanus. Polio, diphtheria, and leprosy still flourish, but ordinary diarrhea is still the biggest killer.

Soon enough, health officials warn, AIDS will worry Africans a great deal. World Health Organization specialists said in early 1987 that as many as five million Africans are believed to carry the AIDS virus, and a million of them may die. In isolated parts of Uganda, whole villages are threatened. But the disease is widely reported elsewhere.

At first, some African health authorities underplayed AIDS, fearing discrimination and a loss of tourism. When scientists began tracing the disease to Africa, some governments said they were victims of racism. Although most have admitted the problem and are helping Western doctors with research, more familiar health problems still take priority.

By 1987, health authorities in West Africa acknowledged that the virus was spreading from Central Africa. In Abidjan, the fast-paced capital of Ivory Coast, the government issued firm warnings. Reaction was mixed. A French reporter saw crowds of children run-ning after a prostitute, stoning her and chanting: "AIDS, AIDS!"

But a more common response came from a young woman in a waterfront bar: "Each week, boatloads of sailors come for sex here and no one has ever complained. Who has seen AIDS? Nobody. Not even on TV. A disease you can't see, with no treatment, does not exist."

Basic hygiene education can save a lot of lives. Private volunteer agencies often concentrate on mother-child nutrition care. A simple dime bag of oral rehydration salts can restore essential liquids to a child stricken with severe diarrhea. But most endangered African children suffer the same crippling deficiency: lack of food. Even in Zimbabwe when crops are good, nearly 36,000 children die each year from malnutrition. UNICEF estimates 30 to 48 percent of Zimbabwean children under five are malnourished. Among the worst off are farm workers' children. The problem is poverty.

James P. Grant, executive director of UNICEF, calls the annual death of 4 million African children "the silent emergency." The cost of malnutrition is incalculable, he notes, since 90 percent of the growth of the human brain, and much of the body, takes place in the first five years. And the World Bank has even found an argument for the cold-blooded: "Better health and nutrition are not only humanitarian imperatives . . . they are also basic requirements for sustained economic growth."

This last point is no small one. Africa cannot possibly develop effectively with so much of its energy sapped by disease. The commonly known ailments and malnutrition are bad enough. But there is more.

Africa suffers from virulent, endemic diseases most Westerners cannot even pronounce: onchocerciasis and schistosomiasis, among others. The first is river blindness, spread by black flies along swift-moving rivers, which starts with a painful swelling and ends often in total blindness. The second is an invasion of microscopic parasites that bore into the body to debilitate and kill.

Malaria attacks and recurs all over Africa. "We used to call malaria 'weeks' because when you got it, you knew that's how long you would be in bed," Djibril Diallo remembers. "People in Europe and America sometimes think Africans grow immune to malaria. Hardly."

In the first wave of development aid, donors built hospitals and clinics. The idea was to reduce the number of miles the average African had to travel to a health facility. But not enough thought was given to what happened when he got there.

An hour up a paved road from Bamako, is the provincial town of Segou. For centuries, Segou has been a major Sahelian crossroads and river port. In 1986, I stopped at the central clinic and found Dr. Mbayi Babambiba. She was twenty-six years old, tending a long line of people stoically waiting their turn. "We are out of aspirin, malaria tablets, and antibiotics," she told me. "We are supposed to be supplied every three months, but the ministry has nothing."

At least, the clinic had a doctor. At the time, a number of Malian doctors were out of work because the government had no money to pay them. In some countries, young doctors back from medical school abroad refuse to leave the capital cities. They worked hard to escape the bush, many felt, and they were anxious to reap the rewards.

At Diré, an Italian doctor sweated in the heat. He was hard at work learning to deal with challenges he never faced in Italy. "The Malian doctors," he said, "they just don't have the experience." A European aid official with me muttered under his breath: "And how are they going to get it?" Mali, he felt, needed fewer foreign doctors and more wherewithal to equip its own.

As a general rule for Africa, in almost all fields, it was not a bad thought.

14 A WORKING MISUNDERSTANDING

The African elephant eats up to a tenth of his weight a day, crashing through every obstacle to get to new sources of sustenance. He sweeps his trunk to test feeding grounds and thrusts it neatly toward what is most tempting. And then whatever else he finds—green or brown— is ingested in great scoops. All of it passes quickly through the simplest sort of digestive tract. Some benefit is extracted, but most of what the elephant consumes ends up behind him on the trail.

This also applies, in too many cases, to the African government.

The metaphor is inelegant but distressingly apt. What economists call "ODA"—overseas development assistance—is like the forests where elephants feed. Each donor government and organization propagates its own species of growth, with a dazzling variety of tempting blossoms and berries. Success is not measured in healthy elephants but, rather, in the alacrity with which the elephant swings its trunk in any particular direction.

Like African underbrush, ODA grants suffer abrupt changes. In lean times, vegetation is scarce. Elephants are less picky; they grow thin, work hard to find food, and sometimes starve. When the bush is thick, elephants are fat and slow. But the comparison stops here. African ecosystems are worked out by nature in fine detail. Each species fits into a grander scheme. When elephants eat too much in one place, they must diet or move on. African governments are more fortunate.

*F*oreign donors gave Africa $116 billion during its first twenty-five years of independence. By the end of 1986, outstanding loans to Africa totaled $175 billion. A lot of that was to buy geopolitical concessions, commercial advantages, or United Nations votes. Some was to reward the embracing of a religion, whether Islam or International Monetary Fundism. But much of it was given to better Africans' lives. And there is damned little to show for it.

When numbers surpass the few thousand dollars a month that most people have to budget, they enter a numbing no man's land. Try as I might, I cannot form a picture of the $3 billion a year earmarked for African development. Instead, I keep on my desk a single dollar bill sent to me by Mr. J. A. Kysel, of Somerset, New Jersey. It came with a six-word note typed across a cutting of a story I wrote on African hunger: "Enclosed for the poor in Mali." When I think of what could happen to that particular dollar, I am forced to leave it on my desk until I find the most effective way to spend it. When I do, Mr. Kysel, I will add my own to it, along with all accrued interest.

It is difficult to pick apart generosity. As French actor Richard Berry replied to criticism of Bob Geldof's hoopla tactics, "A franc is a franc." But it is not so simple. That people and their governments want to help is one thing; it is another when, for all their good intentions, they worsen things in the process.

Generosity alone will not rescue Africa. Nor will emotion. There are pragmatic imperatives behind helping Africans survive, and what matters is what is known in the jargon as the modalities of aid.

In the first flush of independence, foreign aid was simple and enthusiastic. Developed nations felt they had the magic wand of success and the resources with which to wield it. Africans would prosper and gratefully remember their benefactors. Aid fell into four broad categories:

—The United States and the Soviet Union scampered into every window of opportunity. The Soviets bartered arms for commodities, implanting Russian advisers in the bargain. Americans also armed their allies. But where Moscow went for circuses, Washington favored bread. In Mali, the Russians built a stadium; the Americans tried to grow millet on a grand scale. Both philosophies helped African leaders increase their hold over people whose real needs went unmet.

—France and Britain spent heavily in their former territories. Each called it fulfillment of a moral responsibility. Some Africans called it neocolonialism. Mostly, aid subsidized the fast-paced ballet among the ruling elites.

—Other donors contributed within their possibilities and according to their ideologies. The Scandinavians, for instance, funded Julius Nyerere's socialist dream in Tanzania. Israel and Taiwan worked hard to win friends they later lost and then won back. North Korea got farther giving guns than did South Korea growing grain.

—The "multilaterals" offered more general aid with less specific goals. Each had its own guidelines. The World Bank sought to generate wealth meant to be diffused throughout local economies. A panoply of United Nations agencies concentrated on projects defined by the recipients. During the 1970s, these main lines changed. Soviet clients discovered they did not like Russians. The Kremlin began to pick its friends more selectively, based on mutual need. It spent less on circuses and more on MIG fighters, Cuban troops, and East German intelligence advisers. Americans, their initial optimism dimmed, tightened aid budgets. Donors had shifted from fad to fad, and most wondered if they would ever find the "road to development" that had dominated early rhetoric.

A new catchphrase emerged in the 1980s: "Small is beautiful." Donors had seen private voluntary agencies rescue starving Biafrans and then beat back effects of drought. They saw successful little village-level projects that allowed Africans to help themselves. Small programs could skirt the edges of bureaucracy and adapt to change. The big official donors explored ways to contract privately funded independent organizations.

But aid specialists realized that was not enough. James Fenton, reporting from Mali in 1986, noted: "Small is beautiful, but the desert is thinking big." Tidy little projects worked well in places, but were seldom, in the jargon, replicable. When small independent agencies expanded to tackle Africa-sized problems, they faced the same difficulties as everyone else.

After a quarter-century of floundering, official and private donors reached the conclusion that they must coordinate. Each has to fit together with the others in a flexible apparatus capable of meeting emergencies while continuing basic development. It is a noble goal, shared by most. And nearly everyone is finding it impossible.

*B*efore donors can coordinate, each needs to define its own objectives and perfect its ability to achieve them. A close look almost anywhere in Africa suggests what a job this can be. Take, for example, the Norwegian fisheries project at Lake Turkana in Kenya.

The Scandinavians are good donors. They owe little to the developing world but give more per capita than anyone else. Like others, they make serious mistakes; no one has long experience in development. But unlike most, they study their mistakes and admit them. The Turkana disaster is described in excruciating, anguished detail in an evaluation report ordered by the Norwegian aid agency.

The Turkana are cattle herders, numbering 220,000, who are especially susceptible to drought on their bare hills of northern Kenya. What they needed, the Norwegians decided, was a fishery. The first step was a handsome cold-storage plant, at a cost of $2 million, and a $20-million road to connect it to the nearest highway. All things being equal, the Turkana Fisherman's Cooperative Society would sell Nile perch and tilapia to cities down south.

But freezing the fish, from Turkana room temperature (about 100 degrees), took more electricity than the region could provide. After a few days, operators cut the power and created, as the Washington *Post*'s Blaine Harden put it, "Africa's most handsome dried-fish warehouse."

Then, part of the lake vanished, the part where 80 percent of the fish were caught. Norwegian planners had been thrown off by a temporary boom. "When we see a lake, we think in fairly static terms," remarked an official from Norad, the Norwegian aid agency. "We see a lake, we assume it will be there for 100 million years." In fact, the lake dried every few decades, whenever the Omo River from Ethiopia ran low because of the drought against which the fishery was supposed to protect the Turkana.

But officials had already herded 20,000 Turkanas to the shores of the lake, where they were given nets, boats, and fishing lessons. They had lost their livestock—victim of overcrowding and disease along the inhospitable lake banks—and they were destitute. Like so many Africans in so many other such failed schemes, they turned to food aid.

As a symbolic white elephant, the Norwegian research vessel *Iji* sits in the mud and, according to the donors' report, "appears to be damaged beyond the possibility of repair."

There was also irrigation. The U.N. Development Program and FAO decided in the 1960s to make the Turkana desert bloom. They brought water pumps, heavy machinery, chemicals, and specialists. But the rivers, as the Turkanas might have told them, did not co-operate. They shifted course and periodically dried up. In 1980, when U.N. money also dried up, the Norwegians took over. Later, Norad looked closely at the Katilu project, where 10,000 Turkana herders had been converted to farmers. In all, $25,000 had been spent on each farmer so he could earn $100 a year, one-quarter of Kenya's average per-capita income.

A Norad official told Harden: "They make that much if they are lucky. If they are not so lucky, then we have to go in and give them food aid."

As in the Sahel, Kenyan authorities favor projects to settle their nomadic herders. But major schemes are pushed also by donors. In 1986, President Daniel arap Moi swooped down on Kenya's most ambitious development project, at Bura, and declared it a corrupt and mismanaged disaster. It was funded largely by the World Bank, and had Kenyan administrators.

The Bura irrigation scheme was designed for 35,000 settlers to grow cotton and staple crops on 35,000 acres. It was to breathe life into the Somali border district, a day's drive north of Nairobi. With tradesmen and families, Bura would have a population of 65,000. After seven years, 6,500 acres were planted; only 2,000 families had moved in. Capital costs, planned at $98.4 million in 1977, rose to $110 million. But irrigation was still erratic. Engineers did not develop the gravity system Bura depended upon. Instead, temporary pumps provided the only water—when they worked.

The World Bank concluded that the project's management was incompetent. A new team was sought, along with money for gravity irrigation. And a bank official compiled a forty-page bibliography of analyses of the Bura scheme.

The World Bank contributes 10 to 15 percent of African aid, concentrating on agriculture, education, public works, and private entrepreneurs. In tandem with the International Monetary Fund, the bank works hard at "structural reform," to create a framework for aid and private investment to lead to development. And the Bank has taken on a major role in directing traffic.

In regular meetings, donors try to fit their aid into an overall pattern, following the recipients' priorities rather than the donors' goals. I asked a senior World Bank official how the system worked, and he threw up his hands.

Take Somalia, he said. A consultative group worked out aid of $430 million for 1986, largely for the Juba River dam, to supply power to Mogadishu, the capital. That was all Somalia could handle; the government was to adhere tightly to an economic recovery program. "And then the Italians came along and gave them $300 million for roads leading nowhere, ruining the whole package," he said. "Not exactly nowhere. They helped defend the border with Ethiopia."

It was a classic situation: Somalia had come up with yet more wherewithal to, in effect, cheat on its diet.

The World Bank set up a Special Facility for Africa to channel funds toward main priorities. But the United States demurred, preferring to give bilateral aid, which could be aimed more specifically at nudging governments toward free-market systems. But all U.S. aid was cut as pressure mounted from the growing deficit.

As soon as famine appeared to ease in Ethiopia, the U.S. government looked hungrily at African aid funds needed to support policies in Central America. That undermined its public expressions of continuing concern for Africa's plight. But people had stopped watching.

American wariness of multilateral aid has also hamstrung the International Fund for Agricultural Development, IFAD, which tries hard to get aid to Africa's neediest farmers. Although affiliated with the United Nations, it operates quickly, with a minimum of paperwork. Projects are designed to get tools and simple production systems into the hands of peasants who have shown they will use them. During the height of the famine, IFAD remained paralyzed over a test of wills. Neither the U.S. government nor Arab oil states would budge on the principle of who would give slightly more or slightly less.

The most consistent, and often most effective, commitments to African aid have been from private volunteer organizations. By the mid-1980s, their role was changing. Big donors, which had regarded them as amateurs with more enthusiasm than money to spend, began to solicit their help. The PVOs had credibility and efficiency; USAID and others hired them on contract to spend money wisely.

Sometimes the contractors' bureaucracy strangled the smaller agencies, negating their advantage. But often it worked well. In Niger, a young forester working for CARE organized farmers to plant a row of trees to block wind that howled down from the north and eroded their fields. The windbreaks grew wider and longer, and new villages realized their value. Once CARE convinced farmers they could sell or burn harvested wood, enthusiasm soared. Small amounts of USAID helped expand the project.

The biggest problem came from local officials. Despite clear agreements that farmers who planted and tended the trees kept the rights to them, someone with power often tried to collect his share. The trees, after all, were wherewithal.

In theory, guidance should come from the United Nations system. It is an even-handed directorate, representing everyone, with specialized agencies for every problem troubling Africa: health, population, labor, environment, children, general development, disasters, refugees, cities. But it does not work that way. One difficulty is the agency dealing with the two biggest concerns of Africa today: food and agriculture.

People with business at the FAO find it is like picking pearls out of crankcase sludge. Some useful, even brilliant, work goes on in the overpadded headquarters buildings in Rome, Mussolini's old Ministry of the Colonies. Lukas Brader's team of "locust busters," for example, can get planes in the air to head off swarms with blinding speed. Long-suffering experts work hard in the African bush on fisheries and forestry and livestock diseases.

But what was conceived as a technical agency has grown into a vast political apparatus, with layers of bureaucrats charged with defending its power and glory.

Edouard Saouma, director general since 1976, inspires strong reactions. "I think he is a charming man, quite capable," Millicent Fenwick told me after she took up her post as U.S. ambassador to the FAO. Some other senior American officials, less convinced, backed a growing campaign to vote Saouma out of office at the end of 1987. A European deeply involved in African development sputtered when I mentioned his name: "That demagogue!"

The European critic complained that Saouma sought African support by pushing for more food aid than was needed, institutionalizing handouts. "The FAO cried 'Wolf!' so many times that no one listened when famine grew really serious," he said.

Ronald MacIntosh, a Canadian official who monitors the FAO, told the *Wall Street Journal* that "Canada is absolutely baffled" as to why the United States did not join in criticizing Saouma's management. He said the problems were at least as serious as those in

UNESCO from which the United States withdrew in 1984. The FAO handles $500 million a year in operating expenses and programs. It is also a clearing house for $2 billion a year in other donors' agricultural projects.

In Rome, a friendly and efficient—and large—press section churns out texts of Saouma's every utterance. He sweeps into conferences like a head of state, surrounded by a heavy entourage. Aides lobby ceaselessly toward his reelection.

An FAO insider explained: "Saouma began establishing his own representatives in each country, with a primary mission of looking out for his interests. At first political appointees were only at top levels, to P-5. Now they are down to P-2 (support staff)."

Politically expedient people are not always competent. The FAO in Rome can grind along at a snail's pace, pushing programs through the pipeline after their purpose is past. As a result, good work can be lost. The early-warning system estimates harvests and food deficits. But some donors wait for their own estimates, not wanting to trust what they consider a cumbersome and politically oriented system.

Some bilateral and private aid officials dismiss FAO advice out of hand, even when it is useful advice. The result is controversy swirling around the organization that could take the lead in African development. It is a needless complication for a continent with enough trouble already.

Within the organization, morale suffers. In a small city of the Sahel, I found an FAO representative almost in tears. "Look out the window," he said. I saw a gigantic mound of potatoes, filling most of a large courtyard. He explained that experts had discovered potatoes would grow well in the neighboring hills, and farmers were encouraged to plant them. Just as predicted, the crop was excellent. But FAO had not thought about marketing. No one would touch the bizarre brown globs of starch. Anyone with money bought real food. While people starved to death not 200 yards away, farmers struggled to keep their crops from rotting. They might have given away the potatoes. But then how would they cover their costs?

An FAO agronomist, a good man who knows Africa well, told me how he survived. "You must develop a thick skin against things you cannot change and be happy with the little things you can," he said, with a philosophical spread of the fingers. "You know your bosses are incompetent and the organization is impossible, and there is political pressure. But once you understand it, and can work within it, you are free. Then you are able to accomplish some good."

That is frustrating, he acknowledged. "You have to pat yourself on the back; no one else can. You have to bend the rules and do things quietly, so you cannot take credit. But you look at yourself in the mirror at night, and it is worth it."

As pressure mounts against FAO, paranoia and defensiveness deepen. Privilege is carefully guarded. When Perez de Cuellar set up the U.N. Office for Emergency Operations in Africa, its fast-moving staff ordered seed for farmers in Chad. Saouma protested vehemently in a cable that reached the papers. Seeds were his business.

Unwitting outsiders are classed as friends or enemies. During 1985, for instance, I found myself caught in the Great Pole Controversy.

In the Sudan, I spoke to separate sources "close to the FAO," in the parlance, who were outraged over an FAO project to build a fence across rangeland. The plan was harebrained to begin with, they said; a fence would do no good. Worse, the FAO was to import $186,000 worth of untreated wooden fence poles. Desperate peasants would grab them for timber and firewood. Herders would knock them down. In any case, termites would eat them within months.

I wrote about this, and the FAO called me irresponsible, in a press release and in a letter. The poles were metal. How could I be so sloppy with facts? I replied that my sources had said wood; there was a mistake somewhere. No mistake, the FAO insisted; I was a lousy reporter. Finally, in Rome, I was told, off the record, what the FAO would not admit in public: wooden poles had been ordered. At the very last minute, someone had discovered that a local official had minimized the threat of termites in hopes of winning the contract. The order was then changed to metal poles.

The point is that development is new to all agencies, and all are subject to pressures beyond their control. When reporters call attention to shortcomings, agencies should find out what went wrong and add to everyone's experience for the next time. But the FAO ignored my sources' main concern—that it was a harmful and wasteful project. And I was put on the list. Press officers were warned about me; my FAO meetings were screened.

My access, nonetheless, remained unimpaired. Press officials were unfailingly helpful. Raymond Lloyd was not so fortunate.

Lloyd, who resigned a senior FAO post, makes no bones about what he thinks of Saouma. He is now a free-lance journalist, and the World Food Council accredited him to cover a meeting on its premises, which happen to be at FAO headquarters. Building guards refused to let him enter. The WFC apologized to him but could not get FAO officials to budge. Officially, the FAO said Lloyd was a security risk. Unofficially, FAO officials sought to smear his character. I pushed for details. What kind of security risk? No details could be given. If there was real cause for concern, why isn't some other action being taken? No response.

"Is Lloyd dangerous?" I asked a well-placed person at headquarters. His answer was a single expletive, a synonym for the sort of organic fertilizer of which the FAO is so fond. "He pissed off Saouma, that's all," the man replied. Since Lloyd was too mild-mannered to pull the pin on a hand grenade, my supposition ruled out the threat of personal violence. What deep secrets, then, was this U.N.-funded agency keeping that it could trample on a journalist's rights in a way even UNESCO could not get away with?

A high-ranking insider articulated the answer I had heard frequently for years:

"Saouma is not corrupt in the usual sense; he doesn't steal money. But the trouble is his use of politics, the dealing to line up people who will support him. He is God, and no one had better say anything. His is not like an elected government, where he has to answer to anyone. All he has to do is line up the votes, and he's in."

This might be just another case of U.N. paralysis. Politics and personal vendettas are common in the ponderous system. An alphabet soup of specialized agencies and related organs often overlap and compete in developing countries. But in Africa today, it is life and death.

The FAO is supposed to deal in wheat and fish and trees and human beings. It is not a Third World state or a private source of power. Even the large color photographs of Saouma that hang in FAO field offices cost money and staff time to produce. Each time I see some new folly from Rome, I think about Mr. Kysel's dollar sitting on my desk.

At the other extreme is the U.N. Children's Fund. UNICEF has its waste, bureaucracy, and failings, but its image is gold-plated. It starts with an advantage: children are easier to sell than legumes and Nile perch. But the difference goes farther. Director James Grant's high-profile politicking is less on behalf of himself than for those he is charged with assisting.

UNICEF gets its cut of the pot, but also generates funds on its own. Christmas card sales provide cash but also keep the plight of children in the public eye. Grant believes in publicity, and he is right.

Reporters in Africa head straight for UNICEF, because its officials are seldom afraid to make waves. Most admit their disasters and let outsiders see for themselves whether successes are as good as they claim. And, perhaps more than any U.N. agency, UNICEF people push to involve Africans in planning and management of projects.

Field director Leo de Vos, in Mali, for example, argued hard against colleagues who insisted on importing outsiders. "If they just tried to use more Malian administrators," he said, "they would realize."

Whoever donates what, it is up to African leaders to coordinate aid and see that it is used according to local needs. That so many people have forgotten this—Africans and donors—is a serious problem. During 1985, heads of state got together to confront this. They had announced that they had had enough of economic calamity.

African leaders produced a document they called "APPER," the African Priority Program for Economic Recovery. In May, the U.N. General Assembly held a four-day Special Session for Africa, the first such meeting ever on the problems of a region.

Africa needed $128 billion over five years, the leaders said. They promised to find $80 billion of it from their own hard-pressed re- sources. That was more earnest money than they could realistically produce, but it was taken as a sign of good faith.

Just before the meeting, the World Bank issued its fourth study on development in sub-Saharan Africa. Just to inch forward, it said, Black Africa needed $2.5 billion a year in new aid, beyond what could be scraped together from rescheduling and accountants' hoop tricks.

In some ways, the special session was Africa's last chance. The U.N. had not done such a thing before. It would be years before Africans could whip up so much concern and attention to their plight. Certainly it would take another calamity.

The response was dramatic. British promoters came up with Sport Aid on the Sunday before the meeting. Around the world, perhaps 20 million people jogged six miles for Africa. A global tele- vision hookup showed President Thomas Sankara trotting through the streets of Ouagadougou, and then it cut to packs of runners from Paris to Melbourne. The big moment was in New York. Sudanese runner Omar Khalifa brought a torch he had carried aloft, with some help from airlines, across Africa and Europe and then through the streets of New York. With people watching around the world, he touched off a giant flame in front of the towering U.N. Secretariat building at Turtle Bay.

But it would take more than that to light a fire under the United Nations.

In four days of speeches, new optimism infused the old themes. Africans admitted past mistakes and promised to do things differently. They accepted primary responsibility for their own peoples' welfare; they only wanted reasonable help from the outside.

U.S. Secretary of State George Shultz lauded Africans for, in effect, proving the West right. "Now-discredited orthodoxies about state-directed development" were giving way to a "greater scope to individual initiative," he said. "I think we can agree that successful development in any nation—Africa as anywhere else—lies most fundamentally in the expansion of individual human opportunity."

Shultz praised Washington's generosity in emergency relief but warned that was only a stopgap. States would have to reform. With a final rabbit punch to African sensibilities, he said: "The United States firmly believes that our development experience is a useful guide to productive economic policies."

Like the United States, other Western donors committed themselves to meeting the Africans' challenge, and they carefully skirted specific figures.

In the immediate euphoria, a somewhat condescending *Wall Street Journal* editorial suggested that Africans had finally grown up and realized the wisdom of free marketry. The New York *Times* and the Washington *Post* each applauded what both called a new realism.

But then I went to see Pierre-Claver Damiba, Africa director for the U.N. Development Program, whose corner office overlooks the General Assembly. A banker and an economist from Burkina Faso, he is a sound thinker on development. He did not expect the meeting to bring much more from Western donors. "It was a U.N. event, a matter of one week in New York, and then the rain is over," he said. Nor, he said, would the public shift from its basic perception: "These poor Africans cannot feed themselves. They need charity to remain as human beings."

Above all, he was worried about what that suggested. "The syndrome of dependence is now shaping basic thinking," he said. "Some people have the feeling that African people have lost forever something in their personality." Unless donors and recipients found a way to shift to serious development, he warned, that might well be the case.

"The African crisis is not the failure of the people nor the failure of Americans to feed a starving continent," he said. "It is basically the failure of state-oriented enterprises. How can we ask the state to find a solution to a problem where basically they have failed? Are we asking states not only to publicly recognize their failure but also to commit hara kiri?"

"Africans need to express themselves, he said. Democracy is to politics what the free market is to the economy. People are afraid of states, of governments. And governments are afraid to make decisions without Western advice. This kind of passivity has to go. Unless we free these people, not only economically, not only from emergencies, it will not happen."

Potential abounds, Damiba said. "How can we believe that some of these countries which are so rich, a scandal of riches, cannot make it? That these regions, developing for two thousand years, are so bleak? What do we expect when a young boy looks around and sees nothing to encourage him to build a life and make it profitable?"

He was also worried about waste. "You can't imagine the waste in the system," he said. "We are becoming unable to serve developing countries. If we cannot work this out within the organization, we will be part of the problem and not the solution." The Special Session showed no sign of changing all that. He paused a moment and pressed on: "It is time to unveil the facts for people who don't know them."

*D*amiba was right about the donors, of course. Some African leaders put their economies under the knife only to find in mid-operation that the surgeon had gone off to play golf. A year after the special session, Canada's ambassador to the U.N., Stephen Lewis, was pointedly reminding colleagues of their commitment. "There has been no significant change," he said. "I see a critical delinquency among donors." African ambassadors were even more pointed.

But any donor choosing to plead extenuating circumstances could have made a good case. After the special session ended, I went to three follow-up meetings so I could determine what impact the special session had on business-as-usual.

The first was in Rome, a meeting of the U.N. World Food Council. The thirty-seven-member council and its skilled professional staff keeps tabs on who grows food, who eats it, and who starves to death. It recommends policy, makes studies, and battles valiantly to remain independent of the U.N. Food and Agriculture Organization.

Mostly it is ignored, and its 1986 meeting was no exception. Two African questions had seized the world's conscience. South

Africa was seen as a simple conflict in black and white that was building into the year's major issue. And there was a catchall concern for starvation on the continent; this was referred to widely and simply as "Ethiopia," and interest was eroding with each fresh drop of rain. Immediately after the special session, there were two simultaneous U.N.-sponsored conferences: "South Africa" in Paris; "Ethiopia" in Rome. Perez de Cuellar and hundreds of reporters chose the first. Five other reporters and I chose the second.

That meeting focused on a bitter free-for-all among grain exporters. American farmers were losing their market share, and the U.S. government was subsidizing foreign sales to make them competitive. European Community officials argued that all markets were shrinking—former importers were growing their own grain. American subsidies drove down prices, and European farmers were howling for blood. Meanwhile, the Australians, Canadians, Argentines and Chinese, among others, were caught in between. Their economies depended upon grain sales at reasonable rates, and the U.S.-EEC price war was killing them. WFC figures showed that by the year's end, 370 to 390 million tons of grain would be stored around the world.

The minor concern, as fate would have it, was a direct consequence of all that. Africa, believed widely to be starving, was in fact choking to death on excess grain. Because of good rains in southern Africa, in Sudan, and in parts of West Africa, farmers had grown bumper crops of corn, sorghum, and millet. Other African countries were in desperate need of food, but none could afford to buy it from their neighbors. Shipping distances were great, and few countries had the foreign currency to spend. But, worse, Western countries had long ago figured out that one way to dispose of excess grain was to give it away and call it foreign aid.

WFC officials tried to persuade Americans and Europeans to pay for transport so African governments could sell their surpluses on their own continent. I asked U.S. Secretary of Agriculture Richard Lyng what he thought. "Quite frankly," he replied, "we had not thought much about the possibility of African food surpluses." He added: "We have our own surpluses."

In the end, it was more words on the same themes by the same people. There were the nattily dressed African civil servants. Some skipped a meeting to arrange for a Toshiba refrigerator to be shipped home with their luggage. A jolly minister of agriculture answered my questions about family planning by seizing my elbow and directing me into a noisy crowd: "Come, let's have a drink."

But there was also M. S. Swaminathan, director of the International Rice Research Institute, in the Philippines, who Alain Vidal-Naquet, of the WFC, calls the Karajan of development. It is an apt image. Swaminathan has it all together. He speaks of "symphonic agriculture," fitting the disparate pieces together in an eminently sensible, practical—nearly musical—way. The Indian expert was brought to Rome by the U.S.–based Hunger Project for a lecture on Asian lessons for Africa. He reminded his audience of Mahatma Gandhi's warning: Unless development helps the poorest and most destitute, it will only increase misery.

By the time he finished, most WFC delegates felt they could stride out of the Grand Hotel ballroom and go sort out Africa. But it was dinnertime.

The next meeting was in Niger. William Draper III, the new administrator of the U.N. Development Program, was meeting with all of his resident representatives in Africa. Pierre-Claver Damiba, UNDP Africa director and once the ranking African at the World Bank, chaired the meeting. I was the only reporter who showed up, and Damiba asked me in to all meetings. It was a change from Saouma's blacklist in Rome. The UNDP was straightforward about its problems and honest about its failures.

One problem it faced was that it could not give money away fast enough. Funds were budgeted, but African governments and local representatives could not get together the paperwork needed to start projects. Partly, it was because U.N. paperwork is serious business. More, it was because many governments are too disorganized to make use of help when it is available.

Speakers delicately avoided questions of turf fights with other U.N. agencies. Most often, UNDP's role is to coordinate projects of other agencies. But one senior official mentioned "a dynamic orientation from Rome" and brought down the house.

In some meetings, I was paralyzed by the jargon. I swatted a mosquito and then couched that action into U.N.–talk: a pilot project to ascertain negative impact on the propagation of potential malarial vectors in the semiarid zone of the Republic of Niger. People kept talking about a NATCAP. It had something to do with national programs and priorities. To me, it sounded like Texan for the last drink of the evening.

One field director complained he had not yet received a copy of the African leader's urgent Lagos Plan of Action. It had been drafted six years earlier.

As a senior UNDP officer had told me in New York, "We have forty-three representatives in Africa, and if this was a private enterprise, I'd fire all but about eleven of them." I tried to guess which ones he might keep.

One man likely to stay was Alexander Rotival, U.N. coordinator in the Ivory Coast. Rotival, an American, had worked in Mali for USAID just after independence. He joined the U.N. and, when drought struck in the early 1970s, he was called from Romania to Niger to take charge of relief activities. He was about to leave West Africa after watching the same mistakes over and over again.

His theme, repeated at every meeting for years, was regional development. It is impossible to talk about irrigation and Niger River flow without dealing with the watersheds of the coastal states. There was no way to develop cattle industries in the Sahel unless there were also markets to the south. Borders had to be crossed with good roads and rail links. Small industries needed bigger markets than any one state could offer. Food security meant growing surpluses in some places and moving them swiftly to deficit areas. In short, simple common sense.

"There is a lack of strategy, and we are moving toward a major disaster," he said, telling me nothing I had not seen for myself. He recounted the meetings where he had spoken out and was politely told to sit down. Most development planning is on a country-by-country basis, and few people are anxious to change that.

"It is an absolute travesty. We are not saying what we have to say. How can one just acquiesce and participate in this parody? We are aiding and abetting African governments that have been closing their eyes to what is coming. All of the rest of the things we're doing, it's peanuts."

We were sitting along the Niger River, lunching on capitaine poached with fennel. Starving Africans were some distance away. He ran a hand through gray hair and chuckled at the reputation he was getting as Crazy Sandy. But he knew he was talking to someone who had looked closely at the same problems and could not agree more with his conclusion.

"What makes it worse," he said, "is that we know what should be done to prevent the disaster. And we are just sitting here letting it happen."

The last meeting was the twenty-first summit of the Organization of African Unity in Addis Ababa. I went with high hopes. African leaders had summoned the world to the United Nations, and a historic compact had emerged. Africa had admitted its own faults; the international community had accepted the responsibility to help turn the crisis around. And this was the big meeting that would take stock of the new promise and shift the faltering continent into high gear. I should have known better.

African leaders were back home again, and the hard new reality of New York melted away. The departing chairman of the preliminary ministers' meeting was Madun Dulloo, of the little island of Mauritius.

Africa's problems, he said, were someone else's fault. He denounced outsiders' "blind eagerness to further their so-called supremacy." In a hectoring, accusing voice, he declaimed:

"We have long been told or made to believe that most of our economic ills derive from mismanagement or bad planning, inappropriate technology or prestige projects. I ask our critics: Is it not largely their responsibility? Have we not inherited their management techniques? Have we not been imposed upon with planning models and experts for the implementation of alien development strategies? Is it not fair and just for us then to assume that such assistance was merely a disguised way to vehicle old ideas within new formulas? They knew it. I believe they knew it."

I tried to get a copy of the speech, but none was available. It was just more words, pitched upon an ever-growing pile. Dulloo was partly correct. But how exactly was Africa forced to acquiesce to unwelcome advice? It is like the "debt burden." Who forced the money upon governments' shoulders? There is enough blame for everyone; that is no longer the issue.

The other opening speech was by Mengistu Haile Mariam whose country has been independent since before the Bible was written. He would have to find another excuse. Mengistu managed well. He dismissed economic matters in a few sentences. His message was South Africa.

Did people realize that the racist Pretoria regime imposed a curfew? That people could be held six months without a trial? That there was no free press? Mengistu was outraged at such a regime, and he heaped abuse upon it. I reflected on his message that night, between midnight and 5:00 A.M. There was nothing else to do; you can be shot for breaking curfew in Ethiopia. Prisoners have been waiting twelve years to see a judge for the first time. Every word in the papers is rigidly controlled.

Kenneth Kaunda of Zambia, roundly applauded as the grand old statesman each time he emerged from his Mercedes-Benz, delivered a ringing tribute to Mengistu. He praised Mengistu's "humanity" in delivering peasants from the tyranny of feudalism and in bringing Ethiopia into a modern age. Kaunda offered a somewhat eccentric version of history. It was too much for a veteran Western diplomat watching from the wings.

"The U.N. special session was one thing," he said. "But here you see them as they really are, with no pressure to play to the audience. They're ignoring the fact that they took rich countries and ran them into the ground, every damned one of them. A few leaders tried to talk some sense, some economic reality, but nobody listened. Kaunda is a fine orator, but I wonder how many of them know he is full of crap." He overstated his case, perhaps, but he demonstrated the gulf in thinking between those seeking help and those in a position to give it.

There were a few fleeting moments of encouragement during the summit. President Seyni Kountche, of Niger, made a brief speech: "Our people now expect from us urgent and concrete action. It is up to us not to let them down." Abdou Diouf, of Senegal, the departing OAU president, took it further: "At stake is our credibility, before our own people, before the entire world, indeed, before history."

Yoweri Museveni, fresh from restoring order in Uganda, demanded to know where African leaders were for fifteen years when a string of tyrants massacred three-quarters of a million of his people. Such negligence hardly strengthens their moral stance to criticize South Africa, he said.

But most of the rest was the usual hypocrisy, evasion of issues, and silliness. Each day I watched the fifty-one royal-purple Mercedes-Benz limousines disgorge their contents. Men in silk suits and brocaded robes swaggered up the steps, surrounded by fluttering knots of secretaries, military officers, and security thugs. I waited for tidbits to filter out of closed meetings: an OAU anthem was being selected after thirteen years of deliberation; Liberation Committee members were $15 million in arrears. Then I returned to the Hilton and watched the squalid, unchanging slums of Addis Ababa from my window.

But I was thrown out of the Hilton with the rest of the press corps. The Ethiopians had asked each OAU member state to limit its delegation to eighteen people. The Egyptians said they would total 198, and they liked the Hilton. More material for reflection. U.S. economic aid to Egypt alone was more than that given to all of Black Africa combined. Who was paying for well over 100 Egyptians to come to Ethiopia for a meeting at which they had little business to discuss?

There were, to be fair, some signs of new frugality. Basile Guissou, foreign minister of Burkina Faso, shared a seedy room at the Blue Nile Hotel, with neither bath nor telephone. His per diem was

$42, the price of lunch at the Hilton, and he was proud of it. But Burkina Faso was a rare example.

*D*uring the OAU summit, I was buying a bottle of rum at the duty-free shop for delegates when a short but energetic man elbowed his way to the counter. "All right, all right, I want a case of Chivas Regal," he said. That was twenty-four bottles. He shoved his order form ahead of mine, commanding attention. With it, he slapped down his United Nations passport. I wrote the name in my notebook: Sammy Kum Buo, of Cameroon.

I waited. Suddenly, he confronted me: "Why have you written my name?" I replied, "Why are you reading my notes?" A discussion ensued. It was Ethiopia, and I was a mere American journalist. I made a show of crossing out the name. He was not satisfied. I tore the page out of my book. As I walked away, his friend followed. In a menacing tone, he lectured me: "You are allowed to report on the meeting, but you cannot write down people's names without their permission."

In fact, Sammy Kum Buo and his case of scotch, and all the others whose expenses were paid to consider ways of rescuing Africa, were part of the meeting. A major part. I thought of Mr. Kysel and his dollar bill.

15 WHAT TO DO

A United Nations official leaving Africa once plotted out a novel. It was about a U.N. expert who died in his seventh-floor office, crushed when his shelves collapsed and buried him in reports on how to save Africa.

It is not so funny. The trees slain in the service of printing advice to Africa, if restored to life, would likely stretch from Mauritania to Mozambique. The authors' files would fill the home of an average African family of twelve. At the FAO alone, stored printed matter would likely cook meals for the population of Niger until the next century.

And it is more than paper. Eighty thousand foreign "experts" help in Africa, Ghanaian botanist Eddy Ayensu calculated, at an annual cost of $8 billion. Some do hard, essential work; many do not. Each year, more African graduates search in vain for work. Every crisis brings more outsiders to feel Africa's pulse and change its sheets. If Africans are to prosper, they must stop feeding famine groupies like us and start feeding themselves.

Outsiders can only help in certain ways, however motivated they may be; their money alone will not do it. Africans, as much as they may need aid, must develop themselves. The process never was as first presented: a painless, effortless elevator ride from poverty to prosperity.

Africa needs action, not more blueprints. It is long past the time to dust off the solemn compacts and sort out the collected wisdom. Perhaps the soundest advice came at the beginning, from Kwame Nkrumah, when he was hard at work ignoring his own counsel. In _Africa Must Unite_, he recalled some ancient Chinese wisdom:

> Go to the people
> Live among them
> Learn from them
> Love them
> Serve them
> Plan with them
> Start with what they know
> Build on what they have.

Anywhere in Africa, there is plenty to build on. African farmers grow grain in soils a Nebraskan would not use for cement. Long before foreigners arrived, Africans figured out how to keep grain, or harvest water, or find alternate foods during drought. Market women may not apply for McDonald's franchises, but they need no lessons from George Shultz on private enterprise. Yet outsiders and African leaders alike have treated the people on whom development depends as passive bystanders. Outside assistance has overwhelmed some of their skills, and the young are not learning them.

"No one is paying attention to African peasants," says Jamie Wickens, an American working for the U.N. World Food Program. "Every time an old man dies, a whole library burns."

The result is a paralyzing lack of confidence. Peasants don't produce in a system that exploits them. Young leaders don't emerge when fearful governments neutralize them. African ministers follow Western advice too closely or not at all. Constructive criticism is silenced. "Here you can write facts as you see them—if you want to commit suicide," one Ghanaian editor observed. Without confidence, there is little organization. And things fall apart.

In such a situation, Africa is lost, warns Chadli Ayari, president of the Arab Bank for African Development. He put it as well as anyone: "Even if an African country received $20 billion, it could not use them effectively if its people are badly organized."

Without confidence and organization, aid to Africa is so much water spilled into the sand.

The picture, though bleak, is no cause for despair. Among the shifting dunes of words on Africa are these from Lester R. Brown of the Worldwatch Institute: "The greatest risk in Africa is that there will be a loss of hope."

Our purpose, rather than producing yet another blunt instrument to imperil the frustrated U.N. novelist, is to explore the reasons for hope.

Africa now depends more on new values and attitudes than on new sources of capital. And values and attitudes are free. Kenyan journalist Fleur Ng'weno identifies a major one that might be changed: "If the world is to achieve equality . . . the industrialized countries must abandon their current view that economic superiority means moral superiority." Or other sorts of superiority.

Utopian fantasies can be exchanged for feasible objectives, with priorities on performance. It might be realized finally that articulating a problem is not solving it; nor is simply setting up a body to deal with it. Useless government jobs cost more than wasted salaries; they can paralyze growth. These are the bases of "structural reform."

By now, outsiders and Africans have learned the hard way. There are enough tools waiting to be used. "By and large, the continent has become one great composite case of development not working," wrote John Lewis in *Development Strategies Reconsidered*. Lewis has seen it all. As a USAID officer, he learned from the mistakes. As chairman of the Development Assistance Committee of the Organization for Economic Cooperation and Development, he sought to impose order among donors. Now he is at Princeton University.

Lewis puts equal blame on donors and recipients. "There can be no reason but a loss of purpose or nerve for either group not to pursue the effort vigorously," Lewis wrote. More aid would be better, he allowed. But just as important, he argued, is the philosophy with which aid is given—and received.

No single strategy will fix things, Lewis warns. Failure in one area is no cause for slacking in others. And wasted aid cannot be an excuse for mean-spirited politicians to demand cuts. Aid often works better than it seems; you just can't prove it. Lewis concludes, "If one is looking for bad news in this field, it can always be found."

Mainly, experts like Lewis conclude, aid must be designed to help people, whether or not it also brings the donor political advantage. Any effective aid is important; the most meager budgets are stretched when there is willing support from people who benefit. Without local enthusiasm, money buys only physical structures, not development.

Not everyone is hopeful. Jacques-Yves Cousteau just heaves a sigh. "It is too late for Africa," he told me. "Individually, men have the wisdom to save Africa. Unfortunately, when men get together in a society, they act with more stupidity than dinosaurs."

But it is not a matter of "saving," or "not saving," the continent. Africa—as biomass and matter—will not be destroyed. Whatever the remedies, some Africans will still suffer. But any progress saves lives and land, and it is worth the effort. For Abdul Rahman Diku and the Kalahari wildebeest, it may be too late. For Mohammed ag Hamed and Nax, it is not.

*F*or outsiders, a first step might be to take a closer look at the Dark Continent. Some people have yet to replace Ptolemy's map from the second century. He divided Africa into two countries: Libya across the top, with Ethiopia lying beneath it. He missed only South Africa. Too often, the word African conjures the image of a hungry half-formed soul in need of saving. We must get far beyond that, fast.

In the Middle Ages, one West African caravan dumped so much gold into Cairo it nearly collapsed the market. African private business flourished long before even the first Arabs came south to trade. Entrepreneurs made fortunes selling human beings and ivory tusks to enthusiastic buyers. And then they shifted to the commodity trade. During colonial times, Africans' own enterprise was the basis for much of the wealth. Ghanaians organized the cocoa industry and handled marketing.

Today, urban and rural businessmen generate huge sums which, for lack of confidence, never make it into the official economies. When a country's economic figures plummet, it often means that production continues but peasants are successfully hiding it from the tax collectors and the International Monetary Fund. No outsider has yet transplanted Asia's green revolution successfully into Africa. But in West Africa, specialist Paul Richards notes, farmers are on the verge of their own indigenous agricultural revolution.

And no one with any feel at all for Africa suspects Africans of lacking the skills and vitality essential to development.

"I wouldn't have the nerve to tell a Bozo fisherman about fishing, or a Tuareg about herding," says Wickens. "When you go into the villages and see the amazing strength and resilience of these people, you realize it is the character of strong people that will make the difference."

Wickens is a Guppy, a Grown-up Peace Corps Person, as consultant Kathy Hall Foster coined the grammar. He lived among Malian nomads, and he listened. Later, as director of the World Food Program in Chad, he helped Africans save their own lives. He knows the continent's strengths. And he knows its limitations.

Mali's Bozo tribesmen, for example, do not need to hear the visitors' favorite Chinese aphorism about not giving a man a fish but teaching him to catch his own. They know fishing like few people in the world. The first thing they know is that fish do badly when the river has no water. "Everybody who comes here has to invent the wheel and drive it down his road," observed Paul Vlek, a soils specialist from Muscle Shoals, Alabama. "And so no one gets anywhere."

Societies in Africa, in fact, are not so different from those anywhere else. Each ethnic group has its customs, ideals and superstitions. Tribes are nations, with separate cultures, languages and blood loyalties. Flemings and Basques, in this regard, resemble Balubas or Ndebeles. Most European nations have reached compromises over the centuries to live in relative peace within their common lines on the map. Africans are just starting.

African nations urge unity with slogans. But few have the civil service examinations, the anticorruption enforcement or the judiciary essential to unity. Tribalism—internal nationalism—undermines efforts to create a responsible citizenry. To survive, a man in power favors his own people. Otherwise, he risks downfall. He scrambles to put his wealth beyond the reach of outsiders he does not trust. Time has worn away some tribal divisions. But now powerful men are quicker to plunder within their own tribes.

When past chiefs rose above their people, the gap was often narrow: more cattle, larger huts, fly whisks and fancy stools. Today, the trappings of wealth and power have few limits. Leaders, if they choose, are free to indulge in ruthless greed. The people around them, in turn, plunder quickly before someone else's relatives take over.

None of this is news to Africans who have seen something close to a hundred coups since 1960. Few put much credence in the three weird sisters beloved by orators: colonialism, neo-colonialism and imperialism. Africa is dominated not only by international forces but also by a small group of Africans. Hilary Ng'weno, married to Fleur, wrote: "Many (leaders) mismanaged economies, squandered national wealth and literally threw away the future of their people as they jostled with one another for personal power and gain. When it was not greed that moved them, it was folly and gullibility."

Outsiders can help change this, indirectly. If donors cannot meddle in sovereign states, they at least can decide how to help them. Should a leader receive aid if he does not first consult his people? When aid perpetuates misery, should it continue? Fantu Cheru, among many others, thinks not. Traditional rulers, farmers, herders, academics, professionals all know what they need. Their participation is vital to turning money into development. Eventually, they will be part of the process, like it or not. Only if their role is peaceful and constructive can Africa benefit.

If an outside government objects to a leader's mistreatment of his people, it can say so clearly. This is seldom the case. American diplomats might suggest quietly to Mobutu Sese Seko that free markets are skewed without free societies. But if Mobutu can fly off to the White House for a bearhug from the President, the effect is blunted. For all the hand-wringing about Zaire's debt, no one seems to have thought of asking Mobutu to write a personal check.

At the same time, donors should loosen the collars of well-intentioned leaders strangling from debt. No one forced Africans to borrow heavily. Nor did bankers demand collateral. Africa is past worrying about who squandered what, or why. The numbers simply do not add up. Chandra Hardy, a senior World Bank economist, noted that Latin America's debt is a cash flow problem; Africa's is a matter of life and death.

The debt can neither be written off nor paid. Principal and interest already consume too much new aid. Africa, paying back creditor governments, is running to standstill. Donors might allow needy countries to repay in a new currency: development dollars. Instead of repaying dollars, debtors might spend their own currency on development; donors could budget that much less aid.

This could help donors impose accountability, not only for recipients but also for themselves. When a corporate executive wastes $3 million on foolishness, or loses it in the books, he is out on the street. A U.N. official, or a USAID director, or an African minister can usually get by with a nervous cough and a memo in triplicate. Public money, in essence, is no one's money. You might go to jail for stealing it but not for frittering it away.

Accountability, organization and careful priorities can make better use of aid funds already available. But the total is far too small. In early 1987, Shultz took his message on a tour of Africa: African states were finally realizing that only the American way offered them the promise of prosperity. But the U.S. State Department 1988 requests for all of sub-Saharan Africa were $500 million in development assistance and $100 million in economic support funds. And Congress balked at that.

Domestic farm subsidies of $25 billion against African aid of $600 million do little credit to the American way. U.S. aid to Israel is twice that. Egypt alone receives more than all of Black Africa. In Africa, aid rises substantially only when there is famine, and Americans are watching how their government responds.

Robert McNamara, a past World Bank president and former secretary of defense, has a simple enough description for U.S. aid to Africa: "perfectly disgraceful."

The Soviet Union long since dismissed the idea of helping Africa. The continent's troubles are because of Western imperialism, the Kremlin argues. That is tragic irresponsibility, but what to do? Scandinavian states are the most generous, per capita, but their help is not enough. France has the largest stake in Africa. In a recent interview with writer Marguerite Duras, French President François Mitterrand spoke eloquently of his feeling for Africa. "It is a continent in perpetual imbalance, but the game is not lost for those who live there," he said. It suffers badly for lack of a serious long-term plan "to treat the problem of development in its broad scope." Nonetheless, France targets much of its aid toward former colonies whose loyalty needs solidifying.

Taken together, world contributions through all channels approach $9 billion a year to sub-Saharan Africa. Used effectively, that should be enough to help Africa lurch forward. More is needed for real development. However Western officials juggle the figures, African specialists know the truth: Their money is not where their rhetoric is.

*F*or Africans, a first step might be to stop the squandering, whoever is at fault. Africa badly needs what resources it has left; and it must allow land and wildlife to recover. Strictly speaking, no one owes Africa anything. If anyone did, Africans would not collect without some goodwill from those asked to share their wherewithal. Development assistance and relief are no more than an adjunct to local resources. Philosophically and psychologically, this is a vital distinction.

"Adversity is our everyday lot," President Seyni Kountche of Niger once remarked. "Dignity is the most precious quality of our people." Aid or not, he was saying, Africa is the affair of Africans.

Leaders such as Kountche know the size of the job they face. His neighbor, Thomas Sankara of Burkina Faso, bridles at twin stereotypes of presidents in limousines and peasants with beggar's bowls; he drives a tiny Renault. "Those who colonized us had the means to set up a system so that we could survive. But we don't have the right now to sit around and plead for help every time our crops fail. We must develop ourselves, according to our old ways which are being lost." And in Mali, the next country over, President Moussa Traoré has few illusions. "Our civil service is characterized by corruption, nepotism and absenteeism," he told his nation.

No figure represents "enough" aid, explained Xavier de la Renaudière, director of the World Bank's special African section. "We have found that whenever we discuss budgets with African leaders on the basis of a fixed envelope, there is always agreement on priorities. But if they think the sky is the limit, why shouldn't they go for the sky?"

By focusing on priorities, Africans can use huge amounts of aid that otherwise would go unclaimed. Tens of millions of dollars are approved in grants—by U.N. agencies, development banks and bilateral agencies—but are not paid because recipients do not do their part. Sometimes donors' requests delay the paperwork. Often the money is lost as budget periods change.

De la Renaudière admitted that some World Bank funds had been badly spent, and sometimes stolen. But, he said, there are limits on what donors can do. For example, outsiders can design a system to pay farmers fairly. But what if police at roadblocks insist on buying crops at the old prices? "There is no way the Bank would inspect all obstacles as it would a nuclear site," he said. "This must come from Africans." He is right, of course.

At the same time, it is up to Africans to ensure that neither the World Bank nor anyone else damages their environment in the name of development. Very few short-term gains are worth the price Africans will have to pay if their farmlands, rangelands, forests and watersheds continue to disappear. Africa once seemed to be of infinite space. It is not.

The words and promises are already in place. In 1980, a Declaration of Environmental Policies was signed by the World Bank, the African Development Bank, four other such banks, the Commission of European Communities, the Organization of American States and the United Nations. It said that development "should be pursued in such a manner as to avoid or minimize environmental problems peculiar to it."

Barber Conable took over as World Bank president in 1986 and almost immediately made an appeal to protect fragile environment. And in May 1987, he pledged to give the issue far more attention. People will be watching.

According to experts within the World Bank—and it is clear from the record—environment has been essentially an afterthought. Projects lumber onward before anyone knows what their effect might be. Studies are made and then ignored. Even when controls are ordered, they are seldom put into regular practice. Mainly, the burden of proof is still on nature.

"We don't take the environment seriously," a senior World Bank official told me in Washington. "It is something tacked on later which is not part of mainstream planning." He was rebelling quietly against the system. "The Bank responds to pressure, to publicity. People have to understand this. A fundamental systemic change must be made, or there will be no improvement." I later came upon an internal Bank report that concluded exactly the same thing: "As a matter of routine, environmental issues are not considered but . . . are taken into account in specific instances when . . . pointed out by the Bank's environmental advisor, the press, or special interest groups."

The same is true within the U.N. system or bilateral aid agencies. Most are beginning to understand the economic cost of environmental loss. Public pressure is the reason.

Africans can create new wealth by peeling away the layers that stifle initiative. "Structural reforms" offer some promise. But in their quest for a rapid cure, IMF pharmacologists often prescribe an overdose. Food riots do more to block development than numbers that spill out of neatly ordered columns on a page. Reform is essential, but only in the context of the people being reformed.

Often governments that complain the loudest about miserly aid are those that make aid impossible. I met a foreign agronomist in Ethiopia who had discovered hybrid citrus strains that promised to revolutionize production. But he had to send off soil samples for analysis. He spent two weeks of constant labor collecting the signatures necessary to mail dirt to London.

African governments can grant land tenure to peasants. "Who's going to plant a tree, take care of land, unless he knows he will be around to benefit?" boomed Philip Leakey, a junior minister in the Kenya government. "It's obvious, isn't it?"

And they can open the floor to their own citizens. "The most effective assistance the U.N. can give is to help reinstitute native African traditions of free speech and trade," the Ghanaian academic George Ayittey wrote. "There are millions of Africans who have ideas about solving Africa's problems, but they cannot speak out. If they had been allowed to, Africans would not now be starving."

Africa needs more than the reordering of individual countries. The food question is typical, and fundamental. At the end of 1986, Zimbabwe alone could have made up the 1.6 million tons needed in the eighteen countries short of grain. Zimbabwean farmers were desperate to sell. But who would pay the transport? In what currency would grain be purchased? Zambian kwachas, for example, buy little enough in Zambia; across the border, they are worthless.

"Triangular transactions" are the answer. But Western countries have their own farmers to mollify. For 1986–1987, the United States arranged to buy 11,400 tons of Zimbabwean and Malawian corn for Mozambique, about the same amount as Austria. The European Community was a little more generous. But all triangular transactions and local purchases totalled 233,299 tons, about 5 percent of African grain surpluses.

It is one thing to urge African farmers to produce. It is another to help them sell their crops when they do. Rather than expected profits, food-growers are saddled with debts and storage costs. As John Laurie, head of the Commercial Farmers Union in Zimbabwe, put it: "It is a nuisance to be a breadbasket in Africa."

A USAID official in Harare told me in 1986, "The only answer for food security is to concentrate on the dozen or so countries that can produce food and then find a way to distribute it within Africa. But if I said that in public, American farmers would kill me." It is easier to give away food than to help Africans grow it—or worse, to transport it.

But a basic human side is too often forgotten in the argument over food supplies. Technical tourists work out calorie requirements and tonnage, and then they push the numbers into the rigid columns of their work sheets. Shortfalls, they assume, can be made up with food shipments. But during the 1980s emergency, it took the EEC up to 419 days from the time food was ordered for stricken regions until it actually got there. And that was because it was urgent. American officials can move fast with food aid, but they seldom do. With the best of planning, trucks break down and people starve while their lunch sits stranded by the side of a road.

War and famine left Mozambique in desperate need of 700,000 tons of grain by mid-1987. Plenty was available just up the rail line in Zimbabwe. But food aid doesn't work that way.

Africans need to grow their own food so it is where they need it at mealtimes. There is no way around that. Because rains—and every other factor—are so erratic in Africa, farmers must be given the margin to produce more food than they need. This requires creating domestic and regional grain markets, with realistic prices, storage, and transportation systems.

Similar problems restrict general intra-African trade to a fraction of overall commerce. Unless neighbors combine their markets and means of production—and agree on agricultural policies—they have no comparative advantages in a rough world. Terms of trade are weighted against Africa. But "the West" does not determine commodity prices; the market does. I spend two dollars for a Venezuelan mango in Paris when I know fatter, juicier mangoes rot unsold in Mali. This is not conspiracy; Venezuela is better organized.

With cooperation, Africans can build the economic diversity they need to protect themselves from abrupt shifts in the market. Profits can be channeled into light manufacturing for import substitutes and eventual exports. That is simple enough, and almost any African official will say the same thing over a quiet whisky. It is more urgent to identify and confront the political causes preventing this from taking place.

New regional organizations struggle to lower tariffs, bureaucratic obstacles and mistrust across borders. Slowly, highways are appearing, and the old colonial rail system is being augmented. But it is an uphill fight. A decade ago, it took a truck three days to jolt over the potholes between Niamey, Niger, and the port at Lomé, Togo. Now the road is paved, and the trip takes a week. Truckers blame customs checks and roadblocks in Burkina Faso on the way.

Africa would gain by coordinating trade and development with the rest of the Third World. Southeast Asians produce three rice crops a year; Senegal can buy Thai rice more cheaply than Senegalese farmers can grow it at home. The World Food Council is working hard to arrange for Asians to help Africans in "South-South development." China is already doing a lot on its own.

One point of comparison shows the difference: fertilizer use in Asia increased over a decade by 19.2 million metric tons; in Africa, it increased by 1.5 million tons.

African officials are learning from Asians that they need neither huge grants nor miracles. A Chinese team in Dakar to build a football stadium was given a small barren empty lot for a housing compound. Within six months, at the height of a drought, the Chinese were growing all their own food, with lush greens left over.

*W*hen famine strikes, the niceties must sometimes fall away. At times, peoples' lives outweigh sovereignty. The Independent Commission on International Humanitarian Issues, a panel of statesmen and specialists headed by Sadruddin Aga Khan, made this point in 1985: "Bluntly, the U.N. should be prepared to trespass on states' rights when these are in conflict with the rights of disaster victims."

U.N. officials and voluntary agencies found ways around Ethiopia's refusal to allow food to famine victims, and simultaneously rebels, in Eritrea and Tigray. In 1985, Nigeria held up two hundred trucks with food desperately needed in Chad. Finally, World Food

Program officials decided to roll the trucks, whether Nigeria liked it or not. "We forced the borders," a WFP friend exulted to me at the time. "It worked."

WFP stretches what limits it can. One emergency logistics man in Rome has a neat trick. Whenever some official throws up an obstacle, he says, "Just a minute, I've got BBC on the other line." It seldom fails.

Late in 1986, a garrulous Italian named Staffan de Mistura, a WFP hit man, put together Operation Rainbow to fly food to starving people isolated in southern Sudan. Rebels threatened to shoot down his planes unless he obtained their clearance. Sudanese officials, who wanted food to go only to government-controlled towns, called him sneaky and crooked. One wrote to his boss, "It is almost impudent to say that 'because I am a humanitarian, I can supersede the government.' "

If people like de Mistura did not supersede governments sometimes, death tolls would be higher. More often, prudent U.N. officials stick to the rules and, as a result, are party to mass murder.

While people are starving, food aid sparks little debate. A priest once remarked dryly to me in Burkina Faso, "I know food aid is a terrible thing, but it prevents having to bury all those people." Massive amounts of food to Ethiopia saved millions of lives in 1984 and 1985. It was worth it.

But free food can be a crutch, or worse. When the United States cut off grain shipments to punish India for its stand on the Vietnam War, India grew its own. Too often, ill-timed food aid floods African markets just as farmers harvest their crops.

A World Bank report on hunger offered this sensible advice: "Only a multi-year commitment by food aid donors, with flexible drawings in accord with a recipient country's needs, could make food aid a reliable instrument for relieving transitory food insecurity. . . . Food aid should be planned and managed with as much care as other forms of financial aid; but often it is not."

Reaction time must be faster. "The nature of the system is that you raise money after someone is dead," Fred Cuny observed.

George Simon, a senior WFP coordinator, wrestles with the

system. "Governments generally ship food when they have the money budgeted, not according to need," he said. "The result is chaotic. This gives me a job, and more staff for next year, but does not help starving people."

If donors could agree on a reliable early-warning system—one that combines satellite and aerial spotting with on-the-ground assessments of what farmers are thinking—then small, swift interventions from security stocks could maintain market stability. If families can be spared from uprooting themselves in desperation, the worst part will be avoided.

For successful longer term development, examples can be found. Almost always, they involve small amounts of money or equipment put directly in the hands of those who will benefit. They require a committed organizer, with the confidence of the people involved. When they work well, they frequently expand naturally as people elsewhere imitate them. But often they provide little place for a donor to stick a self-congratulatory plaque. The big agencies seldom bother with them; they are too small and isolated for standardized control.

CARE's Majjia Valley project in Niger, for example, cost only a million dollars over twelve years. Nearly two hundred miles a year of acacias are planted as windbreaks. Millet yields have multiplied, and farmers sell wood for cash. In shaded villages, life is immeasurably better. Michael Ahearn, a young forester from Bethesda, Maryland uses local staff. Villages run their own nurseries; the project's success is contagious. CARE took the trouble to enlist villagers' support and protect them from local authorities who wanted their wood.

With similar goals, U.S. aid, European governments and the World Bank have spent scores of millions to do more harm than good. Official projects, through local government channels, ruined huge tracts of the best riceland for failed eucalyptus plantations, and farmers were often not compensated.

"To start a project, you can't just roll up in a jeep and bang on a tam-tam while people are working," said Amadou Maiga, Ahearn's assistant. "They will just nod politely and forget about you the minute you drive away. You have to stay with them." Ahearn was more direct: "It's amazing how easy it is to make people worse off with your best intentions."

Each time I visit an African country, I am struck by the difference among outsiders contracted to help. Optimism brims among the international civil servants who arrive fresh from their pep talks at home. The old hands, almost invariably, come down to the same basic lessons.

Sir Michael Blundell, a Kenyan agricultural official and a life-long settler, watches aid donors with growing frustration: "They need to act in concert and decide what items will be bought from each other instead of scheming against one another," he said. "If they are not going to feed Africa for the rest of the century, they had better get a firm grasp of the nettle."

Jean-Pierre Noblet, an agronomist who grew up in the Belgian Congo and now works for the World Food Program, agrees. He has seen rich Sudanese with foreign aid grants clear trees from ten thousand acres of rangeland at a time to plant crops; after three years, the land had to be abandoned as barren desert. And he has seen African hunters burn 100,000 acres to corner a gazelle. Rather than condemn nature, he said, donors should realize what they are doing wrong themselves—and help Africans avoid damaging mistakes. "Africa destroys itself," he said. "Everyone says desert, desert, desert. But it is man who is at fault."

Joanny Guillard, a blunt French specialist who has seen it all, observes: "We always push for better yields. But the African seeks to minimize risk. He would rather have one ton every year than three in one year and zero the next. His life depends on it." His view was echoed in a different way by Annick Miské of UNICEF, also French but married to a Mauritanian: "The most important thing is not to import the West. We must bring understanding."

A World Bank veteran who prefers anonymity worries that understanding is often overshadowed by greed and egos. "There is no end to dirty deals being done in the name of development," he said. "As long as the Third World is a dumping ground for spare parts, and any aid officer can design a project no matter what he does not know, things will not work. The whole system is sick."

Damning judgments come from René Dumont, who has never stopped ringing the alarm. His first book was *False Start in Africa*. His next, he reflected in 1987, at age 82, could be called "A Very Bad Finish." He calculates that with just the 800 million dollars in aid wasted on a gigantic—and now dry—Senegal River dam, 200 smaller dams and hand tools could have brought new life to 40,000 villages from Senegal to Chad. Aid in Africa, he says, has enriched foreigners, entrenched corrupt states and alienated peasants. And now, he warns, populations burgeon unchecked.

Such advice is starting to sink in, but putting it into practice requires revolution. First, donors need flexibility. "One cannot always avoid the mistakes of tomorrow, but one can avoid the mistakes of yesterday," says de la Renaudière of the World Bank. "The faster the reaction time, the better off you are likely to be."

But that leaves coordination and priorities.

Coordinating aid requires agreement on basic philosophies. Mrs. Gro Brundtland, prime minister of Norway and chairman of the World Commission on Environment and Development, warned that far too much aid was designed for the donor rather than the recipient.

She wrote: "We have to ask whether the structure of international trade and finance is either equitable or effective when, as at present, it leads to a net annual export of capital from Africa. In these circumstances, who is really aiding whom?" Donors, she argued, must anticipate and prevent problems. "That means making environmental concern and protection a built-in requirement for all . . . economic development."

African veterans agree with the outsiders. "It is a joke to talk of food self-sufficiency or anything else in the Sahel until we can master the water," says Bertin Borna, a Senegalese who directed the U.N. Sahel-Sudan Office. "You can do nothing without it."

Samba Sabally, agriculture minister of the Gambia, supports his point. "Of course, rain-fed agriculture is cheaper, and donors prefer it," he told me. "But what good is it if you spend all your resources and all you can do is pray for rain?" Sabally is a familiar figure on the development circuit. He is articulate and thoughtful. But, like his colleagues elsewhere, he is underpaid; a travel per diem helps him make ends meet. At international conferences, the same things are said again and again to little visible effect. But they are lucrative.

Some weeks, up to a third of African cabinet ministers might be dispersed outside their capitals talking about problems they could be home solving. Some, like Sabally, keep track of their real work. Others spend time at home on their expense accounts.

This is part of a larger problem. Too often in Africa, talking about a crisis is equal to solving it. Words are deeds. It is a luxury Africa can no longer afford. Each meeting consumes air fares, hotels, duty-free purchases and nameless personal expenses. On a continent living on artificial life support, much of that comes from dollar bills like Mr. Kysel's.

*T*his dollar-bill theme came up in Paris, early in 1987, at a seminar on African health organized by Médecins Sans Frontières. André Laurent, head of the School of Public Health at the Free University of Brussels, stirred applause in answering someone who suggested that lost aid was inevitable. In parts of Africa, he said, health expenditure per inhabitant is one dollar a year. "A dollar goes a long way in such circumstances," he said. "Not a single one should be spent without its donor knowing exactly where it is going."

If someone had to explain all the broken-down jeeps, all the inspection trips, or the color photographs of Edouard Saouma, the dollars would go farther.

All of these themes repeat themselves, in fact. That is the problem. Maurice Williams, former executive director of the World Food Council, is exasperated with all the fumbling and excuses for delay. "We have already taken too many shortcuts," he said. "The more we wait, the greater the problems we are creating." The WFC was supposed to be a world food authority to channel donors' efforts, he said. Instead, it is a committee. "All the partial approaches don't add up to a comprehensive approach," Williams warned. "Donors break up old structures but don't follow up with resource flows. If we fail to coordinate, we will prolong the crisis rather than solve it."

In 1987, his successor, Gerald Trant, was still trying to get donors to pull together. "Look," he said. "We're like the toothpaste commercial. We're not looking for miracles, just fewer cavities."

*W*ildlife is a separate problem. In many areas, the point of no return is fast approaching. Without dynamic new initiatives, animals will be killed off across wide sweeps of Africa, their ranges occupied by people. A balance must be found. Parks are still part of an answer, but government must look beyond them. David Western warned against trying to separate wild game into delineated areas: "The trouble is that species segregation, like racial segregation, gives the subordinate party, nature, a raw deal."

Governments can be helped not only to manage their parklands but also to create other areas where man and his livestock can coexist with wildlife. But costs and benefits must be analyzed fairly. Conservation is expensive, and it should not fall to the poorer nations alone to pay. African wildlife is part of the world's wealth. The world has a responsibility to share the cost of protecting it.

This principle applies within African countries. Often the people displaced by parks, or those whose crops and cattle suffer from wildlife, derive no benefit from income the parks attract. Esthetic value is no argument to a man who prefers to look at cattle, or whose survival depends on his herds.

Wildlife ecology and science in general need far more attention than they receive. UNESCO estimates that 3,000 African scientists are working outside of Africa. Eddie Ayensu, established in Washington, says many would like to go back but cannot find institutions to absorb them. In Africa, too few civil servants are interested in science.

Twenty-six founding fellows established the African Academy of Sciences in 1985. Its chairman, Thomas Odhiambo of Kenya, said it needed time to develop coherent long-term programs for research on drought, desertification and famine.

But there is a long way to go. At the height of famine, researchers at the International Livestock Center for Africa, outside of Addis Ababa, watched relief money pour into Ethiopia. But none found its way to ILCA. "We're really very frustrated," director Peter Brumby told me. "As far as we're concerned, it's all rhetoric. Next year our budget will be cut. We have to listen to a lot of garbage about how Africa is a major priority, but the people who insist on this are the ones who walk away when you ask for help. We have no resources to tackle these enormous problems. We're doing it with bloody peanuts."

Earlier, Abdul Saleh, a former minister of health in Sudan, told the BBC why donors should stop walking away:

"It is not just an African problem, but a world problem. Something is happening to this planet. It is dying somewhere. People ought to think about it that way. The parts that are now healthy must think about why the periphery, the limbs, are dying."

*P*rogress depends heavily on strengthening African institutions. Every outsider's recipe comes down to this; "institutions," like "structural reform," is a development fad word for the 1980s. What is as important as the institution itself is the philosophy by which it functions.

Too often Africans use a blueprint approach, which plans development from the top. Specific goals and procedures are followed blindly, whatever obstacles appear. Such plans almost never work. The alternative is a learning process, flexible enough to adapt to changing circumstances. For this to work, people who carry out the plan must add their judgment on an equal basis. As initial mistakes are found, and as unforeseen hitches arise, people at both ends can find the best way to adapt.

There was no blueprint for Britain's Industrial Revolution. Individuals set their own goals and worked within their capabilities. Today, Africans are confronted constantly by their own failure to meet objectives set by outsiders. Confidence, in such cases, is invariably undermined.

African institutions are mostly hierarchical and authoritarian. Someone is in charge, and no one questions him. Robert Chambers, a rural development specialist, notes, "most departments in most countries face inwards, upwards and away from rural clients." Their style, he adds, is often punitive. For urban clients, there is little difference.

If they cannot reverse the thrust of African institutions, outsiders can work in that direction. Structural reform depends heavily on slimming and limbering up ossified institutions.

D. K. Fieldhouse offers startling figures from Ghana to show how a useless state apparatus can stifle growth. Peasants working on their own produced crop yields that were five times greater than the state farms'.

Ghana demonstrated a paradox of power: an attempt to build power by political control of the economy crippled the country. But American scholars Nathan Rosenberg and L. E. Birdzell show that where economies have operated freely, government power increased.

Most governments are so paralyzed with institutions, they cannot move with agility even when motivated. The effect is like a muscle-bound weight lifter trying to play racquetball.

While waiting for systems to change, even small amounts of aid can be applied effectively. There is need for low-level thankless work: primary schools, back roads, mother-child nutritional programs, village water supplies. Hundreds of private voluntary agencies beaver away at these sorts of things with little credit: Oxfam, Save the Children, CARE, Lutheran World Relief. The list is long.

There are initiatives from people who want to do something with their money. The Japanese shipbuilding mogul Ryoichi Sasakawa funds Global 2000. Jimmy Carter is its spokesman. In Sudan, he told cheering peasants, "I am not President of the United States of America. I am a farmer." The idea, Carter said, is to "take some action to prevent famine . . . instead of just handing out thousands of tons of wheat after people had begun to starve." The driving force is Norman Borlaug, who signed up former frontline officers from the Asian Green Revolution. His teams understand not only seed but also farmers. On 420 sample plots in Sudan, they increased sorghum yields up to six times.

The showiest aid is seldom the most effective. One night in Paris, I watched on television as a huge Renault truck rumbled toward

Timbuktu. It was bought with contributions collected by the journalist-adventurers who had taken it to Africa. Six months later, I saw the same truck in Timbuktu. It was up on blocks where it had been almost since its arrival. A small spare part was missing, and the truck was corroding to uselessness without it. More than trucks, Mali needs mechanics.

Great publicity heralded the "music bridge" in Chad, a small span erected with funds from USA for Africa and Live Aid. Less was heard about the vital Dogon bridge, in Mali, which was destroyed by the annual motor rally from Paris to Dakar. That same year, at the height of the Sahel food crisis, relief workers complained that Paris-Dakar rally vehicles left Timbuktu dry of fuel for two weeks.

Education is a particular problem. The needs are so vast, and the result so difficult to measure, that donors are tempted to throw up their hands in despair. But nothing is more basic than teaching young Africans to reason and find answers to their own problems. African youngsters should first learn literacy in their own languages and then, with that psychological and educational base, move on to an international lingua franca. Too many Africans have been traumatized by the conflict between what Ayi Kwei Armah calls *l'enracinement* and *l'ouverture*.

Other effective aid, like teaching, is hard to measure, and often invisible: farm advice; small dams and dikes; social work. At times, donors must decide whether to take credit or to help.

Largesse can be lost in a flash; it is part of the problem. In Chad, Beramgoto Baiemroe waited more than a year for his own four-wheel drive truck so he could stop hitchhiking to agricultural projects he supervises at the edge of the Sahara. A few weeks after a grant made it possible for him to get one, the truck was demolished by a bazooka. Government troops commandeered it to push back Libyan-supported rebels.

When effective aid is impossible through official channels, donors can find ways of reaching the people directly. Government donors—those with the money—can fund private voluntary agencies with the capacity to reach the most needy.

More can be done to support indigenous non-governmental African agencies. Effective work is done by volunteer, or poorly paid, Africans who know what their people need. "London, Paris and New York are full of Africans who would love to come home and help if they could make a difference," Djibril Diallo insists. But African initiatives are often blocked by governments who fear their popularity. Outside donors seldom give them the resources they need.

During the height of drought in Burkina Faso, relief operations in Dori were dominated by a jovial bearlike man who spoke American slang with a light Virginia drawl, the local representative of Save the Children. His name was Abdoulaye, and he was a Burkinabe. He had no prejudices about relief versus development. As an African, he knew they were both the same thing. Babacissé Fanta Diallo in Djenné is another example. There are countless thousands in the wings.

In 1987, the Hunger Project initiated an annual prize of $100,000 to the African who did the most against hunger on his continent. The jury included McNamara, Swaminathan and Borlaug.

Trained Africans are not technical tourists; they grew up in the countries they advise. Foreign foresters in the Sahel spent a decade on thirsty and temperamental exotic trees before returning to the good old acacias they found in the first place. Any African could have told them about the acacia, the nomads' *gao*. It fixes nitrogen. Cattle, fond of its pods, leave fertilizer at its base. But mainly, it grows leaves in the dry season in defiance of nature. Herders assume the tree is protected by Allah; it is worth a goat's life to eat a *gao* seedling.

Returning development to Africans builds pride in their cultures. And that can help develop a feeling of nationhood based on more than empty slogans. They can be Ewe and Ghanaian at the same time. Mutual respect and confidence will allow development to start from the bottom, at individual and village level, rather than coming from some abstract center of power.

Africans, far more than outsiders, understand the continent's pace. Michael Andrews of the BBC quoted an old African hand as observing: "It takes a hen twenty-one days to hatch an egg. The World Bank thinks that if you put twenty-one hens on the same egg, it will hatch in one day."

Outsiders, in the end, are outsiders. After twenty-two years of noble effort, Pan American gave up on the "African Queen"; it cancelled twice-weekly service that hopped down the West African coast between Nairobi and New York. One incident of many: Just before Christmas, diverted to Togo, the flight spent eight hours on the ground while the captain argued with authorities who wanted landing fees and fuel paid in cash. It was yet another case of WAWA: West Africa Wins Again. In most of Africa, it is often still easier to fly to Paris and London and back again when flying to the next country over.

It is time outsiders stepped back and let Africans take the lead. When musicians took up the cause of famine, the world paid attention. From Southampton to the South Bronx, Western kids thought about hungry children far away. But then what?

What Africa needs is not a sharp tug at the heartstrings but rather a steady strumming that does not stop. A consistent level of steady support can help Africans regain their confidence, pick up their own rhythm and rescue their own future.

In Mali, I traveled with a U.N. accountant to visit Food for Work projects, where Africans receive food to do things for themselves that outsiders decide need doing. If better than a handout, Food for Work suggests to people that their wellbeing is someone else's responsibility. At each stop, the accountant surveyed the expatriates on hand: French veterinarians, Belgian doctors, German health specialists, American reporters, and himself. He looked around and grunted: "Food for Work. For us."

With outsiders laying the plans and paying the wages, Djibril Diallo's allegorical African bird cannot break loose. Africa remains at its eternal beginning.

By 1986, the latest development catchphrase was: "There is a new political will." African leaders were beginning to listen to their own people. Their options, in fact, were dwindling. People like a U.N. official I met from Uganda were making themselves heard. He would probably let me name him, but why should he risk it? He is hardly alone.

"We have had enough of these verandah boys who become ministers and don't give a shit for the people in the bush," he said, his voice rising in anger. "Once they get sugar and enough to eat, they are satisfied. They can fly it in. All of this worries me as an African and as someone who has seen something better in years gone by. It worries me that I don't know the future of my children when I go. This begging for food, it is bullshit."

He stopped a moment and slowly shook his head. "You know, we tried so hard to break apart even the little bit that we had."

Whatever is to be done, we had better get started.

Robert McNamara warned in 1985: "The whole range of Africa's extraordinarily rich and diverse ecological inheritance is threatened. It is Africa's future that is in jeopardy."

And he added: "Further delay, further temporizing with reform, further weakening of external support—in effect, further failure to recognize and confront this crisis head-on—will condemn an entire continent to unimaginable human misery. We cannot let this happen."

But, of course, we are letting it happen. Piles of tiny corpses brought only a spasm of concern and then the usual apathy. Bob Geldof whipped up compassion and later dismissed development as boring. But publicizing calamity is not the stuff of a Nobel prize. The prize awaits the person who devises a six-letter headline-writer's word for "sustainable development."

How often, in how many ways, must the same thing be said? Should senators and members of Parliament and philanthropists be left overnight, one by one, in an Ethiopian *tukul* or a Tanzanian *shamba* in a "normal" year, when no FAO red lights are flashing? Must hearings and conferences be set up as in *Clockwork Orange*, with eyes taped open and misery made real by electrodes?

Or must we wait for a cloud of African dust to foul the air beyond the Mediterranean and the Atlantic? Or World War III?

Rhetoric has built-in limits. It dissolves into purple haze and becomes a parody of itself. It numbs and oversimplifies, and it provokes, in the end, a helpless throwing up of the hands.

Simple reason should be enough.

BIBLIOGRAPHY

Africa South of the Sahara 1987. London: Europa Publications.

Achebe, Chinua. *The Trouble with Nigeria*. London: Heinemann Educational Books, 1984.

Adams, Herbert, and Koglia Moodley. *South Africa Without Apartheid*. Berkeley, Los Angeles: University of California Press, 1986.

Allen, Charles. *Tales from the Dark Continent*. London: Andre Deutsch, 1979.

Alverson, Hoyt. *Mind in the Heart of Darkness*. Princeton: Princeton University Press, 1976.

Arnold, Guy. *Aid and the Third World*. London: Robert Royce, 1985.

Babatope, Ebenezer. *Coups: Africa and the Barracks Revolts*. Enugu, Nigeria: Fourth Dimension, 1981.

Bauer, P. T. *Equality, the Third World and Economic Delusion*. London: Weidenfeld and Nicolson, 1981.

———. *Reality and Rhetoric*. London: Weidenfeld and Nicolson, 1984.

Bell, Morag. *Contemporary Africa*. New York: Longman, 1986.

Benson, Mary. *Nelson Mandela*. Harmondsworth: Penguin, 1986.

Berman, Edgar. *In Africa With Schweitzer*. Far Hills, N.J.: New Horizon, 1986.

Bernus, Edmond. *Touaregs*. Paris: l'Harmattan, 1983.

Biko, Steve. *I Write What I Like*. London: Heinemann Educational Books, 1978.

Blaikie, Piers. *The Political Economy of Soil Erosion in Developing Countries*. Harlow: Longman, 1985.

Blomström, Magnus and Björn Hettne. *Development Theory in Transition*. London: Zed, 1984.

Boorstin, Daniel J. *The Discoverers*. New York: Random House, 1983.

Borgin, Karl and Kathleen Corbett. *Destruction of a Continent*. San Diego, New York, London: Harcourt Brace Jovanovich, 1982.

Briault, Maurice. *Sur les Pistes de l'A.E.F.* Paris: Alsatia, 1945.

Brown, Lester R. and Edward C. Wolff. *Reversing Africa's Decline*. Washington: Worldwatch, 1986.

Brunschwig, Henri. *Noirs et Blancs dans l'Afrique Noire Française*. Paris: Flammarion, 1983.

Caillié, René. *Voyage á Tombouctou*. Paris: Imprimerie Royale, 1830.

Campbell, Bernard. *Human Ecology*. New York: Aldine, 1985.

Cassen, Robert. *Does Aid Work?* Oxford: Oxford University Press, 1986.

Chambers, Robert. *Rural Development*. Harlow: Longman, 1983.

Chapelle, Jean. *Nomades Noirs du Sahara*. Paris: l'Harmattan, 1982.

Cohen, Robin. *Endgame in South Africa*. Paris: UNESCO, 1986.

Colinveaux, Paul. *Why Big Fierce Animals Are Rare*. London: George Allen & Unwin, 1980.

Conquest, Robert. *Harvest of Sorrow*. London: Hutchinson, 1986.

Crapanzano, Vincent. *Waiting*. London: Granada, 1985.

Curtin, Philip, et al. *African History*. Boston: Little, Brown, 1985.

Davidson, Basil. *Africa in History*. New York: Macmillan, 1968.

———. *The Story of Africa*. London: Mitchell Beazley, 1984.

Davis, David Brion. *Slavery*. New York: Oxford University Press, 1984.

Dayrell, Elphinstone. *Folk Stories from Southern Nigeria*. London: Longmans, Green, 1910.

De Gramont, Sanche. *Strong Brown God*. Boston: Houghton Mifflin, 1976.

Delpey, Roger. *Affaires Centrafricaine*. Paris: Jacques Grancher, 1985.

Dinham, Barbara, and Colin Hines. *Agribusiness in Africa*. London: Earth Resources, 1983.

Dodge, Cole P., and Paul D. Wiebe, eds. *Crisis in Uganda*. Oxford: Pergamon, 1985.

Dorgelés, Roland. *Sous le Casque Blanc*. Paris: Editions de France, 1941.

Dumont, René. *False Start in Africa*. London: Andre Deutsch, 1966.

———. *Pour l'Afrique j'accuse*. Paris: Plon, 1986.

————. *Les Raisons de la Colère*. Paris: Entente, 1986.

Dybowski, Jean. *La Route du Tchad*. Paris: Librairie de Paris, no date.

Ewane, F. Kange. *Semence et Moisson Coloniales*. Yaounde: Cle, 1985.

Fieldhouse, D. K. *Black Africa 1945–1980*. London: George Allen & Unwin, 1986.

Fossey, Dian. *Gorillas in the Mist*. Boston: Houghton Mifflin, 1983.

Fuggle, R. F. and M. A. Rabie. *Environmental Concerns in South Africa*. Cape Town: Juta & Co., 1983.

Gbagbo, Laurent. *Côte d'Ivoire*. Paris: L'Harmattan, 1982.

Giri, Jacques. *l'Afrique en panne*. Paris: Karthala, 1986.

————. *le Sahel demain*. Paris: Karthala, 1983.

Grove, A. T. *Africa*. Oxford: Oxford University Press, 1978.

Grzimek, Bernhard and Michael. *Serengeti Shall Not Die*. New York: Dutton, 1961.

Harrison, Paul. *Inside the Third World*. Harmondsmith: Penguin, 1979.

Haski, Pierre. *L'Afrique Blanche*. Paris: Seuil, 1987.

Hay, Margaret Jean, ed. *African Women*. London: Longman, 1984.

Hoagland, Edward. *African Calliope*. New York: Random House, 1979.

Howe, Sonia E. *Les Heros du Sahara*. Paris: Armand Colin, 1931.

Hyden, Goren. *Beyond Ujamaa in Tanzania, Underdevelopment and Uncaptured Peasantry*. London: Heinemann, 1980.

————. *No Shortcuts to Progress*. London: Heinemann, 1983.

Independent Commission on International Humanitarian Issues. *Famine: A Man-Made Disaster?* London, Sydney: Pan, 1985.

Jacquemot, Pierre. *Mali, le Paysan et l'Etat*. Paris: l'Harmattan, 1981.

Jaffe, Hosea. *A History of Africa*. London: Zed, 1985.

Kabué, Buana. *Citoyen Président*. Paris: l'Harmattan, 1978.

Khalid, Mansour. *Nimeiri and the Revolution of Dis-May*. London: KPI, 1985.

King, Preston. *An African Winter*. Harmondsworth: Penguin, 1986.

Kingsley, Mary. *Travels in West Africa*. London: Macmillan, 1897.

Kjekshus, Helge. *Ecology Control and Economic Development in East African History*. London: Heinemann Educational Books, 1974.

Kodjo, Edem. . . . *et Demain l'Afrique*. Paris: Stock, 1985.

Kouchner, Bernard. *Charité Business*. Paris: Pré aux Clercs, 1986.

Lamb, David. *The Africans*. New York: Random House, 1982.

Lelyveld, Joseph. *Move Your Shadow*. New York: Times Books, 1985.

Lewis, John P. and Valeriana Kallab, eds. *Development Strategies Reconsidered*. New Brunswick, N.J.: Transaction Books, 1986.

Linear, Marcus. *Zapping the Third World*. London: Pluto, 1985.

Lipton, Merle. *Capitalism and Apartheid*. London: Wildwood House, 1986.

Loubat, Bernard. *L'Ogre de Berengo*. Paris: Alain Febeuvre, 1981.

Mahuzier, Albert. *A la poursuite des Gorilles*. Paris: Amiot Dumont, 1953.

Mandela, Nelson. *No Easy Walk to Freedom*. London: Heinemann, 1965.

Mangin, Charles. *Lettres du Soudan*. Paris: Portiques, 1930.

Manue, Georges. *Méditerranée Niger*. Clermont: Sorlot, 1941.

Markham, Beryl. *West with the Night*. San Francisco: North Point, 1983. Reprint.

Marnham, Patrick. *Fantastic Invasion*. London: Jonathan Cape, 1980.

Marseille, Jacques. *Empire coloniale et capitalisme français*. Paris: Albin Michel, 1984.

Mathias, Peter. *The First Industrial Nation*. London: Methuen, 1983.

Mazrui, Ali. *The Africans*. Boston: Little, Brown, 1986.

Meillassoux, Claude. *Anthropologie de l'Esclavage*. Paris: Presses Universitaires de France, 1986.

Melady, Thomas P. *Burundi: The Tragic Years*. Maryknoll, N.Y.: Orbis, 1974.

Meredith, Martin. *First Dance of Freedom*. London: Hamish Hamilton, 1984.

Mokgatle, Naboth. *The Autobiography of an Unknown South African*. Berkeley, Los Angeles: University of California Press, 1971.

Moorehead, Alan. *The Blue Nile*. London: Hamish Hamilton, 1962.

———. *The White Nile*. New York: Harper and Brothers, 1960.

Moss, Cynthia. *Portraits in the Wild*. Chicago: University of Chicago, 1975.

Newitt, Malyn. *Portugal in Africa*. London: C. Hurst, 1981.

Nguza, Karl i Bond. *Mobutu*. London: Rex Collings, 1982.

Nkrumah, Kwame. *Africa Must Unite*. New York: International Publishers, 1963.

North, James. *Freedom Rising*. New York: Macmillan, 1985.

North, Richard. *The Real Cost*. London: Chatto & Windus, 1986.

Owens, Mark and Delia. *Cry of the Kalahari*. Boston: Houghton Mifflin, 1984.

Palmer, Robert and Robert Parsons. *The Roots of Rural Poverty in Central and Southern Africa*. London: Heinemann, 1977.

Paton, Alan. *Cry, the Beloved Country*. London: Jonathan Cape, 1948.

Pean, Pierre. *Affaires Africaines*. Paris: Fayard, 1983.

———. *Bokassa Ier*. Paris: Alain Moreau, 1977.

Pomonti, Jean-Claude. *L'Afrique Trahie*. Paris: Hachette, 1979.

Pringle, John. *The Conservationists and the Killers*. Cape Town: T.V. Bulpin, 1982.

Rawley, James A. *The Transatlantic Slave Trade*. New York: W. W. Norton, 1981.

Richards, Paul. *Indigenous Agricultural Revolution*. London: Hutchinson, 1985.

Rodney, Walter. *How Europe Underdeveloped Africa*. Washington: Howard University, 1982.

Rosenberg, Nathan and L. E. Birdzell. *How the West Grew Rich*. London: Tauris, 1986.

Sandford, Stephen. *Management of Pastoral Development in the Third World*. New York: John Wiley & Sons, 1983.

Schaller, George. *The Serengeti Lions*. Chicago: University of Chicago Press, 1972.

Schreyer, Emil. *L'Office du Niger au Mali*. Wiesbaden: Steiner, 1984.

Schweitzer, Albert. *Ma Vie et Ma Pensée*. Paris : Albin Michel, 1960.

Simon, J. L. *The Ultimate Resource*. Princeton: Princeton University Press, 1981.

Smuts, J. C. *J. C. Smuts*. London: Cassel, 1952.

Soyinka, Wole. *The Man Died*. London: Rex Collings, 1972.

Stanley, H. M. *How I Found Livingstone*. New York: Scribner's, 1913.

Sylvester, Anthony. *Arabs and Africans*. London: Bodley Head, 1981.

Thesinger, Wilfred. *Arabian Sands*. London: Longmans, Green, 1959.

Thomas, Elizabeth Marshall. *The Harmless People*. New York: Random House, 1958.

Tickell, Crispin. *Climatic Change and World Affairs*. Lanham, M.D.: University Press of America, 1986.

Timberlake, Lloyd. *Africa in Crisis*. London: International Institute for Environment and Development, 1985.

Tranter, N. L. *Population and Society 1750–1940*. London: Longmans, 1985.

Trial, Georges. *Okoume*. Paris: Je Sers, 1939.

Ungar, Sanford J. *Africa*. New York: Simon and Schuster, 1985.

Van der Post, Laurens. *Lost World of the Kalahari*. London: The Hogarth Press, 1958.

———— and Jane Taylor. *Testament to the Bushmen*. New York: Viking, 1984.

Wakana, Katambo. *Coups d'état, Revolutions and Power Struggles in Post-Independence Africa*. Nairobi: Afriscript, 1985.

Wästberg, Per. *Assignments in Africa*. New York: Farrar, Straus & Giroux, 1986.

World Commission on Environment and Development. *Our Common Future*. Oxford and New York: Oxford University Press, 1987.

World Resources Institute. *World Resources 1986*. New York: Basic Books, 1986.

Wrigley, E. A. and R. S. Schofield. *The Population History of England 1571–1871*. London: Edward Arnold, 1981.

Zakara, Mohammed. *Traditions Touaregues Nigeriennes*. Paris: L'Harmattan, 1979.

INDEX

Abu Kimbal, Saaed, 84, 85, 86
Achebe, Chinua, 18, 149
Adedeji, Adebayo, 11
Aepyornis (bird), 178
African Academy of Sciences, 302
African Priority Program for
    Economic Recovery, 274
Africare, 69
Aga Khan, Sadruddin, 296
Agriculture in Africa
    cash-crop economies, 244
    colonial failures, 243–44
    food-growing potential, 5, 246
    sale and transportation of crops,
        294–95
    short-term focus of aid programs,
        244–46
    successes of, 246
    women's responsibility for, 256,
        257
    See also Cattle-raising;
        Irrigation projects;
        specific countries
Agroforestry programs, 108–10
Ahearn, Michael, 298
Ahidjo, Ahmadou, 174
AIDS (acquired immune deficiency
    syndrome), 259–60
Alverson, Hoyt, 17, 24–25
Amin, Mohammed, 90
Amin Dada, Idi, 117, 119–20
Amobi, Igwe, 157
Andrews, Michael, 306
Angola, 184
    civil war, 188
    economic potential, 185–87, 194
    environmental problems, 188
    South Africa, conflict with, 189
    U.S. involvement in, 112, 188
    war for independence, 185
Armah, Ayi Kwei, 180–81, 305
Ayari, Chadli, 286

Ayensu, Eddy, 284, 302
Ayittey, George, 17–18, 294

Babambiba, Mbayi, 261
Babangida, Gen. Ibrahim, 155–56,
    162
Baiemroe, Beramgoto, 305
Balewa, Sir Abubakar Tafawa, 150
Bamiléké tribe, 174
Banda, Hastings Kamuzu, 191,
    208–9
Band Aid, 7, 81
Banks, Pat, 95
Bantustans, 219–22, 227
Barre, Siad, 92
Barrett, Lindsay, 156, 157
Belgian colonialism, 13, 14
Bell, Morag, 206, 207
Benin, 167, 172–73
Berry, Richard, 263
Biafra, 151–53
Birdzell, L. E., 304
Birth-control programs, 251, 252–53
Biya, Paul, 174
Blundell, Sir Michael, 299
Bokassa, Jean-Bedel, 176–77
Bongo, Omar, 175
Borlaug, Norman, 134, 304
Borna, Bertin, 300
Botswana, 25, 242
    Bushmen, treatment of, 44
    cattle-raising in, 37–40, 234
    drought in, 34–35, 36
    foreign aid to, 29–31, 39–40
    South Africa and, 206–7
Bozo tribe, 288
Brader, Lucas, 38, 269
Brady, Nyle, 246
Brass, William, 252
Brett-Smith, Sarah, 71
British colonialism, 13, 14, 143,
    243–44
British foreign aid, 264
Brooke, James, 112–13
Brown, Lester R., 286
Bruce, David, 240

Brumby, Peter, 303
Brundtland, Mrs. Gro, 300
Buerk, Michael, 90, 192
Buffalo fence, 37–38
Bura irrigation scheme, 266–67
Burkina Faso, 167, 173–74
Burton, Sir Richard, 12
Burundi, 106, 111
Bushmen (San tribe), 40–41
    destruction of their culture, 1, 2,
        46–47, 48
    economic exploitation of, 45–46
    ethnic prejudice against, 44–45
    modern transformation of, 43–44
    nature, relation to, 41–43
Busia, Kofi A., 145
Buthelezi, Mangosuthu, 221–22

Cabral, Amilcar, 193
Cabral, Luis, 193
Caillié, René, 49–50
Cameroon, 174
Cape Verde islands, 193–94
CARE, 268, 298
Carrefour du Développement, 182
Carter, Jimmy, 133, 198, 304
Catholic Relief Services (CRS), 89
Cattle-raising
    Africans' uses for cattle, 232, 238
    balance with nature, 232, 238
    environmental destruction from,
        29, 35–36, 37, 40, 233–36
    excess of cattle, 233–34
    financial failures, 39, 237
    governmental mismanagement, 238
    meat sales from, 37
    rinderpest pandemics, 232–33,
        239–40
    tsetse-fly eradication for, 38,
        240–41
    wildlife and, 16, 30–31, 40,
        240–42
Central African Republic, 175–77
CFA franc, 167
Chad, 19–20, 59, 74, 179–80
Chambers, Robert, 303–4

Cheru, Fantu, 11–12, 23, 25, 289
Children
  malnutrition among, 260
  militarization of, 123–24, 125–26
Chimpanzees, 135
Chirac, Jacques, 112
Chissano, Joaquim, 189, 191
Christian Relief and Development
    Agency, 89, 90
Climatic effects of environmental
    destruction, 235–36
Colonialism, 12–15. *See also* British;
    French; Portuguese *headings*
Colvin, Ian, 16, 220–21
Commerson, Philibert, 178
Conable, Barber, 293
Congo, 173
Copeland, Richard, 77
Correa, Paulo, 193
Cossins, Noel, 235
Cousteau, Jacques-Yves, 246, 287
Cowell, Alan, 230
Cross, Edward G., 205
Cumming, David, 16
Cuny, Fred, 80, 297

Dacko, David, 176
Dahab, Abdel-Rahman Swar al-, 78
Damiba, Pierre-Claver, 275–76, 278
Davidson, Basil, 26
Debre-Michael, Yemane Berhan, 96
Debts of African nations, 10–11
Declaration of Environmental
    Policies, 293
De Gaulle, Charles, 152, 165–66,
    176
De Klerk, Wimpie, 229
De la Renaudière, Xavier, 292, 300
De Marenches, Alexandre, 176
De Mistura, Staffan, 297
Demographics of Africa, 9
Desertification, 35–36, 50–51,
    236–37
Development in Africa
  "appropriate technology" for, 56
  debt payments used for, 290

disastrous projects, 265–67
environmental destruction due to,
    29–30, 108–10, 292–93
peasant involvement, importance
    of, 22, 285–86, 289, 304–5
peasants excluded from planning,
    15, 25
successful projects, 298
See also Sahel development program
DeVilliers, David, 229
De Vos, Leo, 273
Diakite, Noumou, 60, 61
Diallo, Djibril, 21–22, 24, 26–27,
    28, 260, 306
Diallo, Fanta Babacissé, 257–58
Diamond, Jared, 247–48
Diori, Hamani, 71
Diouf, Abdou, 161–62, 168, 169, 282
Diseases of Africa, 260
Djibouti, 17
Dlamini, Bhekimpi Alpheus, 208
Dodge, Cole, 124, 125
Dodson, Andrew, 239
Doe, Sgt. Samuel K., 159–61
Dogon bridge, 305
Dogon tribe, 70–71
Dos Santos, Jose Eduardo, 188
Douglas-Hamilton, Iain, 106
Draper, William, III, 278
Drought, 34–35, 61
Dulloo, Madun, 280–81
Dumont, René, 15, 256, 300
Duras, Marguerite, 291
Dust storms, 35

East African Community, 118–19,
    120, 127, 129
Ecaré, Desiré, 256
Economic Community of West
    African States (Ecowas), 162
Edlin, John, 204
Educational programs, 259–61, 305
Effiong, Maj. Philip, 153
Elands, 42
Elephants, 106–7, 262
Enquist, Nils, 80–81

Environmental destruction, 1–2
  cattle-raising and, 29, 35–36, 37,
    40, 233–36
  climatic effects of, 235–36
  development and, 29–30, 108–10,
    292–93
  political aspects, 16
  wood cut for fuel, 235
  See also Desertification
Equatorial Guinea, 192–93
Estes, Richard, 247
Ethiopia, 10
  population growth, 250–51
  resettlement program, 92–93, 94
  villagization program, 93–94
Ethiopian famine, 7, 8, 87–88
  civil war and, 88–89
  forecasts of famine, 89
  government's handling of, 88, 89
  media publicity for, 90–91
  recurrence, possible, 95–96
  relief efforts, 89–90, 91
  soil erosion and, 87, 88
  U.S. politicization of, 97
European attitudes toward Africa,
    20–21
Everett, Richard, 174
Eyadema, Gnassingbé, 182

Famine
  in Biafra, 152
  drought, relation to, 61
  as man-made phenomenon, 6,
    71–72
  relief efforts in the West, 7–8
  relief efforts to supersede political
    concerns, 296–97
  sale and transportation of crops as
    solution to, 294–95
  structural food deficits, 96
  See also Ethiopian famine;
    Sudan famine relief effort
FAO. *See* Food and Agriculture
    Organization, U.N.
Fenton, James, 265
Fenwick, Millicent, 269

Fieldhouse, D. K., 304
Food aid
  donors' attitudes toward, 277
  in Ethiopian famine, 89–90, 91
  management improvements, need
    for, 61–62, 80–81, 297–98
  unnecessary aid, 39, 277
  See also Sudan famine relief effort
Food and Agriculture Organization,
    U.N. (FAO), 6, 28, 269–73
Food for Work projects, 64, 307
Foreign aid, 11, 262–63
  accountability, need for, 301
  African leaders' attitude toward,
    273–74, 280–83
  bilateral aid, 27
  consistent, steady support, 307–8
  coordination among donors, need
    for, 28, 265, 277, 298–300
  dependence syndrome, 8, 23, 275
  disastrous projects, 265–67
  fund-raising efforts, 7–8
  indigenous non-governmental
    African agencies, support for,
    305–8
  insufficiency of, 290–91
  leaders, donors' consideration of,
    289–90
  manpower and paperwork of, 284
  misuse of, 6–7, 9, 23, 59
  multilateral aid, 27, 264, 268
  the people as appropriate targets
    for, 287, 289, 305
  political nature of, 27, 56, 264
  private volunteer organizations,
    268–69
  recipient initiative and
    responsibility, 29, 273–76
  regional focus, 279–80
  self-development alternative,
    284–86
  smaller projects, 264–65, 304–5
  See also Development in Africa;
    Food aid; *specific countries and
    agencies*
Fossey, Dian, 99–103, 135

Foster, Kathy Hall, 288
Franco-African summit of 1984, 182
Franjola, Matt, 200
French presence in Africa
  "associations," 166–68, 180–82
  colonialism, 3, 13, 14, 163–66,
    244
  commitment to Africa, 291
  foreign aid, 264
Fryxel, J. M., 234

Gabon, 166, 175
Gambia, 143, 161–62
Gapare, Robinson, 16
Gautier, Emile, 54
Gbedemah, Komla, 145
Geldof, Bob, 7, 8, 308
Gemsboks, 42
Gerster, George, 67, 71–72
Gezira cotton project, 85–86
Ghana, 173
  economic situation, 145, 146, 149
  independence for, 10, 143–45
  political situation, 144–46
Gimpel, Jean, 17
Giscard d'Estaing, Valéry, 176
Giwa, Dele, 157
Goodall, Jane, 135
Gordon, Charles "Chinese," 84
Gorillas, mountain, 99–104, 108
Gowon, Lt. Col. Yakubu, 150
Grant, James P., 260, 273
Gregory, Elbert, 77
Grove, Brandon H., Jr., 112–13
Guillard, Joanny, 299
Guinea, 166, 171–72
Guinea-Bissau, 193
Guissou, Basile, 282
Gwynne, Michael, 236, 237, 238–39

Habré, Hissène, 179, 180
Haidalla, Mohamed Khouna, 59
Haile Selassie, 10, 87, 88
Harden, Blaine, 138, 266
Hardy, Chandra, 290
Harris, Ray, 235–36

Hash House Harriers, 131–32
Health education, need for, 259–61
Heglund, Norman C., 258–59
Henri, Pierre-Olivier, 70
Houphouët-Boigny, Félix, 169, 171,
  176
Howe, Sir Geoffrey, 204
Hugo, Victor, 13
Humanity of the Africans, 11–12
Hunger Project, 306
Husain, Ishrat, 155
Hutu tribe, 111
Hyden, Goran, 25

Ibo tribe, 150
Improvement of the African
    condition, prerequisites for
  debt payments used for
    development, 290
  deeds instead of words, 301
  economic diversification, 295–96
  educational programs, 259–61, 305
  famine relief to supersede political
    concerns, 296–97
  food aid management, 80–81,
    297–98
  foreign aid
    accountability in, 301
    consistent support, 307–8
    coordination of, 298–300
    indigenous, non-governmental
      control of, 305–8
  free speech and trade, 294
  institutional reforms, 303–4
  outsiders' ideas about Africa,
    changing of, 20–21, 287–91
  peasant involvement in
    development efforts, 22, 285–86,
      289, 304–5
  sale and transportation of African
    crops, 294–95
  Third World, trade with, 296
  triangular transactions, 294–95
  unity within nations, 289
  values and attitudes of Africans,
    286–87

Improvement of the African
condition (*cont.*)
  waste of money and resources,
    ending of, 291–94
  wildlife, ecological-scientific
    approach to, 302–3
Independent Commission on
    International Humanitarian
    Issues, 296
International Fund for Agricultural
    Development, U.N. (IFAD),
    174, 268
International Labor Organization
    (ILO), 121
International Livestock Center for
    Africa (ILCA), 39, 240, 302–3
International Monetary Fund (IMF),
    27, 267
  economic measures, 113, 114, 147,
    203
Iona National Park, 186–88
Ireland, 253
Irrigation projects, 55, 56–57,
    68–70, 164, 267
Israel, foreign aid by, 264
Ivory Coast, 167, 169–71, 259–60
Ivory trade, 106–7

Jackson, Glenda, 8
Jacobson, Philip, 19–20
Jawara, Sir Dawda, 161
Jaycox, Edward V. K., 236
Jenden, Kevin, 81–82
Johnson-Sirleaf, Ellen, 160, 256
Jonathan, Leabua, 207
Jonglei Canal program, 245–46

Kader, Abbas, 50
Kaunda, Kenneth, 202, 203, 204,
    281
Keita, Modibo, 54
Kemp, Jan, 241
Kennedy, Edward M., 161
Kenya, 135, 265–67
  agricultural situation, 136, 141
  East African Community, 118, 129

  human rights abuses, 137, 138
  political situation, 136–37, 138
  population growth, 139–40, 252
  tribal conflicts, 139
  U.S., relations with, 137–38
  wildlife in, 140, 243
Kenyatta, Jomo, 129, 135, 136, 137
Kerekou, Maj. Mathieu, 172
Khalifa, Omar, 7, 274
Khat imports, 17
Kigozi, Freddie, 123, 124
Kikuyu tribe, 141
Kjekshus, Helge, 233
Knight, Ridgway, 185
Kodjo, Edem, 15
Kolingba, André, 176, 177, 248
Korea, North, 264
Korea, South, 264
Kountche, Gen. Seyni, 71, 72, 282,
    291–92
Kragen, Ken, 82
Kum Buo, Sammy, 283
Kuti, Fela Anikulapo, 19, 150
KwaNdebele homeland, 223
KwaThema township, 225–26
KwaZulu homeland, 219, 220

Land protection measures, 237–38
Laurent, André, 301
Laurie, John, 294
Leakey, Louis, 100
Leakey, Philip, 294
Lemurs, 178
Lesotho, 207–8
Levinson, Olga, 46–47
Lewis, John, 286–87
Lewis, Stephen, 276
Liberia, 10, 159–61, 256
Lingoupou, Gen. Martin, 177
Linguissa, Philippe, 177
Lions, 42, 215
Livingstone, David, 12
Lloyd, Raymond, 272
Lone, Salim, 137
Lucas, C. Payne, 15
Lumumba, Patrice, 100

Lyman, Princeton, 155
Lyng, Richard, 277

McGuire, Wayne, 103
Machel, Samora, 189–90, 191, 195
Macias Nguema, Francisco, 193
MacIntosh, Ronald, 269
Macmillan, Harold, 14
McNamara, Robert, 291, 308
Madagascar, 177–79
Mahdi, Sadiq el, 84
Maiga, Amadou, 298–99
Majjia Valley project, 298
Makerere University, 122–23
Malaria, 260
Malawi, 196, 208–9
Mali, 3–4, 6, 167, 173
    food aid to, 61
    irrigation projects, 54, 68–70
    nomads in, 60
    See also Sahel development
        program; Timbuktu
Malnutrition, 260
Mandala, Gen. Jean-Claude, 177
Mandela, Nelson, 229
Mandela, Winnie, 229
Mansa Musa, 12
Markham, Beryl, 20, 21
Marnham, Patrick, 55
Marshall, John, 46–47
Martin, Esmond Bradley, 105, 106
Masai tribe, 105, 141, 233
Masire, Quett, 29, 39
Massamba-Debat, Alphonse, 113
Maure nomads, 58–59
Mauritania, 58–59, 173
Mazrui, Ali, 23, 144
M'Ba, Léon, 175
Mbisha, Buy-Niembes, 115
Médecins Sans Frontières, 92, 301
Medical facility shortage, 261
Medrala, Bob, 7
Menemencioglu, Ekber, 75, 76
Mengistu Haile Mariam, Col., 88,
    89, 281
Michaud, Mitch, 71

Miller, Elliott W., 137
Miské, Annick, 299
Mitterrand, François, 173, 291
Mobutu Sese Seko, 100, 111–12,
    113, 114, 115–16
Moi, Daniel arap, 136–38, 252, 266
Momoh, Gen. Joseph, 159
Momoh, Tony, 156
Mondlane, Eduardo, 189
Mongella, Gertrude, 134
More, Chris, 222–23
Morrow, Lance, 140–41
Morse, F. Bradford, 28
Moumié, Félix, 174
Mozambique, 184–86, 189–92, 194
Mswati III, King of Swaziland, 208
Mugabe, Robert, 190, 195, 196, 197,
    198, 199, 200, 201, 213
Mulele, Pierre, 111–12
Munz, Monique, 256
Museveni, Yoweri, 26, 118, 120,
    124, 282
"Music bridge," 305
Mwinyi, Hassan, 138
Myers, Norman, 247

Namibia, 10, 44
Nax (Bushman guide), 40–45, 46
Ndaw, Robert, 244
Ndebele tribe, 198–99
N'Dow, Wally, 161
Neogy, Rajat, 118
Neto, Agostinho, 188
Newby, John, 58
New York Zoological Society, 246
Nguza Karl I Bond, 115
Ng'weno, Fleur, 286
Ng'weno, Hilary, 289
Niger, 71–73, 173, 268–69
Nigeria, 18, 25, 143, 251
    agricultural situation, 154–55
    Biafran civil war, 151–53
    corruption in, 153–54, 155
    criminal anarchy, 156–57
    economic reforms, 155–56
    ethnic violence, 150–51

Nigeria (*cont.*)
  national income, mismanagement
    of, 149, 154–55
  press restrictions, 157
  public relations campaign, 156,
    157–58
  regional integration, 72–73, 162
Niger River, 54, 66–68, 164
Njorogeh, Alex, 8–9
Nkala, Enos, 200
Nkoane, Simeon, 227
Nkomo, Joshua, 199
Nkrumah, Kwame, 143–45, 285
Noblet, Jean-Pierre, 299
Nomadic peoples, 3, 62
  co-existence with farmers, 60
  endangerment of, 47–48, 58–59
  government opposition to, 59, 60
  as multinational concern, 60–61
  neighbors' dislike for, 59
  Sahel development and, 57–58
  See also Bushmen; Tuareg tribe
Norton-Griffiths, Michael, 141, 240
Norway, foreign aid by, 265–66
Nyerere, Julius K., 19, 126, 128–31,
  244

Obasanjo, Gen. Olusegun, 158
Obote, Milton, 117, 118, 119, 120
Odaka, Sam, 118
Odhiambo, Thomas, 302
Office for Emergency Operations in
    Africa, U.N. (OEOA), 28, 95,
    271
Ojukwu, Odumegwu, 151, 152, 153
O'Keeffe, Augustine, 89–90, 95–96
Okello, Tito, 117
Olindo, Perez, 247
Oliveira Salazar, Antonio de, 184
Operation Blé (Wheat), 68–70
Operation Rainbow, 297
Organization of African Unity, 15,
    26, 139, 280–83
Osahon, Naiwu, 157
Otieno, Silvano Melea, 139
Oueddei, Goukouni, 179, 180

Ouedraogo, Josephine, 257
Ould El Bah, Abdullah, 58
Ovahimba tribe, 187
Owens, Ken, 229

Parker, Ian, 106
Paton, Alan, 223–24
Pereira, Aristide, 193, 194
Perez de Cuellar, Xavier, 28, 271
Pesticides, 241
Philip, Prince, Duke of Edinburgh,
    178
Poachers, measures against, 248–49
Political situation in Africa
  slave trade and, 26, 148–49
  stability, need for, 147–48
  See also specific countries
Pompidou, Georges, 176
Population growth, 250–54
Portuguese colonialism, 13, 14,
    183–85
Prattley, Winston, 82
Priestley, Michael, 95, 96
Private volunteer organizations
    (PVOs), 268–69

Quaggas, extinction of, 241
QwaQwa homeland, 220

Raath, Jan, 200
Randal, Jonathan, 76–77
Ratsiraka, Didier, 178
Rawlings, Lt. Jerry (J. J.), 146, 147,
    149, 173
Reagan, Ronald, 113, 138, 160, 198
Redmond, Ian, 103
Reitz, Denys, 46
Renamo (Mozambique National
    Resistance), 190–91
Rhinos, black, 16, 105, 201
Rhodes, Cecil, 196
Rhodesia. *See* Zimbabwe
Richards, Paul, 288
Rinderpest pandemics, 232–33,
    239–40
Robert, Serge, 58

Roberto, Holden, 188
Rodd, F. R., 51
Rogol, Marty, 7, 82
Rosenberg, Nathan, 304
Roth, Toby, 97
Rotival, Alexander, 279–80
Rwanda, 99, 104, 108–11

Sabally, Samba, 300–301
Sahara Desert expansion, 236–37
Sahel development program
    foreign aid for, 56–57
    irrigation projects, 55, 56–57, 164
    as multinational concern, 72–73
    Niger River, impact on, 66–68
    nomads, impact on, 57–58
    tree-growing project, 55–56
Sai, Frederick T., 254
Saleh, Abdul, 303
Sandford, Stephen, 233–34
Sand grouses, 42
Sankara, Capt. Thomas, 173–74,
    255, 274, 292
San tribe. *See* Bushmen
São Tomé and Principe islands, 194
Saouma, Edouard, 28, 269–70, 271,
    272
Sasakawa, Ryoichi, 304
Sassou-Nguesso, Denis, 173
Save the Children Fund of Britain,
    77, 89
Savimbi, Jonas, 112, 188
Schaller, George, 107, 247
Schweitzer, Albert, 20, 26
Sékou Touré, Ahmed, 171–72
Self-improvement by Africans,
    barriers to, 17–20
Senegal, 161–62, 167, 168–69
Senghor, Léopold Sédar, 168
Senteze-Kabuji, William, 125
Shona tribe, 198–99
Shultz, George, 137, 160, 274–75,
    290
Sierra Leone, 143, 158–59
Simon, George, 297–98
Simon, Julian, 253, 254

Sinclair A. R. E., 234
Slave trade, 26, 148–49, 183–84
Smith, Ian, 199
Smith, James, 188
Smith, Linda, 68–69
Smuts, Jan, 217
Sobhuza II, King of Swaziland, 208
Somalia, 91–92, 267
South Africa, 10, 210–11
    Afrikaners, 216–18, 230–31
    apartheid policy, 216–18, 227–28
    apartheid protests, 211–12
    Bantustans (homelands), 219–22,
        227
    beauty of, 224
    black-black conflicts, 221–22, 226
    Bushmen, treatment of, 46
    bushveld and wildlife, 214–16
    cattle-raising, 240–42
    corporate pull-outs, 230
    economic situation, 227–28
    governmental corruption, 213
    Immorality Act, 212
    land mismanagement, 15–16,
        219–21
    legal system, 212–13
    neighboring countries and, 189,
        190, 191, 204–5, 206–7
    politics of race, 222–23
    press censorship, 228–29
    radicalization of blacks, 226–27
    sanctions against, 224, 228
    solutions to problems of, 218–19
    townships, 225–27
    whites' arrogance, 214
    whites' unease, 224–25, 228
South African Defense Forces, 46
Southern African Development
    Coordination Conference, 205
Soviet Union, 56, 92, 264, 291
Soyinka, Wole, 18–19, 26, 138, 150
Spirituality of Africans, 19–21
Sport Aid, 7, 274
Stanley, Henry Morton, 12
Stevens, Siaka, 158
Strong, Maurice, 28

Sudan, 14, 84–86
Sudan famine relief effort, 7
  airlifting of food, 79–80, 82
  civil war and, 83–84
  domestic grain production, 83
  forecast of famine, 74–75, 86
  governmental interference, 78, 79,
    82, 86–87
  professional workers, 80–81
  profiteers, 79
  railroad problems, 76–78
  refugees, movement of, 75–76
  as typical African relief operation,
    82–83
Summit meeting of African leaders,
  280–83
Swaminathan, M. S., 278
Swaziland, 207, 208
Sylla, Ibrahim, 60, 62

Taiwan, foreign aid by, 264
Taka, Tarekegne, 87, 98
Tambo, Oliver, 213
Tanzania, 126
  agricultural situation, 128–29,
    132, 133–34, 234
  East African Community, 118,
    127, 129
  economic and political reforms,
    134–35
  economic situation, 127–28, 132
  foreign aid to, 127, 131–32
  potential of, 126–27
  poverty in, 19
  socialist government, 128–31
Thesinger, Wilfred, 239
Thiong'o, Ngugi Wa, 137, 138
Third World trade with Africa, 296
Timberlake, Lloyd, 245
Timbuktu, 3–4, 49–51, 63
Togo, 167, 182
Tolbert, William, 159, 160
Tombalbaye, François, 179
Transgabonese Railway, 175
Transkei homeland, 221
Trant, Gerald, 301–2

Tranter, N. L., 253
Traoré, Moussa, 292
Tree-growing projects, 55–56
Triangular transactions, 294–95
Tribalism, 139, 198–99, 288–89
Tsetse-fly eradication, 38, 240–41
Tuareg tribe, 3–4, 6, 51
  colonization and, 51–52
  farming settlements, 64–66
  game reserve for, 58
  in modern world, 54–55, 58
  poverty of, 53–54
  settlement in cities, 52–53
  tourism, recourse to, 63–64
Tubman, William V. S., 159
Turkman fisheries project, 265–66
Tutsi tribe, 111
Tyson, Harvey, 229

Uganda
  children in, 123–24, 125–26
  East African Community, 118–19,
    120
  economic situation, 120–22
  health facilities, 123–24
  political violence, 117–20
UNICEF. *See* U.N. Children's Fund
Union of Nationalists to Liberate
  Kenya (Mwakenya), 136–37
United Nations
  foreign aid guidance, 27–28, 269
  Special Session for Africa, 274–75,
    276
    follow-up meetings, 276–83
  See also specific agencies, i.e., Food
    and Agriculture Organization,
    U.N.
U.N. Children's Fund (UNICEF),
  62, 64, 70, 260, 273
U.N. Development Program
  (UNDP), 278–79
United States
  aid to Africa, 264, 268, 290–91
  Angola, involvement in, 112, 188
  Ethiopian famine, response to, 91,
    97

Kenya, relations with, 137–38
Liberia, relations with, 160, 161
Somalia, relations with, 92
Zaire, involvement in, 111, 112–13
Zimbabwe, relations with, 198
U.S. Agency for International
    Development (USAID), 68, 69,
    70, 74–75, 76, 77–78
USA for Africa, 7, 8, 81

Vale, Glyn, 201
Van der Post, Sir Laurens, 2, 43
Vaux, Tony, 191
Vedder, Amy, 103–4, 108
Vegetable Outreach, 80
Vidal-Naquet, Alain, 278
Vieira, Joao Bernardo, 193
Villagization programs, 93–94
Vlek, Paul, 288

War casualties (1960–present), 11
Weber, William, 103–4
West Africa
    economic integration, 162, 163
    history of, 142–43
    political systems, development of,
        148–49
    potential for catastrophe, 142
    See also specific countries
Western, David, 105, 106, 238, 247,
    302
Wickens, Jamie, 285, 288
Wilde, James, 20–21
Wildebeests, 30–31, 32–35, 36–37
Wildlife
    Africans' attitudes toward, 16, 104,
        242, 247
    cattle-raising and, 16, 30–31, 40,
        240–42
    drought's impact on, 34–35
    ecological-scientific approach to,
        302–3
    extinction of species, 241, 247
    future for, 247
    hunting of, as business, 105–7

as international responsibility,
    242–43
poachers, measures against,
    248–49
preservation programs, 104, 201
revenue potential of, 240, 241–42,
    245
tourism as savior of, 103–4
See also specific animals
Williams, Maurice, 301
Willis, Ken, 78, 79
Wilson, Allan, 258
Witt, Eric, 74–75
Wolpe, Howard, 137
Women
    agricultural work, 256, 257
    changing attitudes of, 256
    self-help efforts, 257–58
    subordination of, 255–56, 257
World Bank, 27
    agricultural programs, 84–85
    agroforestry programs, 108, 109
    cattle-raising programs, 29, 39
    development studies, 11, 274
    environmental policy, 293
    on food aid, 297
    irrigation projects, 267
    land protection plan, 237–38
    limits of, 292
    on malnutrition, 260
    on population growth, 250, 251
    Sahel development program, 55
    "structural reform" focus, 264,
        267–68
World Food Council, U.N. (WFC),
    89, 272, 276–78, 296, 301
World Food Program, 86, 296–97
World War I, 13
World War II, 13–14
World Wildlife Fund, 58
Worrall, Denis, 228–29

Yoruba tribe, 150

Zaire, 9
    economic situation, 25, 113–15

Zaire (*cont.*)
  human rights abuses, 115
  political situation, 100, 111–12,
    116
  U.S. involvement in, 111, 112–13
Zambia, 127, 196
  economic situation, 25, 202–3
  human rights abuses, 204
  South Africa and, 204–6
Zimbabwe
  agricultural situation, 199

  economic situation, 199–201
  history of, 196–97
  political situation, 197–99, 200
  South Africa and, 205
  tribal tensions, 198–99
  U.S., relations with, 198
  whites' rights in, 195, 196
  wildlife in, 16, 201, 242, 243
Zulu, Grey, 203
Zulu tribe, 221–22